NARRATIVES OF NOSTALGIA, GENDER, AND NATIONALISM

Also by Jean Pickering

UNDERSTANDING DORIS LESSING

Narratives of Nostalgia, Gender, and Nationalism

Edited by

Jean Pickering

and

Suzanne Kehde

NEW YORK UNIVERSITY PRESS
Washington Square, New York

© Macmillan Press Ltd 1997

This book is printed on paper suitable for recycling and
made from fully managed and sustained forest sources.

First published in the U.S.A. in 1997 by
NEW YORK UNIVERSITY PRESS
Washington Square
New York, N.Y. 10003

Library of Congress Cataloging-in-Publication Data
Narratives of nostalgia, gender, and nationalism / edited by Jean
Pickering and Suzanne Kehde.
p.   cm.
Includes bibliographical references and index.
ISBN 0–8147–6635–8 (clothbound). — ISBN 0–8147–6636–6 (pbk.)
1. American literature—History and criticism—Theory, etc.
2. English literature—History and criticism—Theory, etc.   3. Women
and literature—United States—History.   4. Women and literature–
–Great Britain—History.   5. Nationalism in literature.
6. Nostalgia in literature.   7. Sex role in literature.
8. Narration (Rhetoric)   I. Pickering, Jean.   II. Kehde, Suzanne,
1949–   .
PS152.N37   1996
813.009'358—dc20   96–12917
                                                             CIP

Printed in Great Britain

Contents

Contributors

Hema Chari is Assistant Professor of English at California State University, Los Angeles, where she teaches courses in modern and postmodern British, colonial and postcolonial literature and theory, feminist theory, and world literature. She received her PhD in 1994 from the University of Southern California, writing her dissertation on *Fractured Subjects on the Margins of Identity: Race, Gender, and Sexuality in Colonial and Postcolonial Texts*. She has published 'Decentered on the (A)Isle of the Postcolonial: *My Beautiful Laundrette, Sammie and Rosie Get Laid, and Madame Sousatzka'*, *Spectator* 10: 1 (1990), 20–31.

Ellen G. Friedman is Professor of English at Trenton State College, where she directs the women's studies program. She is the author of *Joyce Carol Oates* (Ungar Publishing Company, 1980) and of articles on modernism, postmodernism and women writers in such journals as *Modern Fiction Studies* and *PMLA*. She is the coeditor of *Breaking the Sequence: Women's Experimental Fiction* and *Utterly Other Discourse: The Texts of Christine Brooke-Rose* forthcoming from Dalkey Archive Press. She is working on a book-length study of contemporary representations of morality, as well as essays on Edith Wharton, Jane Bowles, and Christine Brooke-Rose.

Suzanne Kehde has published articles on Bakhtin and Henry James, Walter Van Tilburg Clark, Graham Greene, David Henry Hwang and Bharati Mukherjee, and various short stories.

JoAnn Menezes earned her Ph.D. in Art History and American Studies at Emory University, Georgia, writing her dissertation on visual representation and the construction of American cultural history and historiography. She is now scholar in residence at the University of Maine, Orono, where she has a joint appointment in Art and History.

Jean Pickering is Professor of English at California State University, Fresno. She has published *Understanding Doris Lessing* (University of South Carolina Press, 1990), assorted articles on

Margaret Drabble, Doris Lessing, and Vera Brittain, the British short story and narrative theory, and various short stories.

Sabina Sawhney teaches English at Daemen College, New York, and has published articles on feminism and postcolonial literature. She is currently working on *The Other Colonialists: Imperial Margins of Victorian Literature*, which deals with the impact of colonialism on the narrative structure of nineteenth-century British novels.

Walter Sondey received his PhD in American literature and critical theory from the University of California, Irvine, where he teaches rhetoric and humanities at the Learning Skills Center.

Janet Sorensen is Assistant Professor of English at the University of Indiana, Bloomington. This essay is part of a chapter from her current project, titled *The Grammar of Empire, the Figure of the Nation: Language and Cultural Identity in Eighteenth-Century Britain*.

Loretta Stec is Assistant Professor of English at San Francisco State University, where she teaches twentieth-century British and post-colonial literatures, and specializes in women writers. She received her PhD from Rutgers University in 1993, and is writing a critical study of Rebecca West.

Jonathan Steinwand is Assistant Professor of English at Concordia College in Moorhead, Minnesota where he teaches comparative literature, literary criticism, humanities, and composition. The essay included in this volume is based on research for his recent SUNY-Binghamton dissertation on *Mnemonic Images: The Gender of Modernity in Schiller, Friedrich Schlegel, Hölderlin, and Bettine Brentano-von Arnim*.

John N. Swift teaches in the Department of English and Comparative Literary Studies at Occidental College in Los Angeles. He has written a number of articles on Willa Cather and other modern writers, and is currently interested in early twentieth-century Anglo-American literary perceptions of the 'yellow peril'.

Acknowledgements

For permission to reprint the essay by Ellen Friedman, *Where Are the Missing Contents? (Post)Modernism, Gender, and the Canon,* we want to thank *PMLA.* For permission to quote from Rebecca West's *Black Lamb, Grey Falcon* and from Trooper Lang's letter we want to thank Penguin USA and the Exposition Permanente du Débarquement respectively. For the sabbatical leave and the research grant that made possible her contribution to this book Jean Pickering also wishes to thank the appropriate faculty and administrative committees at California State University, Fresno.

Introduction

Some explanation of how we came to assemble this collection seems appropriate. For the last decade we have engaged in a mutually profitable dialogue about writing, publishing, texts, critical theory and pedagogy. For several months we were engrossed with the connections between constructions of the ideas of nation and gender, and we became interested in the ways in which nostalgia might function to bind these two presumably unrelated constructions together.

We issued a call for proposals for a conference panel to gauge possible interest in studying these imbrications and received many more excellent responses than we could possibly have anticipated, 33 in all. As we had for some time been thinking of collaborating on a professional project, the number and quality of these proposals presented us with a good opportunity to ease into co-authoring. Although each of us was aware of a certain inclination to retain complete control of her own work, for some years we had been reading each other's manuscripts at various stages, so writing collaboratively, it seemed, might mean only that we would begin sharing ideas earlier in the writing process.

We invited seventeen of the proposal writers to submit essays for a prospective anthology. Ultimately we accepted nine, and Jean added an essay she had been working on independently. As for writing this introduction, we began by agreeing on what generally should go into it and the order in which that material should be arranged. Next we considered it paragraph by paragraph, discussing the details that would go into each, finally agreeing which of us would write which paragraph. We then combined our drafts, and finally we each went over the whole thing to establish a reasonable unity of voice, sentence structure, vocabulary and punctuation.

These essays, then, were accepted as proposals. We chose them on the basis of the proposals' coherence, writing, plausibility and interest. We were not consciously pursuing an ideological quarry; in retrospect it seems clear that the terms in which we couched our call for submissions ensured that those whose founding assumptions about either nation or gender were vastly different from ours would not be writing articles in which these terms were interrogated. Thus our submitters were a self-selected group of reasonably like-minded theorists.

ORDERING

When the essays came in, we were faced with the question of how they should be ordered. Ordering inevitably implies a certain kind of narrative. Should we categorize them by nation? This arrangement we rejected because it would perhaps be seen to imply the independent development of nationalisms, an analysis our reading inclined us to reject. Further, we did not wish to give even more importance to the salient fact that the amount of space allotted to various nations is uneven. The proportion of the final selection is approximately that of the total proposals submitted, if we consider the essays in three groups (Britain, the United States, other nations). These divisions are uncomfortable to face, especially the last, but they do reflect the proportions of the national literatures taught in the US academy. Some of the essays we hoped for, on French-Canadian and Jamaican texts for example, did not materialize. The texts of Britain and the United States were much more popular as objects of analysis than those of other countries.

Could we categorize the essays by the writer's gender? This arrangement would emphasize another kind of disparity: most of the essays were written by women. Here also the proportion of included essays reflects the numbers of the submitted proposals. Even so, would we want to endorse the implication that women are more interested in the relationship of gender and nation than men are? Not on such a small sample, although we do believe that women have more to gain by interrogating it. Could we elect a totally arbitrary order, such as date of arrival or alphabetical by author? Either of the latter would give too much weight to the accidental and would furthermore be so unusual as to suggest a certain quirkiness, a willingness to go to extremes to make a point, that readers might find repellent. So although we do not wish in any way to imply a narrative of development, we at last decided on chronological order, according to the date of the text(s) under analysis. Even though there might be a theoretical chance that this order would imply a certain causality, further examination of the essays has led us to believe that this relationship is not likely to be read into them. We wish to stress however that this arrangement should not be construed to imply an ideal order of reading; each essay is self-sufficient. Readers will of course construct their own categories and their own narratives. We hope this chronological ordering will impede them as little as possible.

ESSENCE VS. CONSTRUCTION

In times of change or crisis, nations look to the past and infer a narrative that erases all confusion and contradiction, which is not presented as history but as a figuration of essential Britishness, Americanness, Germanness, Indianness, as the case may be – a mythic national identity that, Platonic fashion, has presumably always existed. While the simplistic versions of these narratives may be rejected by serious writers, the traces of an essential national character may be figured in their texts; in especially serious national crises, artists may knowingly forward these mythic narratives. During World War II for example, H. E. Bates, conscripted into the Royal Air Force, was posted as a commissioned officer to an aerodrome in Sussex, where his only duty was to write fiction – specifically short stories, and only short stories. The release of Laurence Olivier's *Henry V*, financed by the British Government, was timed to coincide with D-Day. Both artists promoted a myth of essential Britishness in the press of the national emergency.

Although nationalist narratives seem to present *nation* as an unchanging essence, these essays all deal with texts that on analysis show nationalism in an evolving response to developments, both political and cultural, that destabilize the idea of nation. Jonathan Steinwand describes Friedrich Schlegel's appropriation of 'the Greeks', at a moment of Germany's transition into modernity, as a model for the superiority of 'humanity above masculinity and femininity'. In Sir Walter Scott's *The Bride of Lammermoor*, written in a period of increased social conflict consequent on a postwar depression, Janet Sorensen traces two representational systems, the oral, fragmentary, and iconic, gendered female, and the written, linear, and arbitrary, gendered male. These two representational systems are in as uneasy a competition as the Scots and the English, with the Scots denied a voice in the official written British history where they figure as object. Walter Sondey argues that, in order to accomplish through the literary press what conservatives had failed to do politically, Washington Irving in *The Sketch Book* promulgates a middle-class national character legitimated by the hierarchical and deferential values of the colonial past. The conjunction of soaring nationalism and the establishment of woman as a fixed domestic presence is neatly illustrated in JoAnn Menezes's analysis of Charles Weisgerber's painting *The Birth of Our Nation's Flag*. Sabina Sawnhey cities Rabindranath Tagore's *Gora* to substantiate her perception that in the colonized nations, the transformation of the anti-imperialist struggle into a national movement exacerbated a crisis of individual and collective identity in terms of gender, class, religion and ethnicity. John Swift demonstrates that while Willa Cather, in response to World War I and 50 years of non-Northern European immigration, ostensibly supports a masculine idea of national identity, her novels in the immediate post-World War I years contain 'counter-energies of an anti-nostalgic pluralism'. Hema Chari argues that R. K. Narayan's *Waiting for the Mahatma*, which traces the trajectory of the Indian nationalist movement through a love story, recommends the restriction of Indian women to the domestic sphere as their contribution to India's freedom from British rule.

Loretta Stec shows that in *Black Lamb and Grey Falcon* Rebecca West, romanticizing national identity, draws a parallel between the Slavs and the British, who are both engaged in withstanding fascist imperialism. Here she represents Britain, like Yugoslavia, as a defending nation as opposed to the aggressive German imperial power, and recommends the submission of (Serbian) women as the cultural price of national preservation. Ellen Friedman argues that British and American (post)modernist men and women writers have very different orientations towards the lost master narratives of Western civilization, the men expressing nostalgia for what Jean-François Lyotard has called the 'missing contents' and the women 'aim[ing] their gaze unashamedly and audaciously forward'. Jean Pickering's reading of the Musée du

Débarquement at Arromanches and the representation of the D-Day ceremonies in the US media leads to an extended exploration of nostalgia.

Collectively these essays suggest that, just as with the onset of hostilities governments prepare to fight the last war rather than the present one, so nations refurbish outworn nationalisms when a crisis arises; culture – serious writers, popular novelists and the electronic media alike – assiduously promotes new narratives to negotiate the gap between the old construction of nation and the one that current events are calling into being. Overall the essays suggest the enormous cultural effort that goes into supporting, maintaining, and renewing the idea of *nation* in the face of all challenges to unity, and the tremendous price nationalism exacts from the nation's citizens.

WHO PAYS?

Nor does the cost fall equally on all citizens. While this anthology concerns itself only with the ways in which gender functions in nationalist discourse, we are well aware that class and ethnicity are constructed as categories of exclusion, for the hero at the center of the nationalist narrative is the generic human being, the humanist individual, gendered male, colored white (at least in First World nations) and endowed with the conviction of individual uniqueness – with all its sense of social separation, competition and entitlement – upon which capitalism depends for its fuel, its fire, its energy. However, we do not wish to suggest that nationalism exacts no price at all from the citizen it places at the center: the ubiquitous monuments to the fallen that have proliferated during this century testify to what many have paid (though it is a truism that the grunts in Vietnam, who suffered by far the most casualties, were drawn in greater proportion from lower-class and ethnic minority groups. They also disproportionately unenfranchised: at the time 21 was the age of suffrage). Nonetheless women seem to pay a special fee on behalf of the nation, even though it is traditionally represented as an honorarium given to them. The essays comment either explicitly or implicitly on the ways in which the nation-state takes as a foundational principle the subordination of women. For example, our contributors have demonstrated the following: Schlegel wishes to recuperate the female domestic sphere as the

expression of an organic principle fixing a stable space to comple-
ment and thus guarantee the progress of male modernity; Irving
predicates American nationality on the domestic sensibility of a
colonial patriarch; Betsy Ross is translated from an independent
businesswoman into a fixed domestic presence, the Mother of the
Nation; Tagore calls on women to provide stability as a counter-
balance to the change embodied in male action. Even as renowned
a feminist as Rebecca West values the preservation of the nation
over the liberty of women.

This theorizing of national duties explains how women can be
seen as essential beings while men are perceived as free to make
identity choices. If *man* and *woman* are defined in relation only to
biology and each other, both must be either essences or constructions. It would seem that if *woman* is an essential identity and is
also *man*'s other, *man* would have to be a fixed identity also. But
nation is a hidden term in this equation. Nationalism is the field
over which gender differences are played out, making possible
what otherwise seems an irrational if common disposition of
putative gender differences: women are determined by biology,
men by their free wills. It is for this reason that Charlotte Bunch
rightly describes nationalism as 'the ultimate expression of the
patriarchal dynamic of domination'.[1]

IMPERIAL ENCOUNTERS

The model of enforced female subordination supports not only nationalism but its international counterpart, imperialism. These two
are so imbricated as to be impossible to disentangle on a theoretical
level; they can perhaps be differentiated in specific instances.
However we can venture that, while nationalism is at home seen
as a defense against other nations' imperialism, it is frequently a
rationale for one's own. Imperial ventures abroad are usually
explained as necessary for the national interest – the US intervention in Vietnam and in the Persian Gulf for example. The object of
colonial encounters is typically feminized, held to be in want of
masculine (imperial) authority. This feminization can be applied
both to geography, as Annette Kolodny's *The Lay of the Land*
amply demonstrates, and to the colonial population, as David
Henry Hwang has acutely theorized in *M. Butterfly*.[2] Sorensen's

analysis of *The Bride of Lammermoor* shows that Scott's gendering the Scottish representational system as female accommodated English expropriation by calling on the model of 'natural' male–female relationships, the model on which imperialism as well as nationalism is based.

AGAIN THE CONTEXT: FURTHER QUESTIONS

Working on this collection alerted us to some questions the essays do not address but which nevertheless hover in the margins. The dynamic of the nuclear family, sometimes overtly recalled as 'the family romance', frequently appears in the texts analyzed in these essays. Granted that the construction of *nation* entails some organizing principle, why should this particular one be so compelling? If nationalism is predicated on the gender relations of the nuclear family, what kinds of relationships to the idea of *nation* might lesbians and gay men establish? Several essays suggest that the idea of *nation* formulated by the imperial West has defined not only First World nationalisms but postcolonial nationalisms also. How then might this perception influence the relationship to *nation* of native-born minorities in First World nations? What effect might fully democratic practices, entailing full participation by all citizens in what Vaclav Havel has recently called a 'civic society'[3] have on the concept of *nation*? This last question in particular cannot be posed in a nostalgic context of recuperated and recirculated master narratives. It can only be approached with a resolute gaze on the unformulated future.

NOTES

1. *Passionate Politics*, New York: St. Martin's Press, 1987: 339.
2. For a full account see Suzanne Kehde, 'Engendering the Imperial Subject: The (De)construction of (Western) Masculinity in David Henry Hwang's *M. Butterfly* (1988) and Graham Greene's *The Quiet American* (1955)', in Peter F. Murphy (ed.), *Fictions of Masculinity*, New York: New York University Press, 1994.
3. 'How Europe Could Fail: Address to the General Assembly of the Council on Europe, Vienna, October 9, 1993', *The New York Review of Books*, 18 November 1993: 3. Havel contrasts 'the values of a civic

society based on the peaceful coexistence of different ethnic groups and cultures' with the 'idea of the nation state as the highest expression of national life'.

1

The Future of Nostalgia in Friedrich Schlegel's Gender Theory: Casting German Aesthetics Beyond Ancient Greece and Modern Europe

JONATHAN STEINWAND

Germanness is probably such a favorite object of the general essayist because the less finished a nation is, the more it is an object of criticism and not for history.

Schlegel

Nostalgia is a sort of homesickness, a pain (*algos*) or longing to return home (*nostos*) or to some lost past. The distress that inclines one homeward uproots the relation to the present by drawing one toward where one remembers feeling a sense of wholeness and belonging. The homeward pain of nostalgia presupposes that one's present place is somehow not homey enough. Nostalgia therefore is generated by a sense of having lost a wholeness only vaguely recollected save for the rare Proustian experience of '*mémoire involontaire*' or through the explicitly political intervention of aesthetic reification or simulation. The vagueness of the recollection often inspires the idealization of this past. Thus nostalgia summons the imagination to supplement memory. Because nostalgia necessarily relies on a distance – temporal or/and spatial – separating the subject from the object of its longing, the imagination is encouraged to gloss over forgetfulness in order to fashion a more aesthetically complete and satisfying recollection of what is longed for. Such a glossing over temporarily relieves the pain by casting a nostalgic image that has been purified, clarified and simplified in order to supplant the vagueness of the imperfect recollection through aesthetic intervention. In a sense the nostalgic image is torn from its temporal and spatial contingencies as it is imported into and appropriated for an alien time and space. The unpresentable loss, painful as it may be, is thus transformed by nostalgic recollection into a beautiful form. The fiction so loosened from the historical constraints of its original space and time offers a consolation allowing the master-project of modernity to stay its progressive course by orienting itself in relation to the nostalgic image it offers as compensation for the forgetfulness, homelessness and alienation of its guilt-ridden conscience.

It must at the same time be admitted, however, that this view of nostalgia as an imaginative forgetfulness perfecting memory with its supplement does not offer a complete representation. The truth hidden in the familiar saying 'absence makes the heart grow fonder' may offer a clue to the paradox of the recollective forgetfulness of nostalgia. The heart grows fonder not only because in the absence imagination gains a perspective from which it can perfect memory, but also because proximity has in its own way already distorted the relation. Both absence and presence distort relations: absence distorts with nostalgic aestheticization while unmediated presence distorts with familiarity. Thus nostalgia cannot be dismissed as merely an imaginative improvement on the lost past. Rather the possibility should be retained that nostalgia offers a compensation for the lost proximity by supplementing a memory invigorated through absence, which displaces forgetfulness brought on by the immediacy of presence. In other words absence makes the heart grow fonder in part because that which is most proximate comes to be taken for granted. Thus we have the conventional wisdom that 'time heals' and that 'getting a little distance' helps 'put things into perspective'. In short nostalgia ought not simply to be dismissed as a distortion of 'the other' because every reflection on where we are going and where we have been depends upon some distortion.

Nations make use of nostalgia in the construction of national identity. The myths of any nation appeal to the national nostalgia and encourage identification with such nostalgic images as the nation's 'founding fathers' or some 'golden age', or decisive events in its history and the culture of the people. Nostalgia is a particularly useful tool for nations at times of crisis, despair, urgency and transition. As Friedrich Hölderlin wrote in 1799:

In good times there are seldom any enthusiasts. Yet when man lacks great, pure objects, then he creates some phantom out of this or that and closes [his] eyes in order to be able to take interest in it and live for it.[2]

(48)

In good times such enthusiasts are rare, says Hölderlin. Thus we must conclude that it is in bad times, times when there are no 'great, pure objects' within grasp, that the appeal to the past through nostalgia is most effective, necessary and welcome. Such times are ripe for enthusiasts who find ways to channel the nation's nostalgia. To make nostalgia work for them, enthusiasts must close their eyes, they must forget their own bad times, their own lack of great, pure objects, in order to live for the better time they bring forth from their imagination and memory. Such enthusiasts appeal to the nostalgia of their times by addressing the sense of loss and longing for reconciliation which is generated out of the contrast between the confusions of the present and the idealization of vague recollections or presentations of the past. National identities are formed by the nostalgic freezing of a particular idealized moment which the enthusiast takes as a model to orient and anticipate the nation's future.

Nostalgia also imprints the history of engenderment. Gender differences are established and re-established through processes of identification. Just as national identity appeals to nostalgic idealizations of the past, so too does gender identity. Girls and boys of any nation are taught about gender identities by having their attention directed to selected masculine and feminine role models. Such models are produced, selected, and publicized by enthusiasts, emulated out of nostalgia, and usually oriented toward a future by some underlying political motive. Thus rather than looking backward with the reverence and preservationist inclinations of Nietzsche's 'antiquarian' kind of history, nostalgia does so primarily to address the needs of the enthusiast's own time. If Hölderlin is right that enthusiasts creatively address the needs of their own bad times by closing their eyes, then by paying attention to how nostalgia advances a critique of the contemporary situation in which it functions we will be able to attend to the collusion between aesthetic and political programs.

Friedrich Schlegel is famous for saying 'the historian is a backward-turned prophet' (KA II, 176; Lucinde 170 ('Athenaeum Fragment' no. 80) – translation modified). Such prophecy is what charts the course for the future of nostalgia. Schlegel is an enthusiast who senses his nation to have reached a point of crisis and transition. What makes Schlegel an enthusiast is that he recognizes the latent potential precisely *in* the fragmentation and chaos of his own time and nation. He contends that it behooves his critical age to close its eyes on account of its lack of 'great, pure objects' and to reach for the best of all possible phantoms it can imagine. As he writes in his first published statement that attempts to seize the post-Kantian moment for the sake of a German aesthetic revolution, 'our deficiencies are themselves our hopes: for they arise directly from the mastery of the understanding, whose gradual perfection knows no bounds' (KA I, 35; 'On the Limits of the Beautiful' 414 – my translation). Schlegel's enthusiasm is charged by his sense that his generation – the generation after Kant and the Enlightenment declare that 'time is out of joint' by establishing the progressive character of modernity in contrast to the organic cycle of antiquity – was born to set modernity right.

The German states in the last decade of the eighteenth century had witnessed the shift from enlightenment to revolution in neighboring France with a mixture of enthusiasm and trepidation. Since Winckelmann declared in 1755 that 'the only way for us to become great or, if this be possible inimitable, is to imitate the ancients' (4–5), the German-speaking culture was becoming conscious of itself in literature, philosophy and aesthetics, and was beginning to proclaim itself among the great cultures of human history. Schlegel and a few of his contemporaries were convinced that political reform would be effective only if it was founded on genuine cultural transformation or 'aesthetic education' (to borrow the language of the most influential statement on this subject). Winckelmann's 'backward-turned prophecy' encouraged the two subsequent generations of Germans to grapple with the Greek character and style in order to cast a national and cultural identity for Germany. The coupling of political and aesthetic ideology is thus deeply embedded in the history of German thought. The generations following Winckelmann revived the quarrel of ancients and moderns from the previous century but found in the arguments the emergence of a new self-conscious or philosophical discourse of modernity which gave the quarrel an unprecedented urgency for German culture around 1795.

Schlegel appeals to this emerging sense of urgency in forging a German national cultural identity. For Schlegel such an identity was to be cast by fusing together the nostalgic idealization of ancient Greek poetry and a critique of modernity with a philosophy of history. He accomplishes this fusion by associating femininity with the natural (but unenlightened) tendencies of antiquity and masculinity with the progressive (but artificial) tendencies of modernity. By ultimately wedding antiquity with modernity, Schlegel hoped to establish a national aesthetic imperative that would only settle for being at one and the same time wholly natural and wholly free. Thus Schlegel promotes a theory of gender roles that has been called the theory of 'complementarity'.

The emergence of such theories of complementarity in the latter part of the eighteenth century has been traced in German feminist theory. Following Karin Hausen, such writers as Barbara Duden, Silvia Bovenschen, Cornelia Klinger and Genevieve Lloyd have found a polarization of the gender spheres according to the specializations of the masculine in the public commercial world and the feminine in the private domestic familial sphere. This patriarchally constructed modern utopia, which takes a firm hold after Hegel and Napoleon, establishes femininity and the private familial sphere as a reservoir preserving a nostalgic idealization of a premodern intimacy with nature. For the women who uphold the idyllic utopia of a home designed to recreate men, the intimacy means hard work which they must do as if it were not work, art and toil at all, but rather mere instinct and 'natural love'. To come home to this beautiful world satisfies the man's yearning for harmony, peace and intimacy with nature. But the whole system depends upon keeping him at a certain distance from the sort of intimacy that (apparently without knowing it) the women of the household have through their dedication to their work. The men repair to this idyll and recreate themselves so that they can return and keep the modern world functioning with a private interest in upholding their own idyll and a public interest in their productivity. Thus the men are inspired to work hard in order to establish and maintain their own version of the modern utopia. The polarization of the gender roles was modernity's strategy for continuing on the path of progress and yet preserving in the family a 'reservoir' of a more 'healthy' and natural humanity, the nostalgic image of premodernity. At the center of this domestic idyll is woman as she is nostalgically produced: she preserves the lost wholeness; she can save modernity precisely by being excluded from society and history; she recalls a better, more human, more natural, more divine existence; she is a mnemonic image in which modern man can see his 'better half' reflected back, a reservoir, so that the alienation that modernity requires (and enjoys) does not totally devastate itself forever.

Several of Schlegel's contemporaries – among whom Schiller stands out – were also producing similar constructions of femininity and masculinity according to their complementary specializations in polarized spheres. But Schlegel's attempt stands apart from his contemporaries in two ways: first, Schlegel's Greeks are much more like those of Hölderlin and Nietzsche than those of Rome, French Neoclassicism, and Winckelmann. Schlegel's Greeks achieve a harmony with nature by developing their natural talents of presentation and by confronting the conflicts of their own inner and outer laws and duties to the point that they achieve the 'high style' of humanity. The second way Schlegel's version of the 'modern utopia' stands apart from those of his contemporaries is in the configuration of the relation between modernity and antiquity and between masculinity and femininity. For Rousseau, Kant, Humboldt, Schiller, and Hegel (and later on to Simmel, Scheffler, and Scheler – Bovenschen 24–43) the modern utopia was to be engendered through the polarization of the gender spheres; men were to specialize in modern cultural progress in the public industrializing world of work, while women were to tend the private hearth and uphold an idyllic retreat preserving the nostalgic idealization of the pre-modern (or ancient) harmony with nature. For Schlegel's contemporaries, these poles were to be kept strictly separate. Through such polarization modern patriarchy continues the tendency of medieval chivalry to put women on a pedestal so that through such idealization masculine courage, fortitude and imagination might find renewal and hope. Schlegel's model also preserves the nostalgic ancient utopia in the 'feminine'. But the young Schlegel was convinced that each pole could achieve its highest manifestation only by 'studying' its other. In other words Schlegel and many of his early Romantic circle insist that at least a certain amount of 'gender bending' or role reversal is essential in maintaining socioeconomic sanity and most of all a healthy and creative humanity. The early Romantic circle recognized more than other theorists of complementarity that the polarization of the gender spheres was an artificial arrangement implemented in order to further the progressive project of modernity. Such a recognition of the polarization of the gender spheres as a social construct marks this moment as rare in the history of engenderment insofar as the Romantic circle opened itself up to the possibility and the potential of women's autonomy as subjects, enthusiasts and poets in their own right. Even though such an opening for Schlegel is ultimately merely a self-serving patriarchal gesture resembling a moment in Hegel's dialectic, it is worth pausing over long enough to consider how Schlegel's program differs from and yet is ultimately complicitous with the modern patriarchal project of reappropriation.

From Schlegel's early work up to and including his work on the *Athenäum* (1798–1800) two central topics emerge that are relevant to this investigation: ancient models of femininity and the modern study of antiquity. As a part of his history of Greek poetry Schlegel shows a great deal of interest in representations of the feminine in Greek poetry and culture. Through such 'backward-turned prophecy' Schlegel hopes to hold up the Greek excellence found in Sophocles' Antigone (KA I, 57–8) and Plato's Diotima (KA I, 70–115) as a model for reconsidering modern failings. Schlegel frequently admits that his interest in antiquity is essentially for the educational value that study affords by allowing the inquirer to confront the foreign in order to correct the one-sidedness of the present moment and thus raise the human spirit to truth (KA I, 45–6). In the essay 'On Diotima' Schlegel proposes that there might also be a similar value in studying the history of the opposite sex. He finds examples in Greek culture which he holds up in support of his critique of the modern exaggerations of gender difference. Whereas the Greek spirit was directed toward the 'higher humanity' in both men and women, the modern spirit polarizes the sexes to the extent that each becomes a self-parody and forgets the 'higher humanity' which requires a harmony of what modernity splinters into 'masculine' and 'feminine' qualities:

> What is uglier than the overladen femininity, what is more disgusting than the exaggerated masculinity that predominates in our morals, in our opinions, and even in our better art? Indeed this corrupting way of thinking exercises its influence even on those artistic representations which are supposed to be ideal and on attempts purely to develop a concept of femininity. ... Even the power-hungry vehemence of the man and the selfless sacrifice of the woman is exaggerated and ugly. Only independent femininity, only gentle masculinity is good and beautiful.
>
> (KA I, 92–3)[3]

The classical ideal of gender difference endorsed by Goethe, Schiller, and Humboldt finds consolation in the contrast between politically active, striving men torn from nature by civilization, and domesticated naive women who unconsciously harmonize all they come into contact with. The Classicists found consolation in the way the nature-bound classical ideal of woman inspires the establishment of a peace among men. Such women are treated merely as means to this end and there is little serious talk of understanding between men and women nor any interest in what women might want or think or say – except insofar as they preserve the traditional pre-modern naive pious idyll of the beautiful soul. For Schlegel, on the other hand, humanity was to be elevated by drawing femininity and masculinity into a more intimate relation based on a more reciprocal rapport rather than driving in the wedge between the two ever more deeply.

Schlegel had hoped to find his ideals of 'independent femininity' and 'gentle masculinity' in Athens, his source for political, aesthetic and philosophical ideals. But Schlegel's hopes are dashed when he is forced to acknowledge that women were excluded from equal education and public life in Athens (KA I, 106–7) despite the examples of Antigone and Diotima (who, not incidentally, were already nostalgic images offered to Athens by Sophocles and Plato). Thus Schlegel begins to consider the possibility that the Greeks might not have attained 'the highest' in every aspect of humanity. Perhaps modernity might still be able to accomplish the ideals of 'independent femininity' and 'gentle masculinity' which are found in such literary figures as Antigone and Diotima on the one hand and in heroic friendships on the other, but which are not completely actualized in the Athenian state and its morals.

Schlegel's essay was inspired by and dedicated to Caroline Böhmer, who latter married first Schlegel's favourite brother and then his friend Schelling. The muse of the Diotima essay, in fact, because she was intimately bound up in the historical and political events of the revolution, embodied the feminist and humanitarian ideals of the French Revolution for Schlegel. For the young Schlegel the emancipation of women was a logical development of the progressive unfolding of enlightened reform – and it may therefore not be insignificant that his Diotima essay was published in what had been the Prussian forum of enlightened thought, the *Berlinische Monatsschrift*. Schlegel learned soon enough however that the establishment had other ideas on this subject. Still struggling to find a way to earn a living from his writing, Schlegel used his connections to be considered as a contributor to Schiller's *Horen*. Schiller's initial skepticism was based primarily on his preference for Wilhelm von Humboldt's treatment of sexual difference. Ironically Humboldt's treatment marks the culmination of the modern exaggeration of sexual difference that Schlegel had argued against. Whether or not he was motivated by the desire to earn Schiller's favor, Schlegel shifts his focus to the study of antiquity in general.

In the drafts and essays that lead up to what Schlegel considered his first real 'contribution' to the discourse of modernity, *On the Study of Greek Poetry*, Schlegel argued his case for the value of studying antiquity. Schlegel holds that antiquity provides 'the best refuge from the seductions or oppressions of the age' (KA I, 623). The 'authority' of antiquity has however fostered a tradition in which one professes the classical creed out of habit and does not even think to ask about the laws and principles upon which this faith is built. Schlegel negotiates his course toward the goal of overcoming both classicism and modernity by having it both ways: to restore Greek perfection without hindering modern progress.

By slicing human history in half and treating each half according to its respective philosophy of history, Schlegel concludes that while ancient natural Bildung[4] is a system of circulation, modern artificial Bildung is a system of infinite progression. By slicing history in half, however, Schlegel wants to show that these halves – though still whole in themselves and never quite symmetrical – constitute one whole. In other words he wants to show how the dissonance of modernity might be resolved into an even higher harmony. Schlegel invokes Kantian language to present his theory:

> there is a double sort of Bildung and thus also a double sort of History: a natural and an artificial Bildung dependent upon whether the presentational or the aspirational capacity gives the first impulse toward Bildung. ... The system of circulation is only possible and necessary in natural Bildung and the system of infinite progression is only possible and necessary in artificial Bildung while the two systems, as perfectly complementary concepts, correspond reciprocally to the most perfect one.
>
> (KA I, 631)

These two possible types of Bildung and history correspond to antiquity and modernity. The Greeks and Romans receive the first determinate impulse toward Bildung from their presentational capacity; the modern Europeans receive the first determinate impulse toward Bildung from their aspirational capacity. Thus, driven by nature, natural Bildung is impelled by an indeterminate desire or drive while, struck by freedom, artificial Bildung tends toward a determinate purpose (KA I, 230–1). Hence the natural Bildung of the ancients satisfies theoretical reason but, because freedom never quite fully takes control of nature, cannot satisfy practical reason (KA I, 631; 636). Conversely modern artificial Bildung by making freedom its creed strives in a way that appeals to practical reason but not theoretical reason (KA I, 631; 640). The task of satisfying both is the crisis opened up by Kant's philosophy and the central stumbling block before Hegel. Schlegel proposes his answer to the crisis as an attempt to wed the ancient system of circulation with the modern system of infinite progression in order to satisfy both (KA I, 631). Once they have been distinguished Schlegel emphasizes the complementary nature of the two systems and insists that they somehow be combined. If they are directly opposed, however, can they both be pursued simultaneously without compromising their respective principal tendencies? This is the problem that will trouble Schlegel over the next few years until he finds a temporary solution in the engenderment of this difference in femininity and masculinity.

At the moment of its highest enthusiasm and freest play of the natural human capacities, the Greek Bildung attains a maximum height and thus the Greeks provide a high 'prototype of humanity' (KA I, 637). For Schlegel the study of this prototype is of 'absolute value' for understanding humanity (KA I, 639). For the best of the Greeks and Romans – and in fact the Greeks and Romans as a whole – were almost 'superhuman beings, human beings in the highest style' (KA I 637). Thus

> the study of the Greeks and Romans is a school of the great, noble, good, and beautiful – a school of humanity: in such study we regain the free abundance, the fervent strength, simplicity, symmetry, harmony, completeness, which the ever yet crude art of modern Bildung restricted, mutilated, confused, disturbed, tore to pieces, and shattered!
>
> (KA I, 639)

Without yet going into a careful analysis of his notion of 'study' Schlegel has argued for its 'absolute value'. Bernd Bräutigam characterizes Schlegel's notion of 'study' as 'the hermeneutic process of recollecting what is one's own in what is past with the goal of gaining an action-oriented concept for universal history' (30–1). Such study requires taking the problematic constellation of the relations between antiquity and modernity, nature and art, and sensuality and spirituality together with a rigorous attentiveness to and consciousness of time. Schlegel suggests that Greek poetry in particular offers a body of material which we moderns might use as a sort of mnemonic image against which to criticize our own idiosyncrasies and begin to raise ourselves up to universal validity. This proper 'use' of antiquity's exemplarity is not a matter of mere imitation followed out of a sense of tradition and uncritical nostalgia. Rather mimesis needs to be rethought along the lines of Schlegel's idea of 'study'. Such a mimetic act for Schlegel is the attempt to grasp the Greek spirit or 'style' as a whole and use it to correct the deficiencies of modernity. Thus the study of antiquity offers criteria with which to judge the admirable goals of modernity's commitments to freedom, emancipation, and enlightenment. Through such study Schlegel hopes that modernity will be able to stay its course and yet restore the more human, more natural, more beautiful sentiments that are often trampled in the progressive march of modernity.

Modernity also has a contribution to make to the way toward a higher resolution. For although ancient Bildung offers a 'high prototype of humanity', it emphasizes for the most part natural humanity over free humanity. Hence modernity's artificial Bildung comes to the rescue by offering guidance toward a better future for humanity. Schlegel thus anticipates Habermas's assertion that modernity is inherently 'an incomplete project' (see KA I, 635–6; Habermas, 'Modernity versus Postmodernity'), for modernity holds on to the principle of infinite progression, the distant goal of which is 'unattainable' because it is 'infinitely great'. Schlegel concludes that while the Greeks provide 'the high prototype behind us', modernity projects 'the higher goal before us' so that we might move beyond ancient and modern and achieve an even better, more complete age in the history of humanity (KA I, 640).[5]

The imperative to study the Greeks developed in *On the Study of Greek Poetry* is further directed toward the overcoming of modernity by holding it up against the objectivity of Greek poetry. In this essay Schlegel formulates the 'aesthetic imperative' with extreme urgency. This urgency is both personal and political. *On the Study of Greek Poetry* can be read as Schlegel's audition to join Schiller's circle since one of the first things Schlegel did immediately after sending off the manuscript was to advertise his essay to Schiller in the letter accompanying his essays on Greek femininity recommended to Schiller by Christian Gottfried Körner and August Wilhelm Schlegel (KA XXIII, 261–2). The urgency of Schlegel's essay may therefore have had something to do with his desire to join Schiller's circle and reunite with his brother. With this in mind, *On the Study of Greek Poetry* can be read as an elaboration of the sixth letter of Schiller's *On the Aesthetic Education of Man*. But the project takes on a life of its own and begins to overtake Schiller's position – and its urgency may have a lot to do with this discovery of disagreement.

Urgency in any case saturates the entire text. But this urgency is not primarily a personal urgency. Rather it is a national urgency to address the modern cultural crisis. *On the Study of Greek Poetry* seizes its day in 1795 – probably drawn toward the turn of the century – as a crisis point in human history. The essay attempts to capture the enthusiastic energy vis-à-vis the recent political developments and revolutions in France and America (KA I, 356). At the same time it attempts to draw together Kant and Fichte's practical philosophy (KA I, 357–8), Kant and Schiller's aesthetic theory (KA I, 272; 357–8), and German classical study after Winckelmann and Herder (KA I, 358; 363–4). 'The time is right', Schlegel repeats over and over with increasing urgency as he counts off these favorable tendencies toward a better poetry which is coming into view on the horizon.

Although Schlegel had planned to restrict his focus to Greek poetry, his first rhetorical reflex to the title *On the Study of Greek Poetry* zeroes in on the word 'study' and launches into a complaint about the depraved state of modern poetry. 'Modern poetry has either not yet reached the goal for which it strives', writes Schlegel, 'or it has no fixed goal of any sort for which to strive' (KA I, 217). Thus modern poetry is characterized by dissatisfaction and yearning for completion, harmony and peace. The modern for Schlegel therefore is fraught with its own imperfection and thus fueled toward its perfectibility by nostalgia. Schlegel complains that modern art and taste have become so relativized that an 'anarchy' of style predominates, and no particular character stands out except 'characterlessness' as such. German poetry in particular offers a 'collection of all national characters of every epoch and every continent: only the German, they say, is missing' (KA I, 222). We moderns therefore – or at least modern Germans – live as if we were in 'an aesthetic junk shop' (KA I, 222) where everybody can find something for their every taste, virtue, and perversion. And yet the disorder of this 'aesthetic junk shop' might be said to resemble the ancient chaos out of which a world sprang into order (KA I, 224). So perhaps modern poetry is not hopelessly lost. Perhaps anarchy will become 'the mother of a benevolent revolution' (KA I, 224). Thus Schlegel considers his time to be at the moment of truth when taste will either improve for good or fall forever back. This is the 'decisive moment' when history will demonstrate which of the two systems, which of the two halves of human history is the stronger: the organic system of circulation or the artificially instigated system of infinite progressivity (KA I, 224). This is the 'decisive moment' when modernity will choose whether it wants to strive toward a set goal even if it is unattainable or if it wants to continue striving with no direction at all.

From out of the chaos of modern poetry however Schlegel discerns in the distance that

> there is also a better art, the works of which jut out from among the common lot like high cliffs from the indeterminate masses of fog of a distant region. We run across poets here and there in modern art history who seem to be strangers from a higher world in the midst of our depressed age. With all the power of their soul these poets want the eternal, and if they do not yet fully attain attunement and satisfaction in their works, then they strive just as mightily after it again. These poets arouse the most legitimate hope that the goal of poetry will not remain eternally unattainable.
>
> (KA I, 218)

Thus from the outset of his essay Schlegel distinguishes an authentic from an inauthentic modern poetry. Goethe is the leader of these 'strangers from a higher world'; he is this Greek amidst the barbarians. Goethe is the beacon of a new epoch for German poetry; he is 'the dawn of authentic art and pure beauty' (KA I, 260). And this is the 'decisive moment' when the authentic and the inauthentic modern poetry will fight for predominance over public taste and the future of modern art.

In order to sort through the 'aesthetic junk shop' and to separate the incidental from the essential, the authentic from the inauthentic in modern poetry, and also to understand the unity among them all, Schlegel proposes searching 'in a double direction: backwards toward the first origins of their emergence and development and forwards toward the ultimate goal of their progression' (KA I, 229). The result of this double strategy is that, in contrast to the objective poetry of the Greeks dedicated to disinterested pleasure in the beautiful, modern poetry can be characterized as 'interested'. In other words modern poetry is always put to some use, be it a philosophical interest in truth or a moral interest in goodness (KA I, 241–4).

Thus modern poetry after Goethe is caught in between the goals of ancient and modern, between circulation and progressivity, between objective and interested art, between 'the high prototype behind us and the higher goal before us'. This 'being-caught-in-between', according to Emil Staiger, is harbored within Schlegel's characterization of modern poetry as *'inter-essant'*. For if we take the word literally, if we separate the components of the word 'interested', we hear *'dazwischensein'* or 'being-in-between' (10). For Schlegel, this means that modernity had come to the 'decisive moment' in its history. Modern poetry in Schlegel's era is caught between the exemplarity of objective Greek poetry and the progressivity of the modern tendency toward an even higher goal.

Schlegel frames his discussion of the difference between ancient and modern poetry in a comparison between ancient 'aesthetic' or 'objective' and modern 'philosophical' or 'interested' tragedy. The fundamental point of this juxtaposition is that the objective tragedies of Sophocles obtain the 'highest harmony' while the philosophical tragedy, 'the highest artwork of didactic poetry', results in an 'irresolvable disharmony' (KA I, 246). Shakespeare's *Hamlet* exemplifies the latter, for here we see the 'eternal, colossal dissonance which infinitely separates humanity and fate' (KA I, 248) turn inward and play itself out within the character of the hero. Hamlet takes the place of Kant here and is internally torn asunder by the 'unlimited disproportion of his thinking and acting powers'. Thus Shakespeare with this presentation of a 'maximum of despair' stands beside Goethe (who also pays tribute to Hamlet in his *Wilhelm Meister's Apprenticeship*, also 1796) and anticipates the age of Enlightenment and the age of Kant in which Schlegel lives (KA I, 248–9).

And yet this 'dominion of the interested is surely only a temporary crisis of taste: for it must in the end destroy itself' (KA I, 254) since self-overcoming progressivity is the nature of modern poetry. But what then will become of poetry? It will either have to sink back into barbarism or it will with a 'sudden leap' spring into a new objectivity (KA I, 255). Here Schlegel problematizes the dilemma facing modern poetry and Bildung at the end of the eighteenth century, between Kant and Hegel. Since modernity is by nature progressive and its goal is sublime, it can never reach its goal and can always only approach it. But this does not mean that the impossible quest itself is worthless. For, as Schlegel asks (KA I, 255–6), is the provisional and preparatory approach not infinitely more worthwhile than sinking back into barbarism? And what if the natural 'catastrophe' (KA I, 224) is not so distant as it at first may seem? At least with a little preparation in the artificially motivated Bildung of taste, we will be in a position ready to ride the cutting edge of such a natural catastrophe. Or perhaps the gap between the infinite unattainability and the infinite striving for it will become so slight that a sudden leap may not be as great a risk as it now seems to be.

Even the ridiculous German predisposition to imitate may have a more positive side when it is seen as a preparatory phase on the way to a higher goal: for this fanatical will to imitate shows 'versatility' which is a 'forerunner of universal validity' and thus infinitely preferable to the national one-sidednesses of other European nations (KA I, 259). This German lack of national identity is for Schlegel a sign for hope. The Greeks themselves, according to Hölderlin (149–50) and Nietzsche (*Philosophy* 30–1), became predecessors primarily on the laurels of the strength with which they were able to organize the chaos of foreign influences and make free use of them. For Schlegel this is the point where Goethe's poetry rises up from the chaotic masses. Goethe excels at this versatility and holds it up toward the goal of objective beauty. Goethe 'stands in the middle between the interested and the beautiful, between the mannered and the objective' (KA I, 261). Put in the language of Kant's *Critique of Judgment*, Goethe brings taste to bear on genius. In fact artificial taste brings Goethe so far that his successors found it impossible to determine whether genius remains a natural capacity, a gift of nature, or whether it is produced out of the artificial desperation of taste.

But in order to bring about the 'aesthetic revolution' that is required, Goethe's spirit must be recognized and become predominant in the public sphere (KA I, 262) and a complete aesthetic theory based on 'objectivity' must become a 'public power' (KA I, 273). A complete and 'universal natural history of art' will aid this process (KA I, 273). And this means, of course, above all else a history and study of Greek poetry (KA I, 275). For the Greeks from Homer to the pinnacle of Sophocles and the decline back into the Alexandrian are the high prototype of all that is 'purely human' (KA I, 277). Here Schlegel pushes the point to say, 'Greekness is nothing other than a higher, purer humanity!' (KA I, 284). In classical Greece poetry was still 'the only teacher of the people' and the poets were the 'holy priests' who transmitted and interpreted divine revelations (KA I, 351).

Thus with Greek poetry and educated public taste as a guide (KA I, 316–18) modern poetry might be directed away from its tendency toward 'sublime ugliness' (as in the more inauthentic modern poetry) and disharmony (as in *Hamlet*) and directed instead toward 'sublime beauty' (KA I, 313). In other words Schlegel is searching for a modernity that combines the ancient art of the beautiful with the modern art of the sublime and equalizes antiquity's subservience to nature and modernity's artificially imposed mastery over nature. He finds a glimpse of this poetry beyond ancient and modern in Goethe.

The personal, national and cultural urgency of this text must have weighed heavily on Schlegel throughout the significant delay of its publication. The work was not published until the end of January 1797, by which time Schlegel's position shifts and the urgency can no longer be read in quite the same way, in part because Schiller had already capitalized on much of the public taste with his *Naive and Sentimental Poetry*. Nevertheless, the urgency for casting aesthetics beyond ancient and modern remains constant even after 1797. Only the recipe for the combination of circulation and progressivity is varied.

Schlegel never pulls the threads of his nostalgia for 'the Greeks' and 'the feminine' together in a convincing way that could pose a challenge to the modern utopia of polarized gender spheres which was taking hold in modern Germany. He was probably too caught up in finding his own niche as a grown-up author and critic of the world, which required that he more or less in one way or another buy into the masculine stereotype. Nevertheless Schlegel's writings between 1795 and 1800 are saturated with gestures that indicate that he is searching for an alternative to the polarized patriarchal model. For example in the 1799 'Letter on Philosophy: To Dorothea'

(KA VIII, 41–62) Schlegel repeats his call for a gentler masculinity and a more independent femininity by proposing that women, whose nature is more poetic, whole and classical, should study philosophy and modernity, while men, whose nature is more philosophical, divided and modern, should study poetry and antiquity. Such a complementary pedagogical program, according to Schlegel, would stay the course of history by using the advantages of both sides of all these dichotomies (ancient/modern, feminine/masculine, poetry/philosophy, nature/art) to bring men and women into a more reciprocal, intimate and complementary relation. Still, the complementarity in the letter to Dorothea and the *Lucinde* of 1799 harbors an asymmetry of relation that leans more toward supporting the modern utopia of Schiller and Hegel than had the more radical essay on Diotima where Schlegel insisted that 'only independent femininity, only gentle masculinity is good and beautiful' (KA I, 93). In these later works gender role exchange and an androgynous utopia are recommended to both genders for their pedagogical value: so long as they are young, masculinity and femininity ought to aspire to learning how to acquire each other's virtues, including the respective propensities for philosophy and poetry of each. In reaction against the polarizing gender theory of Weimar Classicism, Schlegel insists that both genders will benefit by practising gender role versatility rather than specialization. But once life becomes serious, once nature separates the mothers from the boys, the time has come in Schlegel's view for the preordained assignment of men to the public world and women to the private idyll.[6]

For Schlegel the end of the eighteenth century was the appropriate time for moving beyond ancient and modern without having totally to give up either one. In fact there has 'perhaps not yet been a moment in the total history of taste and poetry so characteristic for the whole, so rich in resonances of the past, so pregnant with fruitful seeds for the future' (KA I, 356). Because Schlegel finds the convergence of the study of the Greeks and the history of aesthetics indispensable to this remedy, he posits his program with urgency as a nationalistic opportunity; for 'in Germany and only in Germany have aesthetics and the study of the Greeks reached a height that requires the total transformation of poetry and taste' (KA I, 364). The time is ripe for Germany not only to surpass its European rivals among whom the French come closest to the Greeks (KA I, 362; 365), it is also the 'high vocation' of the age 'to recall the departed shadows of ancient greatness to a new and better order on earth' (KA I, 639) to rival even the Greeks. By distinguishing between ancient Greek and modern European culture, Schlegel tries to deduce what is essential to both. Thus by combining nostalgia for a lost ideal with a critique of present conditions, he hopes to project a future utopia oriented by 'the high example behind us and the higher goal in front of us' (KA I, 640). The strategy of engendering the relation between antiquity and modernity in the feminine and masculine spheres was Schlegel's solution to the national identity crisis of Germany at the end of the eighteenth century. By wedding the timeless and nostalgically ancient and natural harmony of the feminine with the enlightened and historically modern and artificial progressivity of the masculine, Schlegel was determined to forge a new national relationship between aesthetics and politics. By charting the course of the future of nostalgia in such a way, Schlegel wanted to start an aesthetic revolution in Germany.

In effect, however, Schlegel's 'solution' is more of a deferral of the resolution of dissonance, for what Schlegel imagines is that the feminine will preserve in its harmony the nostalgic image as a timeless refuge or reservoir for the future. In the end Schlegel's solution to defer the problem ultimately came very close to the version proposed by Weimar Classicism. The only difference is the pedagogical imperative that insists on a more reciprocal apprenticeship in relation to otherness. What made Schlegel so enthusiastic about the last five or six years of the eighteenth century was the convergence of an aesthetic and political urgency for German culture.

Ultimately Schlegel's gender theory differs only in degree from that of Weimar Classicism. Both project a nostalgic and timeless reserve of a more natural and humane order on to the feminine. Both channel the modern nostalgia for the loss that accompanies the march of perfectibility into the feminine sphere as belonging to and preserving a closer relation to nature and antiquity. We need only think of Goethe's Iphigenia, Hölderlin's Diotima, and Hegel's reflections on Antigone. At the same time this eternalization of the feminine permits masculine striving for perfectibility to be unencumbered by scruples over the loss that historical progress entails, which is nowhere more apparent than in the character of Goethe's Faust. For Schlegel, however, the place of women is not altogether closed off from the mediating artists. Although equality is denied, more of an effort is made to attend to the feminine voice.

Still, this feminine voice is heard not in the voices of women as much as in the nostalgic harmony of nature and antiquity, which women are taught to represent and preserve pure of temporal and spatial contingencies.

NOTES

1. KA II, 169; Lucinde 165 ('Athenaeum Fragment' no. 26; translation modified).
2. Hölderlin's statement represents a growing urgency in Europe after the French Revolution to connect cultural and political progress by reflecting on the dilemmas of modernity. Such reflection and philosophical discourse however was not limited to Germany. William Wordsworth made a similar statement in his Romantic manifesto, the 'Preface to *Lyrical Ballads*' in 1800. Wordsworth describes a poet as

    > a man speaking to men: a man, it is true, endowed with more lively sensibility, more enthusiasm and tenderness, who has a greater knowledge of human nature, and a more comprehensive soul, than are supposed to be common among mankind; a man pleased with his own passions and volitions, and who rejoices more than other men in the spirit of life that is in him; delighting to contemplate similar volitions and passions as manifested in the going-on of the Universe, and habitually impelled to create them where he does not find them. To these qualities he has added a disposition to be affected more than other men by absent things as if they were present; an ability of conjuring up in himself passions, which are indeed far from being the same as those produced by real events, yet ... do more nearly resemble the passions produced by real events, than anything which, from the motions of their minds merely, other men are accustomed to feel in themselves: – whence, and from practice, he has acquired a greater readiness and power in expressing what he thinks and feels, and especially those thoughts and feelings which, by his own choice, or from the structure of his own mind, arise in him without immediate external excitement.

    (264–5).

3. All translations from the *Kritische Friedrich-Schlegel-Ausgabe* (KA) are my own unless otherwise indicated.
4. I have chosen to leave *Bildung* untranslated in order to emphasize the central position this concept occupies in Schlegel's thought as well as in the Zeitgeist of this era. More than in the generations of Kant and Schiller, *Bildung* plays a central role in the terminology of Schlegel, Humboldt, Hölderlin, and Hegel. To translate *Bildung* into English would require using 'culture' at some points, 'education' at other points, or sometimes 'formation', 'cultivation', or 'development'. For

Schlegel, *Bildung* most often refers more to the process of education and culture than to a finished product or an institution.

5. Upon reflection, however, Schlegel will admit that since this 'infinite perfectibility' is by definition open-ended and depends on its incompleteness for its movement, the desire for a synthesis is rather hopeless, as he will say near the end of the essay *On the Study of Greek Poetry*. Such a recognition of the infinite project of perfectibility establishes Classicism and Romanticism according to the distinct artistic programs of promoting an art of completion and restriction on the one hand and an art of incompleteness, fragmentation and openness on the other (see, for example, Strich and Behler). Furthermore, the recognition of the necessary incompleteness of modern art from its very first self-consciousness of its artificiality prepares for the art of high modernism.

6. For a more thorough treatment see Steinward 272–323.

WORKS CITED

Note: KA: Schlegel, *Kritische Friedrich-Schlegel-Ausgabe*.

Behler, Ernst, *Unendliche Perfektibilität. Europäische Romantik und Französische Revolution*, Paderborn: Ferdinand Schöningh, 1989.

Bovenschen, Silvia, *Die imaginierte Weiblichkeit: Exemplarische Untersuchungen zu kulturgeschichtlichen und literarischen Präsentationsformen des Weiblichen*, Frankfurt am Main: Suhrkamp, 1979.

Bräutigam, Bernd, *Leben wie im Roman: Untersuchungen zum ästhetischen Imperativ im Frühwerk Friedrich Schlegels (1794–1800)*, Paderborn: Ferdinand Schöningh, 1986.

Duden, Barbara, 'Das schöne Eigentum: Zur Herausbildung des bürgerlichen Frauenbildes an der Wende vom 18. zum 19. Jahrhundert', *Kursbuch* 47 (March 1977): 125–40.

Habermas, Jürgen, 'Modernity versus Postmodernity', trans. Seyla Ben-Habib, *New German Critique* 22 (Winter 1981): 3–14.

Hausen, Karin, 'Die Polarisierung der "Geschlectscharaktere": Eine Spiegelung der Dissoziation von Erwerbs- und Familienleben', in Werner Conze (ed.), *Sozialgeschichte der Familie in der Neuzeit Europas*, Stuttgart: Ernst Klett, 1976: 363–93. Reprinted as 'Family and Role-Division: The Polarisation of Sexual Stereotypes in the Nineteenth Century: An Aspect of the Dissociation of Work and Family Life', in Richard J. Evans and W. R. Less (eds), *The German Family*, Totowa, New Jersey: Barnes and Noble, 1981: 51–83.

Hölderlin, Friedrich, *Essays and Letters on Theory*, trans. and ed. Thomas Pfau, Albany: State University of New York Press, 1988.

Klinger, Cornelia, 'Frau – Landschaft – Kunstwerk. Gegenwelten oder Reservoire des Patriarchats?', in Herta Nagl-Docekal (ed.), *Feministische Philosophie*, Vienna: Oldenbourg, 1990: 63–94.

Lloyd, Genevieve, *The Man of Reason: 'Male' and 'Female' in Western Philosophy*, Minneapolis: University of Minnesota Press, 1984.

Nietzsche, Friedrich, *Philosophy in the Tragic Age of the Greeks*, trans. Marianne Cowan, Washington, DC: Gateway, 1962.

Schlegel, Friedrich, 'On the Limits of the Beautiful', in E. J. Millington (trans.), *The Aesthetic and Miscellaneous Works of Frederick von Schlegel*, London: Bohn, 1860: 413–24.

——*Kritische Friedrich-Schlegel-Ausgabe*, 35 volumes, ed. Ernst Behler, Paderborn: Ferdinand Schöningh, 1958– .

——*Friedrich Schlegel's* Lucinde *and the Fragments*, trans. Peter Firchow, Minneapolis: University of Minnesota Press, 1971.

Staiger, Emil, *Friedrich Schlegel's Sieg über Schiller: vorgetragen am 13. Dezember 1980*, Heidelberg: Winter, 1981.

Steinwand, Jonathan, 'Mnemonic Images: The Gender of Modernity in Schiller, Friedrich Schlegel, Hölderlin, and Bettine Brentano-von Arnim', unpublished dissertation, Binghamton NY: SUNY-Binghamton, 1993.

Strich, Fritz, *Deutsche Klassik und Romantik oder Vollendung und Unendlichkeit. Ein Vergleich*, 5th edition, Bern: A. Francke, 1962.

Winckelmann, Johann Joachim, *Reflections on the Imitation of Greek Works in Painting and Sculpture*, bilingual edition, trans. Elfriede Heyer and Roger C. Norton, La Salle, Illinois: Open Court Publishing Co., 1987.

Wordsworth, William, *Criticism: Major Statements*, eds Charles Kaplan and William Anderson, 3rd edition, New York: St. Martin's Press, 1991: 256–75.

2

Writing Historically, Speaking Nostalgically: The Competing Languages of Nation in Scott's *The Bride of Lammermoor*

JANET SORENSEN

Walter Scott's *The Bride of Lammermoor* looks backward at a nation that is itself looking backward. Set just before or just after the 1707 Union between England and Scotland, the novel depicts a Scotland anxious about its past – both for what is slipping away unremembered and for what, once forgotten, uncontrollably re-emerges. The novel's anxiety, however, registers that anxiety within Scott's own present. Scott wrote *The Bride* between 1818 and 1819, a period of increasing social conflict, due especially to the post-war drop in wages and an emergent cyclical trade depression. These upheavals reached their high point in the 1820 Glasgow rebellion. This was a period of internal factionalism, and it comes as no surprise that, like the Scotland of 1819, the society depicted in *The Bride* is nostalgic for a past believed to be socially cohesive. In fact Scott invokes and constructs notions of a residual Scottish distinctiveness, a distinctiveness that could function as a means of warding off radicalism in the present. With a view of the rebellions taking place Scott warned of the importance of a distinct Scottish identity: 'if you unscotch us you will find us damned mischievous Englishmen' (P. H. Scott 84). Scott clearly supported the 1707 Treaty of Union between England and Scotland. And yet Scott also displayed weepy moments of nationalist sentiment at the passing of Scottish distinctiveness, evidenced for example in the British legal reforms of Scottish law.[1]

Scott's nationalism, then, maintained a tricky balance between assimilationism and independence. The nationalism he arrived at has been best described by N. T. Philipson (186) as 'noisy inactivity'. This type of nationalism insists on a cultural nationalism but rebukes a parallel official political nationalism. Yet in stopping far short of the trajectory from this cultural nationalism to a political call for a separate state, Scott's identification with this 'other' space is really an appropriation, his speaking it an act of ventriloquy. Cultural nationalism's heightened concern with the nation's past, a past specifically constructed around the details of everyday life, and the location of that pastness of Britain in Scotland form the basis for *The Bride*. Here Scott locates Scots identity within a feminized folk, linked to a consequently unthreatening past in desuetude. From this distance Scott can narrate a discourse of nostalgia – identifying, objectifying and reifying customs of the everyday, the private, and even the marginal to create a nonthreatening space of distinctive national identity. Constructing this space but withholding claims to its status as politically separate from England, Scott creates an idea of the ancient Scottish nation that comes to serve the modern British nation which is subsuming it.

It is precisely in the 'coziness', the containable 'heimlich' space created by this nostalgia, however, that the occult and frightening emerge. *The Bride* fails to control the past entirely. The nonthreatening space of a cultural nationalist language becomes instead the site of a reified history's uncanny repetition; these compexities are writ large as the text is ultimately unable to resolve the contradictions a nationalist discourse produces. These ambivalencies are embodied in two competing representational systems associated with two different temporalities. They are mutually exclusive yet interdependent; they are the fields on which these ambivalencies come to be played out in a nationalist discourse. In the inscription of elements of the everyday world into a nostalgic narrative of the nation, a reification takes place creating in turn an uncanny effect.

In 'recording' a history of the Scottish nation Scott invokes competing representational systems, one associated with ancient Scotland, the other with modern Britain. Scott genders these semiotics: the sign system of official history is gendered male and the semiotic of the 'other' marginalized history female. Attempting to merge the two produces contradictions. Neither the written, arbitrary and linear sign system ascribed to the Whig rulers of the new order nor the oral, iconic language of the feudal old order represents the world adequately, or in a way allowing complete control. *The Bride* turns to a nostalgic narration that attempts to incorporate the feminized sign system into an official narration of the nation. By incorporating this other space into a historical fiction Scott finally re-genders it male as he claims it for a distinct Scottish identity within the British nation. Yet the transformation that occurs when the Scottish oral folk culture is inscribed in a written history leaves a haunting residue.

The elaborate frame provided for the novel in its first chapter foregrounds the consideration of these two alternative semiotic systems. Here Dick Tinto, the peripatetic painter, and Peter Pattieson, a writer and the narrator of *The Bride*, debate the merits of their arts. Tinto argues that his visual, spatial, iconic medium of painting and emblem allows one to 'receiv(e) that instant and vivid flash of conviction, which darts on the mind from seeing the ... single scene, and which gathers ... not only the history of the past lives ... and the business on which they are immediately engaged, but lifts even the veil of futurity' (25). His representational medium is capable of immediacy, directness and an all-at-onceness he would deny to writing. It is also universally accessible as it depicts 'the symbols of good cheer so as to be obvious to all ranks' (15), illustrated in the case of the 'lively effigies' of a pub sign. Writing is 'mere chat and dialogue' (22) filled with encumbering 'said he's and said she's'. It communicates in an excess of words what could have been expressed in a single drawing.

Pattieson receives the information on which he bases the narrative of *The Bride* from Tinto in the form of 'loose scraps, ... where ... sketches of turrets, mills, old gables ... disputed the ground with his written memoranda' (26). Tinto's medium is figured both in his overlapping sketches suggesting the nonlinear, 'all-at-once' character of his medium, and in loose scraps suggesting its fragmentary nature. Like any fragment they point to a larger lost context of wholeness. Such fragments serve as the basis for the nostalgic national narrative. Pattieson, out of respect for his now-dead friend – an allusion to the outdated nature of the medium for which he argues – vows to attempt to incorporate that semiotics into his writing of *The Bride*.

Throughout the novel these two theories of representation play against each other. The terms of the debate would be familiar to any student of aesthetics in the eighteenth century. In such debates the understanding of the verbal sign as arbitrary, transparent and deriving meaning from its place in a linear syntax is counterpoised to an older understanding of the sign as 'natural', merging form and content, and therefore directly linked to the object it represents. As writing, the most obviously conventional medium, was increasingly understood to be arbitrary, other media such as painting, gesture and oration were viewed as 'natural'. While it was taken for granted that writing was the language of business and law, the alternative 'languages' represented in the other media became the language of the heart and sensibility, thus central to the discourse of nostalgia.

WRITING HISTORICALLY

The language of Sir William Ashton suggests the Enlightenment semiotics of the written sign, which regards the sign as arbitrary and linear. Such a view of the sign, developed, as Condillac had argued, through reflective distance, envisions a representational system over which its user has full control. This is the language of power because it gives control over nature. As David Wellbery has put it, the use of arbitrary signs 'necessarily implies an element of free choice: the sign is instituted at that moment when the distance achieved in reflection allows us to attend to representations over which we have free control' (19). *The Bride* highlights this closure and determinate man-made signification and represents this language as the hegemonic language of the rising Whig power.

Ashton, a lawyer, uses this language to authorize his power. He transforms the former Ravenswood dining hall into a library where 'long rows of shelves bend under the weight of legal commentators' (*The Bride* 36) and he is surrounded by 'letters, petitions, and parchments'. *The Bride* is set after the Glorious Revolution, and in this period of Whig ascendancy their new order has usurped the place of the old feudal order; its outward sign is voluminous writing, specifically that of history and law. Here Ashton generates more writing. When Ravenswood defies Ashton's honor and the honor of his state with a Scottish Episcopal funeral service for Lord Ravenswood, Ashton responds not with the physical show of strength associated with an older, martial order but by taking 'careful notes' and writing an account of the proceedings (38).

This prolix response varies from the scene of the crime itself. When an officer of the law attempts to halt the service, he is met by 'an hundred swords at once glitter[ing] in the air' (33). This image, along with the image of the funeral itself with its procession of banners and coats of arms, establishes an order of feudal display, a single visual and immediate frame directly juxtaposed to the temporizing language of Ashton. Analogous to these scenes are two models of power, one which sites authority directly on the body of the king, the other which diffuses power across the abstract and textual notion of a contract.

The Bride characterizes written language as manipulable in part because of the temporal and spatial distance believed to be implicit in writing and the lack of a physical connection between the sign and its object. By emphasizing the use of this language for purposeful obtuseness and deceit, the text highlights the disparity between official written language and the world it would convey. For instance, Ashton plans to confuse Ravenswood, 'justly thinking that it would be difficult for a youth of his age to follow the expositions ... concerning actions of compt and reckoning, and of multiplepoindings, and adjudications ...' (163–4). Part of the power invoked by this language is its inaccessibility to all but those familiar with its jargon. Although this language describes what should be intimately familiar to Ravenswood – his estate – it occludes.

Emphasizing the controlling and linear qualities of the written, the passages of legal language in the novel include the vocabulary of addition and accrual in words such as 'compound' and 'reckoning and compte'. The form of writing produced by arbitrary signs in syntax presents a version of temporality as accrual over time, an understanding of time as continuist and accumulative. Ravenswood refers to the time implied here in his reference to usury and the way it has 'melted away' his lands (165). This is a temporality modeled on the logic of interest; it is the time-consciousness of a ruling order which derives its power from the accretion of value over time.

The temporality of writing is linear. With the emphasis on syntax a linear temporality of progress subsumes the spatial. The figuration of Lucy's calm life as a stream before an impending waterfall and the images of the arrows that hit the bull and the raven all suggest this unidirectional, unstoppable and non-repeating sense of time. Each presents an image of forward movement towards inevitable consequences. Such images of time's movement clearly facilitate an understanding of history as moving in a progressive and coherent order.

The temporality of the language of a rising Whig officialdom embodied in the Scottish Ashtons, then, is not a temporality of custom, of past controlling future to the point of replicating the past, but of linear causality. The temporality inscribed within this language asserts a present causally related to but distinct from the past and leading towards the future. Moments of temporal proximity are theorized and narrated into cause and effect relationships. These relationships are abstracted into principles. Ashton adjudicates through such principles, which are uniformly applicable to various situations and operate outside specific temporal and spatial coordinates. In Ashton's assertions legal principle, in words highly abstract and seemingly divorced from local situation, supersedes 'antique custom and hereditary respect' (133). Lord Ashton, who rules through principle and not custom, is described as coming from a 'young' family; he has no claim to the customary power the Ravenswoods would have. The narrator refers to Ashton as a 'time server', but it is certainly not a feudal customary past that he serves. Instead he anticipates a future sequence of causal relationships he can manipulate.

The representational system of arbitrary linear language is necessary for the conceptualization of the nation's rational progression through history, a subject, as Duncan Forbes has argued, near to Scott's heart. Its ability to reproduce and chart time's movement seems to allow control of time. In *Imagined Communities* Benedict Anderson describes how the arbitrary sign enabled this particular temporality. Secular writing facilitated a temporality of what he calls the 'horizontal simultaneity' of the modern nation state. The horizontal simultaneity of the secularized arbitrary sign perceives time and history as an 'endless chain of cause and effect or of radical separations between past and present' (12). Importantly, it creates an imagined community of people – the nation – who share a 'horizontally' synchronic moment within this language, a community moving linearly forward through 'homogenous empty time'. This is the language in which the nation's 'official history' must be written. It makes progressivist history possible in its emphasis on meaning derived through linearity. Kristeva refers to this as 'linear' time, and sees it as gendered male. It is clear that in *The Bride* this time is associated with a public world of male power.

Scott's historical fictions speak with the authority and temporality of an official history. Homi Bhabha has focused on this particular 'narration' of the nation in his description of the 'pedagogic' temporality of nationalism. In the pedagogic temporality the present exists not as a singular present moment but as the 'rhetorical figure of the national past' (*Nation* 294)[2] which ultimately gives 'authority to a pregiven origin' (297). The pedagogic narrates an event or fragment from the everyday into a causal chain whose telos is the inevitability of the nation. The pedagogic temporality of nationalism assumes a 'teleology of progress' (294). Most significantly 'the people are the historical "objects" of a nationalist pedagogy' (297). Not narrating, they are narrated. They are altered from the subjects of the nation's agency to the objects of a national history.

SPEAKING NOSTALGICALLY: CLOSING THE GAP BETWEEN WORD AND WORLD

Yet Scott maintains an uneasy relationship with that official 'arbitrary' language. The use of standard English spreading throughout Scotland also highlights the post-Union blurring of cultural borders between England and Scotland. Such a disappearance and displacement of a Scots identity into a British one might make the notion of national characters and labels seem all the more arbitrary. What was clearly 'Scottish' one hundred years before exists only vestigially in 1819. And perhaps what is British or Scottish today therefore has no essential claim to that label. It seems however that Scott would cling to, even fervently produce, signs for a narrative insisting that these identities are not arbitrary.

In order to counteract the arbitrary character of the borders of the nation, articulated in an equally arbitrary language, *The Bride* offers alternative language systems. These alternatives take several related shapes. First there is the iconic language of the token. There is also the visual language of the pictorial and the 'natural' language of gesture associated with the novel's female characters. Last there is the oral Scots language, also feminized as it is linked to hearth and home. These languages, as we shall see, have a recursive temporality that arrests or encircles the linear narratives. What these languages share, as *The Bride* represents them, is a seemingly 'motivated' non-arbitrary representation and a rejection of the temporality of linear causality. In their claims to bridge the gap between word and world, they conjure the nation nostalgically.

The operation of the nostalgic is peripheral but indispensable to the discourse of nationalism. While official history is central to the nation's claims of legitimacy, these claims must always be troubled by the gap between the linguistic label 'nation' and the arbitrarily determined sections of peoples and lands which that label seeks to designate. How can the nation invoke a natural national subjectivity with such arbitrariness at its base? Here the work of Susan Stewart on nostalgia is revealing. She argues that nostalgia is produced in and by that troubled juncture between the 'real' and the linguistic label that would describe it. In that juncture in nationalist discourse fragments of 'native' language are inscribed in a narrative that would naturalize the relationship between word and world. This relationship, if now undermined by the writing and arbitrary contract of 'official history', was a relationship claimed to exist in the past. The nostalgic operation in nationalism attempts to erase that arbitrariness and insists on a non-arbitrary relationship between a particular place and people and their label 'nation'. It both laments a past time when these two fields were unified and seeks to re-unify them by an invocation of that past. Of course in nostalgia that motivational field is empty, absent, made possible only through the very narrative of nostalgia. But in its address to the 'lived' and affective, displaced to a mythic past where experience mystically mirrored – even joined – linguistic description, the nationalist nostalgic enables a suturing of the national subject in a way unavailable to official historical discourse.

This cultural nationalism necessitates a representational system which would mitigate, even deny, the gap between experience and expression, between word and world. The iconic symbol presents one alternative, nostalgic both because it conceals its conventional status and because it is outdated in the time of the novel. Consider for instance Ravenswood's 'heathen ceremony' of vengeance in which he cuts off a lock of hair and burns it in a fire, swearing, 'that my ... revenge should pursue enemies until they shriveled before me like that scorched-up symbol of annihilation' (*The Bride* 200). Here an actual part of Ravenswood, contiguously linked to his body, is literally burned, representing through resemblance and contiguity both his own annihilation and that of his enemies. The most important emblem is the gold coin of Lucy's and Ravenswood's betrothal. Alice, the old psychic whose entire perception of the world works in these ancient modes of resemblance and 'natural' language, uses the coin to warn Ravenswood of the dangers of pursuing Lucy. When the coin falls to the ground and Ravenswood stoops to pick it up, she observes that 'gold is an emblem of her whom you love; she is as precious ... but you must stoop even to abasement before you can win her' (194). This is a language predicated on connection to the body. Value is directly inscribed in the gold, the body literally stoops. These emblems, then, simultaneously function at a figural and literal level. It is this very coin which Lucy and Ravenswood break apart, implying the literal two parts of a whole, and then with direct authenticating proximity to the body wear next to their hearts to signify their vow. Both scenes make use of visual, motivated signs which blur the distinction between the figural and literal.[3]

This visual sign system refers back to an old feudal order's fiction of a motivated national body. If Ashton's signs of power are his writing and weighty tomes, Ravenswood's are crests, arms and escutcheons. They invoke the feudal display that once signified power through material signifiers connected to the body. The power of the ruler was directly mapped on to the body for display, and the spectators' consolidation within a social hierarchy seemed naturally, because visually, beyond question. Under the new order this social unity is now abstract, no longer visual, superseded by a sign system of power in the arbitrary writing of contract. The text asserts a nostalgia for that former blazon and its seeming ability to call up the nation 'naturally'.

Further, the novel enlists the feminized language of the hearth, gestural and oral, in a pose of opposition to the language of power. Based on presence, context and an immediate relationship between feeling and expression, it is not open to control and manipulation. This language presents itself, for instance, in its description of countless uncontrollable blushes, in Lucy and Ravenswood's pledge of troth with lip and hand. Blind Alice, the communicator in this language *par excellence* can read these cues; the steps of an approaching visitor or the vague faltering of a voice deliver a message more powerfully than any mere verbal language could.

This language is both gendered female and tied to the emotional economy of domestic space. While Ravenswood is capable of exerting a 'manly' control over his emotions, Lucy can only operate in a 'silent' mode of sudden blanches and blushes. These blushes summon 'naturally' the affections of her family. This sphere of domestic affection and communication is clearly non-arbitrary, almost extralinguistic. Acutely aware of the feelings which circulate around her, Lucy acts as a substitute mother and Lord Ashton at one point even introduces her as Lady Ashton. When her mother, who like Ashton is invested in the verbal language of power, returns to their estate, Lucy is marginalized, even absent, as her mother serves as both her surrogate and her masculinized oppressor. But when her mother is following 'state intrigues' in the cosmopolitan centers, Lucy sets aright the gender inversion of her mother, creating a sentimental model of the domestic. In this scenario, unity is evoked in an unmediated, 'natural' manner.

The blissful scenes at Wolf's-Hope offer additional examples of this domestic world. The scenes at the cooper's house, with two generations of women preparing a bountiful table, contrasts starkly with the space of Wolf's Crag, which offers 'security and not comfort.' At Wolf's Crag the mother is absent, presumably dead, and the only woman, Mysie the servant, is never seen. While the Wolf's-Hope home of the cooper is a scene of reproduction, featuring a christening, Wolf's Crag offers no such hope. There has been no inversion of the gender hierarchy here, for the cooper is 'maister and mair at home' (139). Ravenswood refers to such nostalgic scenes of folksy domestic peace as the hope for a nation that would free it of splintering enemies. He opines, 'As social life is better protected, its comforts will become too dear to be hazarded' (98). This domestic space of the everyday functions as a sign of cultural nationalism, which through affect and sympathy could suppress the antagonisms of class, gender and 'faction'.

The mode of description of Wolf's-Hope, locating it in a world of details of the everyday, has a direct connection to place. The catalogue of the appointments of the cooper's bedroom marks intimate detail, relaying that 'the bed was decorated with linen of most fresh and dazzling whiteness … [:] there mounted guard on the other side of the mirror two stout warders of Scottish lineage; a jug, namely, of double ale, which held a Scotch pint, and a quegh, or bicker, of ivory and ebony, hooped with silver, the work of John Girder's own hands' (271). This passage emphasizes locality, offering vernacular terms and measurements specific to the area. W. F. H. Nicolaisen describes the language and character of this fictional space 'as a forceful alternative to the often pale and stale English of officialdom. … [It is] a vital and vibrant landscape in which the folk who speak Scots and use folklore live in places that have names containing generics like heigh, brae, hope. … Tradition here is anchored to the ground and nurtured in the fertile soil of daily experience and ever repetitive hard work' (136). The direct link between the people and the land suggested in their geographical onomastics again asserts a word–world connectedness and a cultural particularity. The detailed spatial description of the land and the folk's relationship to it marks it as the space of 'the people' and the nation. We can contrast it with the implied inappropriateness of the 'Ashtons' occupying the Castle of 'Ravenswood'.

The spatially-oriented world with its detailed description of quotidian experiences and repeated ritual events is the locus of what Homi Bhabha has termed the 'performative' narrative of the nation, which I would want to link to the 'cultural nationalist' semiotic. In this capacity the 'nation–people ... demonstrate the prodigious living principle of the people as that continual process by which the national life is redeemed and signified as a repeating and reproductive process' (297). Like the cultural nationalist model of language, the performative invokes a temporality of cycle, repetition and custom. Yet in its manifestation of the 'living principle' of the nation this narration will stress the bodily, oral speech and a spatial mode of communication which emphasizes a 'present' moment in a nonlinear cyclical relationship to other moments. The particular details of the seemingly marginal elements of everyday life become the signs of that present and 'lived' quality. Bhabha draws from Bakhtin's notion of the chronotope in his identification of this process as 'national time becom[ing] concrete and visible' (295). Unlike the universal, arbitrary language of official history, cultural nationalism grounds itself in concrete, specific markers of time and history.

Kristeva has associated this spatial semiotic with women. She writes, 'when evoking the name and destiny of women, one thinks more of the space generating and forming the human species than of time, becoming or history' (190). The spatial, picturesque mode of perception in the novel is feminized not only in Alice's character but also in Lucy's. Whereas Lucy's masculinized mother inhabits a realm of action where she attempts to manipulate causal relationships, Lucy sings the merits of detachment from such a world. Hers is a space of reflection, recollection and fairy tales. In contrast to the temporality of linear 'ongoingness' of the pedagogical narration, this gendered spatial world suggests its own temporal coordinates, which Kristeva refers to as a temporality of repetition and of cycles (191). Although Kristeva essentializes this temporality, such associations can have ideological ends. In 'feminizing' the past, Scott attempts to defuse it. It is not clear that he succeeds.

If the formal written English of the Ashtons is inauthentic, the oral Scots speech, phonologically reproduced to mimic the sound of that language, bespeaks an unmistakably 'authentic' language of cultural nationalism, which is also feminized in the novel. Represented as the language of 'the people' it embodies a genuine 'natural' language. Consider for instance a section of Caleb's dialogue, 'I am wae ye suld hae stude waiting at your ain gate; but wha wad hae thought o' seeing ye sae sune, and a strange gentleman with a – Mysie – Mysie woman! stir for dear life' (*The Bride* 83). Departing from the clear linear syntax of the narrator and the noble characters, Caleb emits fragments of sentences. The words themselves are incomplete, missing letters and contracted by dialect. Caleb moves from one digressive track to another, circling rather than straightforwardly stating his points – a replication of an oral mode which seemingly abnegates closure. Here digression, 'dilation', is feminized in the figure of the servant. Caleb's is a quaint marginal dialect, yet the use of such language attempts to represent the real more closely. In addition, the implied presence between speaker and listener supplies a fullness of feeling which, *The Bride* suggests, is lacking in written language. And, unlike Ashton's deceitful written language, Caleb's 'oral' language as he attempts to conceal the lack of food and comfort at the now desolate Wolf's Crag is honest to the point of being humorous.

Scott spells many Scots words in standard English, tempering the remoteness of this world to make it safe for his readers. He constructs a 'cozy' world of the different by mediating between just the right amount of familiarity and distance. The need for the book's attached glossary to translate 'wae' as 'sorry' sadly, that is to say nostalgically, marks the distance between this disappearing language and the reader. This is the sadness that Stewart associates with the writing of oral genres, which 'always results in a residue of lost context and presence that literary culture imbues with a sense of nostalgia and even regret' ('Scandals' 135). Similarly the text's many quotations, adages, sections of ballads and proverbs exist outside of their original context, furtively pointing back towards it.

Yet in as much as it is servants and female characters who speak this language, it is not threatening. It has been displaced to a quaintified language of a marginalized people. The folk, then, speak the nostalgic language of the 'real' nation. That language is a perfect mapping of nature and language, an appropriate semiotic of the nation. Here the folk oral is fetishized precisely because it signifies doubly, both on a sheer semantic level and beyond it, in signifying the very authenticity which it hopes to evoke. In the signification of the act of pointing to that perfect mapping for which the text is nostalgic, it opens up and exposes the constructed nature of the perfect unity that is said to exist there.

Around the time of the novel's publication the Scots language was described in precisely these terms of unification. Scots was rapidly vanishing, remaining at most the private language of the home and hearth in early nineteenth-century Lowlands Scotland. The professional class still spoke Scots informally, but by Scott's time it was associated with the lower class, the elderly, informal oral contexts and domestic space. As such, a rising number of nostalgic nationalists like Scott bound it to a folk, a national identity and an irretrievable past. As Francis Jeffrey put it,

> [Scots] is the language of a whole country, long an independent kingdom, and still separate in laws, in character and in manners. … It is connected in [the] imagination not only with that olden time which is uniformly conceived as more pure, lofty, and simple than the present, but also with all the soft and bright colours of remembered childhood and domestic affection. All its pleasure conjures up images of schoolday innocence, and sports, and friendships which have no part in succeeding years. (178)

It is difficult to imagine a more perfect articulation of the nostalgic light in which Scots was viewed by the early nineteenth-century writers like Jeffrey and Scott. This passage situates the identity of the nation within language. It describes the unbridgeable distance between the past of that language and the contemporary world, and it unashamedly characterizes those 'olden times' as 'more pure'. Most important, it makes explicit the connection between these clearly nostalgic ideas and the domestic and feminine.

In a move similar to Jeffrey's, Scott in *The Bride* constructs a nostalgic space which also conflates the feminine, the domestic and the folk. Pattieson tells us at the novel's opening that Tinto 'became acquainted with the history of the castle' (*The Bride* 26) through an aged goodwife who lived in a nearby farmhouse. Various Scott biographies inform us that 'it was from his mother that Scott heard the story on which he based his novel' (*The Bride* v). Others tell us his great-aunt was the source.[4] In both cases the tale itself is linked to a private, domestic scene where a female relative orally – and compellingly – tells vernacular and marginalized histories. Lucy delights in the 'old legendary tales' too – and here she functions like any 'gudewife' in that she is a repository of the past, its stories, and a site of the nostalgic.

While working on *The Bride* Scott had lamented to Ballantyne, his publisher, 'Query, if I shall make it so effective in two volumes as my mother does in her quarter of an hour's crack by the fireside' (Millgate 194). Here Scott invokes a literal hearth and the 'crack' immediacy of his mother's language in contrast to his own lengthy, written volumes. He suggests that, compared with the official histories generated in the public realm, this private history, oral and feminine, is somehow more authentic. The anecdotal, and the 'living past' available to it, is linked to the maternal, a matrilineal heritage. Closer to the 'real', tied to the body's physical presence in the telling, this history offers an immediate, affective alternative to official history.

CULTURAL NATIONALISM'S UNCANNY DOUBLE

We have seen that the text genders female the spatial world of the detail, the language of affection, the oral Scots language of 'the hearth', and nonlinear temporality. This space of the home and temporality of repetition and cycle are clearly tied to the space and time of reproduction, analogous to the constructed space and time of the folk. Recall again the ritual christening and cozy hearth space of Wolf's-Hope. Lucy figures this semiotic with her knowledge of every bower of the Ravenswood estate and her expression through gesture and music. This world and its way of seeing and speaking, formerly outside the discourse of history, becomes a construction integral to Scott's historiography, a supplement to official history. These alternative languages and their customary cyclical temporality are posed against a masculinized spatial and temporal world of forced homogenization and inauthentic community.

The more authentic language that the novel posits effaces the compositional dilemma of the cultural history Scott wants to construct. It erases the distance between official history, permanent in its form and totalizing in the causality it maps across space and time, and the moment it attempts to record in writing. *The Bride* seems to relinquish official language, yet ultimately recuperates it. The very placing of that folk language – oral, iconic, immediate – within an historical narrative takes it out of the realm of the immediate that the novel would like us to believe the folk inhabits. The failure of *The Bride* ever to capture the 'authentic' realm of the folk points to the problematic of Scott's own compositional practices. Narrated by authoritative third person narrators, his historical fictions speak with the authority and temporality of an official history. The dilemma of the text is its need to represent the 'non-arbitrary', the immediacy of the everyday, within an arbitrarily constructed language of official history. This dilemma takes on a temporal dimension, as the text attempts to convey 'presentness' in a representational system that always comes after the fact.

We have also seen that the linearity of official history, the temporality of the novel, is encircled by the repetitive temporality of cultural nationalism, which places a restriction or impress upon the future, as in promises and vows. These verbal acts are represented generally as sinister – either in the tragic consequences of breaking vows or in the much repeated motif of revenge, curses, and the references to 'legacies' of poverty and vengeance. This recursive economy emphasizes an exchange of evils or wrongdoings, therefore promising in the future a repetition of the initial provocative act. It is a code of behavior which stresses an irrational inevitability of repetition, instanced in the 'hereditary temper' and bequest of misery inherited by Ravenswood. In order to assert the authority of linear official history, the repetitive temporality must be viewed as retrograde. Similarly, the spatial condensation of family history at the fountain is cursed for the Ravenswoods. Ever since an ancestor memorialized his mysteriously murdered 'nymph' there the space has been haunted. The once naturalized relationship between place, history and family is now a nostalgically narrated memory. And much of what is inevitably remembered and/or repeated is frightening.

Consider also the temporality constructed by the artifacts of the Ravenswood family, such as the crests, the portraits, and even the castle. These visual signs of feudal power encircle the linear narrative. This happens quite literally when Ashton, writing his account of the illegal funeral service, stops and looks up 'to see the crest of the family ... It was a black bull's head, with the legend, "I bide my time"' (38). Embedded in these physical and spatial markers of his-

toric time is a temporality of repetition. When Lucy's brother
Henry sees Ravenswood, he fears him because of his resemblance
to the portrait of his ancestor. The visual resemblance precipitates a
fear of repetition, where Ravenswood, like his ancestor, would
reclaim his castle from his usurpers by murdering them, saying, 'I
bide my time' (187). This phrase, a repeating fragment throughout
the text, suggests, not the linear causality which Ashton serves, but
a power based on the knowledge and performance of repetition
and tradition.

Any process of reification, which is what this construction of the
folk and the marking of space and emblem surely is, suppresses
alternative histories. *The Bride* stages these alternative histories as
malevolent forces that, once released, inject catastrophe into the
harmonized cultural space. Alice and her fellow cummers, rumored
to be witches, for instance, function as a shadowy double of reified
feminized language. In the private space of her home Alice and her
fellow gossips receive information through oral tales and attain
power that way. They speak in the broad Scots language which had
been associated with the safe, intimate world of the hearth, and in
spells and adages – a language of prediction and an invocation of
repetition. Their semiotic also opposes the arbitrary linear language
of the new order. Yet their space and language are far from the
nostalgia which the text constructs in folk. In the case of the
cummers, the identification of the oral and the iconic languages
with the feminine proves highly treacherous. The cummers are
'ghastly' and are guilty of 'real crimes under imaginary witchcraft'
(298). When Alice warns Ravenswood to stay away from Lucy and
prophesies his destruction if he stays with her, there is little deferential about her delivery which would make it available for a nostalgic depiction of the old world. This is an address which disobeys
social rules, as the folk woman asserts her superior knowledge over
that of the aristocratic man.[5] Social interaction between the folk and
gentry begins to exceed the comfortable hierarchic bounds
constructed by, and necessary to, the nostalgic.

A similar inversion takes place when Lady Ashton employs Alsie
Gourlay to break Lucy's emotional attachment to Ravenswood.
Gourlay uses mock tenderness to malignant ends, destroying Lucy.
Here the language, the temporality and the affective world of the
nostalgic metamorphose into the tools and space of destruction,
working against the motif of reproduction. Part of what is fearful in
the witches is their gendered control of reproduction and their

choice, given that control, to destroy. In *Letters on Demonology and Witchcraft* Scott describes this as one of the chief powers attributed to witches: 'our ancestors believed' witches could 'destroy human lives, waste the fruits of the earth, or perform feats to alter the face of Nature' and that they had the power to 'rais[e] tempests to ravage the crops of their enemies, … spread pestilence among cattle; infect and blight children' (Scott, *Letters*, 56; 67). Here fertility and conventional notions of the feminine are destroyed.

If the cummers derive their power from gossip and knowledge of private tales, they also achieve power through their ability to read the 'prose of the world', interpreting omens in the natural world, instanced in Alice's abilities to perceive 'extra-verbally'. This world/word coherence, the celebrated semiotic model of cultural nationalism, now takes on malignant overtones. Scott describes this ability in *Letters on Demonology*, asserting that before the Fall world and word corresponded in perfect and apparent harmony, but post-Fall, it is only witches who are able to read the world in this way. He suggests as one example the attempt to prophesy the future by the flight of birds. Ultimately however this attempt to read and use physical objects takes the form of a charm or a fetish, as Scott compares these 'natural signs' to the 'senseless block a heathen worships'. *The Bride*'s own construction or a feminized/ folk space and time of the nation is itself an enactment of the fetish, wanting to impute *natural* meaning and power to *constructed* signs.

How can we account for the text's ambivalence, where the constructed familiarity of the nostalgic brushes against an alternative, double space that speaks the same language but inverts it into the unfamiliar and frightening? The worlds of the witches and of the Ravenswoods are both spaces of terror. I would like to describe this terror as the uncanny double produced by nostalgia. Freud describes the uncanny effect as being 'produced when the distinction between imagination and reality is effaced, as … when a symbol takes over the full functions of the thing it symbolizes' (244). This is analogous to the operation of the nostalgic, especially if we recall the gap between word and world that the nostalgic wants to fill and the actual absence of the 'real' it claims to symbolize. We will not be too far off track to perceive the development of national identity through the nostalgic – with its emphasis on the constructed (reified) spatial details of the folk and their oral language – as contributing to the uncanny effect. Nostalgia reifies the 'everyday' experience of the folk. It inscribes everyday customary practices in a narrative of a non-arbitrary 'natural' national unity which is actually non-existent. The uncanny might emerge in this operation – as the familiar is made alien in its inscription into nostalgia, as the subject is made object, there is every chance, in fact necessity, of it reappearing as a ghostly, *unheimlich* double.[6]

Freud defines the uncanny as 'that class of the frightening which leads back to what is known of old and long familiar' (220). Identity, and the nostalgic narrative of the nation's identity, are constructed through repetition, drawing from and constructing customary cultural practices. Freud links the uncanny, that which is familiar and cozy yet frightening, to the doubling and repetition that form the basis of identity. Consider the repetition implicit in traditionalism. However, in the performative temporality of the nation that Bhabha describes, this double must be surmounted, or at least concealed, in the process of renewal and the performance of a 'lived' present. Further the linear, non-repeating time of pedagogic temporality also suppresses this notion of cyclical repetition. This double that had been surmounted reappears then, taking the form of involuntary repetition, 'fateful and inescapable' (Freud 237). Ravenswood's sense that his every movement in the present or future is doomed to repeat ancestral actions suggests that the attempt to integrate past and present, ancient and modern, and their opposing sign systems and models of authority is not entirely controllable. To put it simply: how can Scott draw upon the ancient ways and rivalries of the feudal clans without returning to the ruinous rivalry; how does one purchase the libidinal pleasures of atavistic repetition without its disastrous consequences?

That double, 'originally an insurance against the destruction of the ego ... an assurance of immortality', becomes when that initial stage is surmounted 'the uncanny harbinger of death' (Freud 235). Most horrifying about the uncanny is its threat of regression to the period before identity. It is 'a regression to a time when the ego had not yet marked itself off sharply from the external word and from other people' (236). It is the horror of recognizing the constructedness of nostalgia – the realization that the narration of cultural identity is arbitrary. Located within the repetition which constructs national identity, then, is the spectral horror of nonidentity, the reality of its fictional constructedness. This is the horror of the 'unmarked grave' such as the one Lucy receives, the decayed and unreadable grave stones of Ravenswood's relatives, and finally the unchartable quicksand of the Kelpie Flow which sucks Ravenswood into an undifferentiated liquid earth.

Amongst this group whose fate ends in loss of identity, Lady Ashton might be said to have the last word, in the form of her 'splendid marble monument [which] records her name, titles, and virtues, while her victims remain undistinguished by tomb or epitaph', the final note of the novel (*The Bride* 334). Inscribed into the future in the permanent language of writing in stone, hers is not the horror of the unmarked grave. Yet neither is it the future-oriented power of a 'textual' model. The writing of the epitaph is fragmentary, linked to one particular time and space, and is therefore non-reproducible. Incapable of initiating dialogue, its carved phrases can only be repeated. The novel suggests that, despite being 'male-identified', as a woman Lady Ashton could never finally master textual power. Abnegating her own 'feminine' qualities of the private sphere and destroying her daughter, who might have carried on such traditions, Lady Ashton is held entirely to blame by the novel. In fact the cummers describe her as the most successful witch of all.

* * *

While Scott's attempt to rein in the oral and spatial might leave echoes of their alternative temporality, their ultimate signification is within a narrative of nostalgic nationalism.[7] This resonance of the oral might be figured, oddly, in the final image of Alice's ghost, whose lips move while her message cannot be heard: the 'original' signification is unknowable, unavailable as Scott constructs it in his novel *The Bride*.

These alternative modes of perception and communication are re-presented as alternatives to the factional Whig order the text constructs in order to oppose. If it is true however as Robert Crawford has argued, that 'Scott's novel (his novels, in fact) is about the construction of a new, culturally eclectic unity – Great Britain – but it is also about the need to preserve the cultures within that unity' (130), the terms of that preservation are highly suspect.[8] While Scott constructs signs of a distinctive culture in the face of a homogenizing official culture, his narration constructs this alternative culture as homogeneous. In doing so the text attempts to resolve contemporary anxieties both about social divisiveness and about the loss of identity. The establishment of a fictional, nonthreatening Scots identity eliminates social division and real difference. That residue of difference, though weak, remains within the space of the novel because the signs and signifying practices of difference are made familiar through Scott's linear narration. Emptied of the signification of their own space and time, they are ghosts, haunting the text. Their reinscription in a linear narrative makes them safe for a nostalgic narrative of a distinct Scottish identity, small and manageable, a diminutive adjunct to England under the auspices of a British nation.

Scott constructs a history out of the oral fragments, ballads and tales. He appropriates an increasingly marginalized oral language, a rapidly disintegrating folk culture and a spatial/iconic semiotic associated with the past. It is that relegation to the past, the characterization of these cultural practices as residual, which allows them to be invoked and displayed without threat to a rising British national identity. Linking them to a feminized domestic sphere is a parallel move meant to render these cultural activities safe. In doing so, Scott re-appropriates the logic of succession. The Bride, at the center of the family and at the center of the history, becomes monument – the 'living' monument of an infinitely reproducible text. She does not reproduce, but is reproduced. She does not narrate but is narrated into a nostalgic narrative that reifies a vestigial oral folk world as it sites a modern Scottish–British nationalism there.

NOTES

1. Lockhart's biography, for instance, describes a scene after an 1806 meeting of the Faculty of Advocates over changes in the administration of justice:

    > Mr. Jeffrey and another of his reforming friends ... would willingly have treated the subject-matter of the discussion playfully. But his [Scott's] feeling had been moved to an extent far beyond their apprehension: he exclaimed, 'No, no – 'tis no laughing matter; little by little, whatever your wishes may be, you will destroy and undermine, until nothing of what makes Scotland Scotland shall remain.' ... Mr. Jeffrey saw tears gushing down his cheek – resting his head until he recovered himself on the wall of the Mound.
    >
    > (P. H. Scott: 70)

    In this sentimental expression of nationalism, Scott turns to the ideologically marked Mound as sanctuary, with its direct link to a Scottish space and Scottish identity, producing an overdetermined sign humorous in its excessiveness.

2. I draw from Bhabha's article in my analysis of pedagogic and performative temporalities. Bhabha sees these temporalities as gendered, but fails to explore how and why in detail.

3. I should point out here, in anticipation of my later argument, that the emblem and symbol are themselves fetishizations. In my use of the term 'fetish' I have in mind Marx's description of the fetish, as 'a definite social relation between men, that assumes, in their eyes, the fantastic form of a relation between things' (72).

4. Introduction to *The Bride of Lammermoor* (Oxford: Oxford UP, 1991).

5. Tzvetan Todorov maintains that 'the function of the supernatural is to except the text from the action of the law, and thereby to transgress that law' (159). This might be analogous to the 'transgressions' of Alice in this passage. *The Bride*, however, recuperates these supernatural incidents as uncanny moments, which I shall discuss below.

6. Instead of locating this process within the logic of the supplement, as Bhabha eventually does, I would like to think of it in terms of the fetish. This operation is more socially and culturally specific, and describes the doubleness that results when customs and language are narrated into the nostalgia of nationalism.

7. Katie Trumpener dislodges Scott from his singular position as purveyor of 'historical explanation' and re-situates him in an especially rich context of 'alternative forms of historical explanation'. At one point she counterpoises Scott, and his textualist antiquarianism (his extensive framing and footnoting of his texts), to contemporary writers who combine the gothic novel with annalistic history. The gothic elements of *The Bride* place it nearer to the practice of these alternative writers.

8. The arguments of my paper should make clear my difference with Crawford's assertion that Scott's 'linguistically daring multiculturalism was his greatest achievement' (133).

WORKS CITED

Anderson, Benedict, *Imagined Communities*, London: Verso, 1987.

Bhabha, Homi K., 'DissemiNation: Time, Narrative, and the Margins of the Modern Nation' in Homi K. Bhabha (ed.), *Nation and Narration*, London: Routledge, 1990.

Crawford, Robert, *Devolving English Literature*, Oxford: Clarendon Press, 1992.

Freud, Sigmund, *The Standard Edition of the Complete Psychological Works of Sigmund Freud*, trans. and ed. James Strachey, vol. 17, London: The Hogarth Press Ltd, 1978.

Jeffrey, Francis, *Contributions to the Edinburgh Review*, quoted in Philipson 'Nationalism'.

Kristeva, Julia, *The Kristeva Reader*, ed. Toril Moi, New York: Columbia University Press, 1986.

Marx, Karl, *Capital*, vol. 1, trans. Samuel Moore and Edward Aveling, New York: International Publishers, 1974.

Millgate, Jane, *Walter Scott: The Making of the Novelist*, Toronto: University of Toronto Press, 1984.

Nicolaisen, W. F. H., 'Scott and the Folk Tradition' in Alan Bold (ed.), *Sir Walter Scott: The Long-forgotten Melody*, London: Vision Press Ltd, 1983.

Philipson, N. T., 'Nationalism and Ideology' in J. N. Wolfe (ed.), *Government and Nationalism in Scotland*, Edinburgh: Edinburgh University Press, 1969.

Scott, Paul Henderson, *Walter Scott and Scotland*, Edinburgh: William Blackwood, 1981.

Scott, Walter, *The Bride of Lammermoor*, preface W. M. Parker, London: J. M. Dent and Sons, 1991.

—— *The Bride of Lammermoor*, Oxford: Oxford University Press, 1991.

—— *Letters on Demonology and Witchcraft*, London: George Routledge and Sons, 1885.

Stewart, Susan, 'Scandals of the Ballad', *Representations* 32 (1990): 134–54.

Todorov, Tzvetan, *The Fantastic*, Cleveland: Case Reserve University Press, 1973.

Wellbery, David, *Lessing's Laocoon: Semiotics and Aesthetics in the Age of Reason*, Cambridge: Cambridge University Press, 1984.

3

From Nation of Virtue to Virtual Nation: Washington Irving and American Nationalism

WALTER SONDEY

Washington Irving (1783–1859) began his literary career in the midst of the national identity crisis prompted by the transition from Federalist republicanism to Jeffersonian democracy. During the first decade of the nineteenth century Americans found themselves at odds over conflicting elitist and populist, public and private conceptions of the masculine persona representative of American nationality. On the one hand conservatives advocated an elitist conception of American character exemplified by the publicly virtuous legislator typical of classical republicanism. Democrats on the other hand advocated a popular conception of national character exemplified by the private liberal–democratic individual. The basic difference between these two personifications may be summed up as that between a corporatism that emphasizes duty to station and hierarchy over individual interests, and an individualism that emphasizes social mobility and self-interest over duty to social and political institutions. In *The Letters of the Republic* Michael Warner notes that the eventual ascendance of liberal democracy prompted the development of the bourgeois domestic character typical of modern American nationalism:

> Modern Nationalism is more at home. It constructs 'Americanness' as a distinctive but privately possessed trait. It allows you to be American in the way you tailor your coat, or the way you sing, or the way you read a book. It does not insist that you regard such activities as public, virtuous actions. I speak of a

modern nationalist imaginary to emphasize that it requires your
public self imagery to develop in a private sphere.

(149)

My aim, insofar as this nationalist imaginary is of a literary nature,
is to analyze how Irving taught his readers to experience national
identity as a matter of reading a book. However in doing so I will
argue that such a nationalism is more usefully discussed as a publicly developed representation that regulates the perception of self
in a private sphere that consists of domestic life and individual
taste or sensibility. More specifically I will argue that Irving was
the first American author to realize that the productions of the literary press, particularly sentimental literature, constituted the
primary means to regulate the nation's self-image. In other words
his books demonstrate how the apparently moribund values of
American conservatism might achieve a renewed influence over
bourgeois individuals if distributed in a capillary fashion via the
press and figured in terms of the domestic sentimentality associated with the private character of liberal democracy.

An examination of the changing role that nostalgia plays in two
of Irving's earliest publications offers an unparalleled opportunity
to trace the various purposes and circumstances that influenced the
formation of the conservative or genteel strain of American nationalism that Irving pioneered. In *Salmagundi* (1807–8), a magazine of
social and political satire, Irving employs nostalgia simultaneously
to mourn and lampoon the decline of conservatism from a socio-
political movement of national scope to a merely private disposition. There the public character of conservatism appears reduced to
the nostalgic figure of an aging Federalist patriarch limited in
power to the personal tastes and authority he exercises within the
confines of family life. It is not until the publication of *The Sketch
Book* (1819), a collection of short stories, literary criticism and travel
essays, that Irving demonstrates how nostalgia and patriarchal domesticity may be used to represent conservatism as a vital influence
upon national character. In this case, rather than sponsoring
mourning among conservatives for the lost public aspects of
Federalist character, his work promotes a desire among liberal democrats to affiliate themselves with it on a private basis. The result
is a literary mode of affiliation that links readers to a textual or
virtual society whose substance is the commonly held desire for a

genteel sensibility that appears as if it must be recovered from the past. In short, by showing how Irving learned to use nostalgia to create desire for a patriarchal representation of domesticity, I will demonstrate that his genteel nationalism provided American conservatism with the Trojan Horse it needed to carry its values into the bourgeois private sphere and regain there as a matter of cultural authority the influence it had lost in the public sphere.[1]

Like many conservatives during the Jefferson administration (1800–8), Irving believed that a hierarchical social order promoting class deference constituted the substance of republican national character and the essence of the public interest. Accordingly he believed that it was the personal duty of virtuous republican citizens and legislators to use national government to maintain that order and prevent the disorderly effects of the laissez-faire progressivism favoured by democrats. Indeed it was Irving's namesake, George Washington, who personified the paternalistic public character that conservatives hoped to institutionalize in the national government and from there impress upon society at large. However, the reelection of Jefferson in 1804 demonstrated that such political paternalism had poor prospects given the social and economic ambitions of the American electorate. Conservatives thus had little choice but to concede the hopelessness of promoting a 'republican' social and political character by means of national government.

In *Salmagundi* Irving attacks representative democracy for destroying the political aspects of republican character, namely the paternalistic rule of those elite few whose property, social standing and leisure allowed them the independence and education needed to serve the public good. He complains that in Jefferson's 'mobocracy' any virtuous candidate 'who possesses superior talents … will always be sacrificed to some creeping insect who will prostitute himself to familiarity with the lowest of mankind' (193). Such corrupt candidates, he continues, 'by administering to [the people's] passions, for the purposes of ambition' will ultimately 'convince them of their power' and thereby make government an instrument of popular interests (195). As the mixture of bestial, sexual and economic metaphors suggests, Irving assumes that democratic candidates have abandoned the cause of reason and morality: they have rejected the rational deliberation and paternalistic administration of the public good (political virtue) in order to give voice and power to the passing desires of an ignorant majority.

Other conservatives, however, trying to be less pessimistic about the prospects of preserving republican values, looked toward the voters for help. In an essay titled 'Phocion', Fisher Ames, a leading Federalist congressman during the Jefferson administration, raises the hope that the virtuous members of the electorate may yet remove the democrats from office. He bases this hope on the assumption that there still exists a sufficient number of voters who 'reverence' the transcendent good of social hierarchy, particularly those 'customs and institutions we derive from our English ancestors' (178). However, the affection among the national electorate for the elitist social institutions and deferential political relations found mainly on the long-settled east coast proved quite limited compared to that for representative democracy and laissez-faire liberalism.[2] Consequently Ames admits that a return to republicanism is in fact unlikely, a view to which he gives pointed expression in an 1805 essay titled 'The Dangers of Liberty'. There, after noting that the republican character of Rome resulted from a 'political virtue' of its people, he turns to the issue of American character: 'Is there any resemblance in [Roman virtue] to the habits and passions that predominate in America? Are not our people wholly engrossed by the pursuit of wealth and pleasure?' He then observes that 'Though grouped together into a society, the propensities of the individual still prevail; and if the nation discovers the rudiments of any character, they are yet to be developed' (*Works* 412–13). As a result, Ames concludes, the nation is 'descending from a supposed orderly and stable republican government into a licentious democracy, with a progress that baffles all means to resist' (429).

In *Salmagundi* Irving addresses the decline of conservative fortunes in his description of Christopher Cockloft, a nostalgic old Federalist whose disgust with liberal democracy drives him to retreat into his ancestral home, Cockloft Hall. There he indulges his 'propensity to save every thing that bears the stamp of family antiquity' (132–3) and attempts to create a refuge free from modern influence where he can preserve the 'little vivid spark of toryism which burns in a secret corner of his heart' (134). But even at home Cockloft must fend off the inroads of parvenu styles that threaten the English and colonial tastes that attest to the historical legitimacy of his character:

The Miss Cocklofts have made several spirited attempts to introduce modern furniture into the hall, but with very indifferent success. Modern *style* has always been an object of great annoyance to honest Christopher, and is ever treated by him with sovereign contempt, as an upstart intruder. It is a common observation of his, that your old-fashioned substantial furniture bespeaks the respectability of one's ancestors, and indicates that the family has been used to hold up its head for more than the present generation; whereas the fragile appendages of modern style seemed to be emblems of mushroom gentility, and to this mind predicted that the family dignity would moulder away and vanish with the finery thus put on of a sudden. The same whim-wham made him averse to having his house surrounded with poplars, which he stigmatizes as mere upstarts, just fit to ornament the shingle palaces of modern gentry, and characteristick of the establishments they decorate.

(241)

Ironically, the use of domestic nostalgia to establish a standard of taste and to transform the illegitimacy of liberal–democratic character also highlights the historical failure of American conservatism. As Irving's satirical tone suggests, Cockloft's nostalgia is ridiculous insofar as it displaces criticism of liberal democracy on to taste and reduces what had been a momentous social and political struggle over national character to a contest of class sensibilities within the home. Thus his struggle to exorcize both liberal tastes and feminine influence from Cockloft Hall portrays a conservatism so socially and politically marginalized that it must retreat to the domestic scene and displace women from their traditional sphere of influence.

Nonetheless it would be incorrect to assume that Irving's satirical treatment of Cockloft implies a thorough detachment from the elitist values he represents. Prior to this passage Irving advises the reader to look kindly upon Cockloft's efforts to preserve in the privacy of his home those curious objects reflecting the values of his grandfather's generation: 'Let no one ridicule the whim-whams of [Cockloft's] grandfather: – If – and of this there is no doubt, for wise men have said it – if life is but a dream, happy is he who can make the most of the illusion' (239). As Irving's wistful comment suggests, nostalgia compensates to some degree for Federalist losses by constituting a private realm of sensibility where conservatives might enjoy an illusion of the paternalistic authority they had hoped to exercise in public.

Irving's use of the private sphere to figure larger social and political issues conforms to Eric Sundquist's observation regarding nineteenth-century American literature that metaphors of 'family or
genealogy ... act as surrogates for a more abstractly envisioned
"past"' that 'stimulate the writer's *desire* to find in the family a
model for the social and political constructs still so much in question for a recently conceived nation' (Sundquist xii). However, in
Irving's case, this desire to find in the past familial models for contemporary social and political constructs was frustrated by conservatism's preemptive historical failure. The Cockloft family, rather
than representing a private model for the character of the nation's
public institutions, merely represents the private character of a
class that had already lost its bid to define them. Moreover in
telling the story of that loss, particularly its political consequences,
Irving depicts a conservatism that also has lost all hope of reassert-
ing any vital national influence.

Sundquist addresses the problem of preserving and distributing
authority under revolutionary circumstances in terms derived from
Freud's understanding of social genesis. He observes that the
liberal–democratic victory over Federalist conservatism prompted
the production of literature whose representation of paternal authority he likens to the ritual of celebration and atonement in
Freud's account of the patricide that establishes fraternal authority
and order. After noting how this guilt engenders a desire to recover
the father's authority through cultural ritual, Sundquist comments
that among American writers 'experiments in authorial desire must
risk the possibility that they ... will either become repetitive commemorations in the name of an overthrown authority, or else find
themselves at a loss before the very absence of that authority' (xii).
Ideally the resolution to this problem is the transfer of the overthrown paternal authority to the commemorative ritual. From
there, it may then be distributed and made present among the
sons as a means to assure the continuity and authority of the
social order founded upon their revolt. However Irving's experiment in authorial desire constitutes a failure to transfer and dis-
tribute paternal authority. As a cultural ritual his nostalgia is
merely a mournful commemoration of the destruction of such authority that leaves his audience at a loss as to how to compensate
for its absence. Thus *Salmagundi*'s nostalgia merely serves to ad-
umbrate the lost public dimension of Federalist ideology and
reduce desire for the patriarchal family to a mournful reminder of

conservatism's failure to impress its character upon the public institutions of the nation.

In *Salmagundi* Irving's nostalgia indicates that he had yet to realize the potential of the press as a means to form the national identity and preserve conservative authority. The disparaging comments he makes there regarding 'Logocracy', or rule by the printed word, indicate that he perceived the press (especially political publications) to be largely responsible for the partisan fighting that had undermined the Federalists' efforts to preserve republican character and public institutions. He notes that because of the political press many Americans 'are at a loss to determine the true nature and proper character of their government' which seems one moment to be a republican 'aristocracy' and another a democratic 'mobocracy'. But in fact the truth is 'a secret which is unknown to these people themselves, their government is a pure unadulterated LOGOCRACY or government of words' (142). Although Irving exaggerates to satirize, conservatives generally were frightened by the power of the press over the opinions of the people and policy of legislators. Ames makes clear the Federalist case against the press:

> The many, who before the art of printing never mistook in a case of oppression, because they complained from their actual sense of it, have become susceptible of every transient enthusiasm and of more than womanish fickleness of caprice. Publick affairs are now transacted on a *stage*, where all the interest and passions grow out of fiction, or are inspired by the art, and often controlled at the pleasure of the actors.
>
> (392)

Ironically Ames' complaint that political publications diminish the authority of experience, create a malleable popular opinion and replace reasoned political deliberation with a popular sentimentalism elicited by fiction anticipates precisely Irving's use of the literary press in *The Sketch Book*. There Ames' bitter observation that many Americans 'learn only from newspapers that they are countrymen' (414) assumes a positive connotation and marks the difference between a republican national character based upon elitist social and political institutions and a modern nationalism founded upon popular participation in a textually propagated sensibility.[3]

In *The Sketch Book*'s first literary essay, 'English Writers on America', Irving states that 'Over no nation does the press hold a more absolute control than over the people of America; for the universal education of the poorest classes, makes every individual a reader' (74). He then addresses directly the role of the press in creating the 'public mind' that forms the substance of the national character when he warns his American readers not to let 'political hostility' arising from the press accounts of the recently concluded War of 1812 bias their attitude toward the English:

> Governed as we are entirely by public opinion, the utmost care should be taken to preserve the purity of the public mind. Knowledge is power, and truth is knowledge; whoever therefore knowingly propagates a prejudice, willfully saps the foundation of his country's strength.
>
> (77)

However the apparent opposition of rational judgment to sentiment (hostility), public interest to private prejudice, breaks down when Irving tries to explain his simple assertion that 'knowledge' governs the formation of the nation's collective 'mind'. On the one hand Irving objects to the use of the press to determine opinion for the public. He insists that its role in the democratic political process should be limited to providing the information that citizens need to make the individual rational judgments from which representative democracy derives popular will. Such citizens, he asserts, 'are individually portions of the sovereign mind and sovereign will, and should be enabled to come to all questions of national concern with calm and unbiassed judgments' (77). But on the other he claims that it is precisely the author's responsibility 'to make [the press] the medium of amiable and magnanimous feeling' (74) and invest the public mind with sentimental fictions that do bias it in matters of 'national concern'. It is in fact this latter approach that corresponds to Irving's use of sentimental literature to create a sensibility conducive to genteel nationalism.[4]

Gaining recognition for the press itself as a basis of modern society was only the begnning of Irving's struggle to promote genteel nationalism among American readers. Establishing the legitimacy and authority of the conservative sensibility he hoped to propagate there constituted his greatest challenge. To accomplish this required the use of English literary models whose patriarchal representations of domestic life sponsored the sort of sensibility from which Irving hoped to construct a genteel American nationalism.

The ongoing anxiety over the legitimacy of the American national character guaranteed Irving a ready audience for the account of his cultural 'pilgrimage' to England in 1815 that constitutes the majority of *The Sketch Book*.[5] There, in the guise of his authorial persona, Geoffrey Crayon, he attempts to elide the historical ruptures that had prevented Americans from looking toward England for models of private, if not social and political, character.[6] His nostalgic desire for English culture thus represents an effort to establish an affiliation with England that will allow that country to serve as 'a perpetual volume of reference ... wherewith to strengthen and embellish [American] national character' (79). As his allusion to textuality and filiopiety implies, he proposes this affiliation in order to provide American literary culture with the genealogy and paternal character it needed to legitimize its own sentimental authority. Moreover in the course of doing so he also demonstrates the figural, narrative and associative techniques that give nostalgic discourse the ability to evoke desire among bourgeois readers for a conservative sensibility. For it is, he suggests, the study of these literary models and techniques, not the outright imitation of English social and political institutions, that will help Americans learn how to create their own nationalism.

In 'English Writers on America' (*Sketch Book*) Irving clearly abandons the republican assumption that national identity depends primarily on its social and political institutions. Instead he emphasizes the spirit, thought, opinion and feeling typical of bourgeois sensibility as the bases of national character. Public institutions, he suggests, are merely the expression of a nation's private character, not vice versa. This change is particularly apparent when Irving advises his American readers not to resent the English for denigrating their character:

We are a young people, necessarily an imitative one, and must take our examples and models, in a great degree, from the existing nations of Europe. There is no country more worthy of our study than England. The spirit of her constitution is most analogous to ours. The manners of her people, – their intellectual activity – their freedom of opinion – their habits of thinking on those subjects which concern the dearest interests and most sacred charities of private life, are all congenial to the American character; and in fact are all intrinsically excellent: for it is in the moral feeling of the people that the deep foundations of English prosperity are laid.

(78)

Irving goes on to conclude that English social order itself, 'an edifice that so long has towered unshaken', owes its durability to 'foundations' in 'private life'. In particular he refers to those 'sacred charities' and 'moral feelings' that originate in the bourgeois family and bind the individual to the father as the source of the patrimony and legitimacy that guarantee social standing. Like Edmund Burke, who claimed that 'We begin our public affections in our families' (315), Irving models the individual's relationship to the nation on patriarchal family life. Thus his domestically figured nationalism offers its readers membership in a virtual family that transforms their private lives into what Burke calls 'so many little images of the great country in which the heart [finds] something it [can] fill' (315). In this manner the modern nation substantiates itself in the mutual identification or recognition that bourgeois individuals realize through a shared desire for the cultural ideal represented by the patriarchal family.

In effect Irving proposes to synchronize and regulate American sentiments by establishing a paternalistic cultural authority modeled upon that of English domestic literature. To this end *The Sketch Book* engages its American readers in a nostalgic ritual meant to invoke the spirit of those days when they approached England 'with a hallowed feeling of tenderness and veneration as the land of our forefathers' and when after 'our own country there was none in whose glory we more delighted, ... none toward which our hearts yearned with such throbbings of warm consanguinity' (75). Irving uses such filial and domestic sentiments to create the sense of impending patrimonial loss and genealogical discontinuity essential to the invocation of nostalgic desire, as is apparent when he reminds Americans who reject their English heritage for political reasons that

there are feelings dearer than interest – closer to the heart than pride – that will still make us cast back a look of regret, as we wander farther and farther from the paternal roof, and lament the waywardness of the parent, that would repel the affections of the child.

(75–6)

Thus the filiopiety that Irving invokes touches upon his most encompassing purpose: to perform a ritual of cultural reconciliation between America and England that will allow Americans to desire the cultural authority and legitimacy associated with their conservative heritage.

Of nearly a dozen literary essays, character sketches and short stories in *The Sketch Book* addressing questions of national identity, the character sketch 'John Bull' offers the most pointed illustration of Irving's transformation of nostalgia. The sketch begins by examining how Bull, the personification of England in a series of political allegories by John Arbuthnot (1667–1735), contributed to the creation of modern English character. Irving observes that the widespread printing and sale of caricatures based on Arbuthnot's texts was a likely reason that Bull became the personification of 'common' or middle-class English character:

> Perhaps the continual contemplation of the character thus drawn of them, has contributed to fix it upon the nation; and thus to give reality to what at first may have been painted in a great measure from the imagination. Men are apt to acquire peculiarities that are continually ascribed to them. The common orders of the English seem wonderfully captivated with the *beau ideal* which they have formed of John Bull, and endeavour to act up to the broad caricature that is perpetually before their eyes.
>
> (379)

However, despite the focus of this passage on the pictorial aspect of Bull as an ego ideal, the main purpose of Irving's sketch is to elaborate a narrative context in which Bull may represent nostalgia as an effective conservative response to the conflict between tradition and progress. Toward this end, Irving sets Bull's story in the midst of a family crisis that poses his paternalism and reverence for tradition against his sons' democratic and progressive interests. But despite the apparent parallels between his story and Cockloft's, Bull's differs significantly in the positive effects it ascribes to nostalgia.

As a paternal figure 'who is given to indulge his veneration for family usages and family incumbrances, to a whimsical extent' (387), Bull maintains his home in a manner redolent of an English monarchism at odds with the progressive values held by his sons. Although he is inclined to listen to their counsel and slowly accommodate their modern tastes and interests, this 'wholesome advice has been completely defeated by the obstreperous conduct of one of his sons'. This impatient younger son sees little purpose in preserving the hierarchy and authoritarianism that characterize relationships among the inhabitants of Bull's estate and threatens to lead 'the poorest of his father's tenants' in revolt: 'No sooner does he hear any of his brothers mention reform or retrenchment, than he jumps up, takes the words out of their mouths, and roars out for an overturn.' Irving emphasizes the democratic or 'leveller' inclinations of the disobedient son by noting that he will not be satisfied until 'the whole family mansion shall be leveled with the ground, and a plain one of brick and mortar built in its place' (388). At this point Bull's story appears likely to be little more than a mournful recapitulation of Cockloft's. However its conclusion does not bear out such an assumption. Instead the older son sides with his father, helps preserve his rule and forestalls revolt 'against paternal authority'.

The story of Bull's relationship to his sons suggests an impending lower-class overthrow of upper-class paternalism much like that which American conservatives perceived in the rise of Jeffersonian democracy. However in this case the story concludes with the promise of reconciliation. The eldest son, though in favor of change, nonetheless seeks to preserve his patrimony and mitigate any outright destruction of paternal authority. As with Freud's account of the totem meal, Irving's story describes an attempt to balance the desire to assert independence from paternal authority with the desire to preserve that authority for the benefit of the sons. The ideal result, the story suggests, should be a 'wholesome' reformism or balance of the old and new.

Typically, Irving illustrates his conception of the proper manner in which to reform national character in terms of Bull's home and the tastes that it reflects:

John had frequently been advised to have the old edifice thoroughly overhauled, and to have some of the useless parts pulled down, and the others strengthened with their materials; but the old gentleman always grows testy on this subject. ... If you point out any part of the building as superfluous, he insists that it is material to the strength or decoration of the rest, and the harmony of the whole, and swears, that the parts are so built into each other, that if you pull down one, you run the risk of having the whole about your ears.

(385)

Again, like Burke, Irving subscribed to the belief that, compared to the simplicity of mere reaction or revolution, 'At once to preserve and reform is quite another thing' (Burke 80). Accordingly, Irving's architectural metaphor represents English nostalgia as an effective means supporting and preserving conservative interests. Bull's home represents the desired result of a communal narrative requiring that the old remain a vital part of the present and that the new not be added at the expense of those long-established interests 'built into' the extant order. Bull's home is thus an image of a patrilineal narrative that promises to confer power and authority (patrimony) upon those who seek at once to reform and to preserve its values rather than depose them through revolution. However, unlike England, the United States had no longstanding conservative social and political institutions to serve as foundations for a reformist narrative of this sort. As Irving's earlier effort to evoke nostalgia in *Salmagundi* indicates, any attempt to ask Americans to recall a desire for a 'traditional' social and political order they never had is ridiculous. Cockloft Hall is an illusory image of a past and a patrimony that American conservatives had merely wished for. It is not, however, ridiculous for Irving to offer his American readers a patrilineal cultural narrative featuring the 'traditional' values he would have them use to 'embellish' their liberal–democratic reality. In this case, it becomes entirely reasonable to suggest that Americans reform their liberal–democratic excesses in a manner consistent with the cultural patrimony represented by Bull and other figures drawn from English letters. It is in this case the 'traditional' sensibility exemplified by models of English private life that constitutes the substance of nostalgic desire. Consequently, the nostalgia and nationalism that Irving offers his American readers is more thoroughly virtual or cultural than that which he ascribes to the English, and the genteel reformism he promotes among Americans thus proceeds from the private realm of sensibility to the public realm via literature.

Irving offers a more personal example of how sensibility itself may constitute a basis for nationalism in his account of Geoffrey Crayon's literary pilgrimage to Stratford-on-Avon. Crayon, though an American, participates in English national community through the associations he has acquired from reading English books, particularly his tourist guide, the 'Stratford Guide Book', and Shakespeare's plays.[7] Crayon announces that 'Indeed the whole country about here is poetic ground: every thing is associated with the idea of Shakespeare' (329). Irving represents the power of textual associations in the way that Crayon participates in English sensibility through his reading. Crayon exclaims at one point that 'My mind had become so completely possessed by the imaginary scenes and characters connected with [Stratford-on-Avon], that I seemed to be actually living among them.' Shakespeare, he goes on to note, 'is indeed the true enchanter, whose spell operates not upon the senses, but upon the imagination and the heart' (339). Despite his recognition that his participation in English society is merely a matter of textually propagated associations of questionable historical validity, he still defends the value of his experience: 'What is it to us whether these stories be true or false, so long as we can persuade ourselves into the belief of them, and enjoy all the charm of the reality?' (320). Unlike in *Salmagundi*, where Cockloft's sensibility constituted a barrier between the individual and community, the sensibility illustrated by Crayon reflects an understanding that a textually regulated sensibility provides a crucial means to link the individual to the larger community of those with similarly organized tastes.[8]

'The Legend of Sleepy Hollow' exemplifies how Irving applied these lessons of English nationalism to the United States. Narrated in the persona of the 'sentimental historian' Diedrich Knickerbocker, the story elaborates representations of prerevolutionary domestic life from vague hints of the Dutch colonial period in New York. As a little-studied group with few controversial historical or political associations, the Dutch offered Irving a relatively neutral set of figures upon which to inscribe the narrative and associations appropriate to a genteel nationalism. As might be expected, the narrative he uses is that of a contest between conservatism and progressivism. The Dutch are associated with the historical legitimacy that Irving ascribes to those who demonstrate a tasteful respect for paternalism, tradition and social hierarchy characteristic of members of the community of genteel sensibility. Their opponent, Ichabod Crane, the Yankee incarnation of modern America, exhibits the individualistic desires for economic gain and social mobility typically associated with liberal–democratic progressivism.[9]

'The Legend of Sleepy Hollow' satirizes these desires by subjecting Crane to Sleepy Hollow, an environment governed by the influence of the past.

From the listless repose of the place, and the peculiar character of its inhabitants, who are descendants from the original Dutch settlers, this sequestered glen has long been known by the name of SLEEPY HOLLOW, and its rustic lads are called the Sleepy Hollow Boys throughout all the neighbouring country. A drowsy, dreamy influence influence seems to hang over the land, and to pervade the very atmosphere.

(*Sketch Book* 417)

Unlike liberal–democratic society, with its fixation upon the future and social mobility, the Dutch village retains its conservative character in the midst of flux:

it is in such little retired Dutch valleys ... that population, manners, and customs remained fixed, while the great torrent of migration and improvement, which is making such incessant changes in other parts of this restless country, sweeps them by unobserved.

(419)

Sleepy Hollow thus represents a nostalgic sensibility that shelters conservative values that no longer find acceptance in the liberal–democratic public sphere. There, ensconced in the privacy of the domestic scene and individual sensibility, they maintain their influence as matters of taste. In effect Irving's story represents a ritual space which permits the members of his audience to exorcize their unmitigated liberal–democratic progressivism through a literary act of sentimental bonding that affirms the paternal authority over the private sphere of a conservative sensibility ostensibly recovered from the past.

The story of Ichabod Crane's invasion of Sleepy Hollow centers upon his desire to marry Katrina Van Tassel and sell the land that forms her dowry to realize an investment scheme: Crane's 'heart yearned after the damsel who was to inherit these domains, and his imagination expanded with the idea, how they might be readily turned into cash, and the money invested in immense tracts of wild land, and shingle palaces in the wilderness' (428). Whereas the value of Katrina and her land to the villagers derives from their role as necessary means to reproduce their patriarchal family and communal values, their value to Crane is primarily economic. Consequently Crane's rival, the village hero, Brom, must defend the integrity of the village by asserting his claim (and that of the village) to Katrina and her land.

This confrontation between nostalgic and progressive modes of national ideology comes to a climax in the encounter between Brom (disguised as the Headless Horseman) and Crane. There the intergrity of conservatism reasserts itself by subjecting the liberal–democratic desires that fire Crane's economic dreams to the conservative sensibility that they threaten. Ultimately, Crane's inability to understand Sleepy Hollow's legends as a virtual basis of the villagers' society causes his downfall. His literal belief in their 'marvellous' ghost stories and 'Mather's direful tales' provides them with a means to turn against him the sensibility that he represses.

Ironically, 'The Legend of Sleepy Hollow' is a gothic ritual of exorcism in which the quotidian Crane represents the evil spirit and the Headless Horseman the figure of communal integrity. Thus the communal sensibility that Crane represses and threatens returns to haunt him and nearly trample underfoot the liberal ideology he represents:

> Ichabod cast a look behind him. … Just then he saw the goblin rising in his stirrups, and in the very act of hurling his head at him. Ichabod endeavoured to dodge the horrible missile, but … he was tumbled headlong into the dust, and … the goblin rider, passed like a whirlwind.
>
> (451–2)

Exiled from the community of genteel sensibility, Crane finds a more congenial home in the institutions of liberal–democratic public life. We are told that he

> had changed his quarters to a distant part of the country; had kept school and studied law at the same time; had been admitted to the bar, turned politician, electioneered, written for newspapers, and finally had been made Justice.
>
> (453–4)

This conclusion, however, may suggest an escapist fantasy isolating conservative sensibility from a liberal democracy that continues to gain power in the public institutions of the nation, as Crane's subsequent career indicates. But insofar as sensibility replaces such institutional bases of national character (educational, legal and political and the publishing system that supports them), their loss is not so great a blow to conservatism. As the conclusion suggests, Irving is willing to cede these institutions to democrats in return for control of sentimental literature (the 'public mind') that regulates the sensibility of American readers.

Although genteel nationalism may appear to be the consolation prize for America's social and political losers, in reality it is a cultural institution of great importance. Irving realized that being a modern American did not require participation in specific social or political institutions. What it did require was participation in a desire organized by a textually propagated sensibility whose tastes and manners constituted the substance of the national character. In *The Sketch Book* Irving defined the genteel aspect of the great imaginary national family that has served for nearly two centuries as the United States' principal cultural mechanism of ideological regulation. He was first among American writers to articulate clearly the narrative and associative strategies by which a culturally defined character (sensibility) might mediate the social and political conflicts of a progressive nation. He was first, in other words, clearly to articulate for Americans how the reading of domestic literature constitutes a socio-aesthetic ritual that fuses elitist and populist, liberal and conservative elements into an enduring basis for national community. However, it is also this same cultural ritual, with its emphasis on genealogy, patrimony and paternal authority, that has promoted and legitimized the white, male and anti-democratic character of American nationalism. In this context, Irving's abandonment of the myth of the republic for the genteel American Dream sets the terms for the subsequent development of the anglocentric and patriarchal culture that continues to exercise a considerable, if not dominant, authority over the representation of American national character in academe and the popular media. And, as the current multicultural trend and conservative reaction to it indicate, we have only recently begun to recognize the extent to which genteel nationalism has contributed to the oppressive exclusions and divisions that characterize class, gender and race relationships in the United States.

NOTES

1. In *Salmagundi* Irving failed to recognize that the United States was becoming a virtual nation founded upon the printed page and that

social and political institutions no longer constituted the principal means of regulating its self-image. Not until the publication of *The Sketch Book* does he finally employ a textually propagated desire for familial representations as a public means to exercise cultural authority over the private sphere. Kaja Silverman discusses this linkage of desire to representation as the 'suture' or ideological bonding 'inherent in all the operations that constitute narrativity' (236). She goes on to note in reference to the work of Lacan and Jacques-Alain Miller that 'Suture can be understood as the process whereby the inadequacy of the subject's position is exposed in order to facilitate (i.e. create the desire for) new insertions into a cultural discourse which promises to make good that lack' (231). Similarly, Irving's nostalgia elicits a sense of lack that it subsequently fulfills.

2.   As Isaac Kramnick notes, Jeffersonian America witnessed the ascendancy of the 'new liberal ideal' of 'a society of achievement, a social order of competitive individualism, in which social mobility was possible and the rightful reward for ingenious people of talent and hard work' (4). Although conservatives accepted the 'improvement' of certain individuals of 'merit' within a given social order, they condemned the self-interest of competitive individualism as antithetical to the character of a republic. From their perspective, social hierarchy constituted the *raison d'être* of American republicanism and the essence of the public good.

3.   Irving's use of literature as a mode of community is a variation on Benedict Anderson's account of how newspapers helped create nationalism. In *Imagined Communities* Anderson observes of newspaper reading that

> the significance of this mass ceremony – Hegel observed that newspapers serve modern man as a substitute for morning prayers – is paradoxical. It is performed in silent privacy, in the lair of the skull. Yet each communicant is well aware that the ceremony he performs is being replicated simultaneously by thousands (or millions) of others of whose existence he is confident, yet of whose identity he has not the slightest notion. Furthermore this ceremony is incessantly repeated at daily or half-daily intervals throughout the calendar. What more vivid figure for the secular, historically-clocked, imagined community can be envisioned ...? [This] remarkable confidence of community in anonymity ... is the hallmark of modern nationalism.

(39–40)

It is precisely the synchronization and regulation that Anderson ascribes to reading newspapers that Irving employs in his attempt to reassert conservative authority by means of sentimental culture. Although *The Sketch Book* does not qualify as a mass media production on the scale of newspapers, it nonetheless represented a prototype of popular prose fiction insofar as it was aimed at an inclusive audience and written in a sentimental style. Nonetheless Michael Gilmore notes in *The Columbia History of the American Novel* that the 5000 copies it

sold made it a best-seller in its day (Elliot 58). He also comments that
The Last of the Mohicans 'qualified as a best-seller in 1826 with 5750
copies in circulation' (54). See Jay Fliegelman's definitive study of
metaphors of paternal authority in popular American publications of
the late eighteenth century.

4. In a passage comparing the bourgeois individual to more traditional
Anglo-American conceptions of the publicly active political subject, J.
G. A. Pocock states that the bourgeois individual lived in an 'increasingly transactional universe of "commerce and the arts"' in which 'he
was more than compensated for his loss of antique virtue by an
indefinite and perhaps infinite enrichment of his personality, the
product of multiplying relationships, with both things and persons, in
which he became progressively involved. Since these new relationships were social and not political in character the capacities that they
led the individual to develop were called not "virtues" but "manners"'
(49). It is my contention that one of the most important manifestations
of these manners is taste, which makes possible an affiliation to a class
and, ultimately, a national community on the basis of sensibility.

5. Stanley T. Williams discusses Irving's life in England and Europe at
great length in the first of his two-volume biography, *The Life of
Washington Irving*. Irving's main residence from 1815 to 1832 was in
England. Scott exercised an important influence upon him there prior
to the publication of *The Sketch Book*. Both shared an enthusiasm for
Edmund Burke's conservative reformism.

6. Irving's collaborator in *Salmagundi*, James Kirke Paulding, had
entered into combat with the English in his 1812 satire *The Diverting
History of John Bull and Brother Jonathan* (see Reynolds, *James Kirke
Paulding*, 40–54). Works such as his contributed to the 'Paper War'
between America and England that Irving hoped to dispel. This jour-
nalistic feud fueled considerable anger and insecurity among
Americans regarding the historical legitimacy of their national character. Many, conservative and democrat alike, responded to English
insults by arguing that the legitimacy of American character resulted
from its radical newness and independence from the corrupt character
of Europeans. Noah Webster takes this position in his *American
Magazine* (1788) when he advises his readers to 'Unshackle your
minds and act like independent beings. You have been children long
enough, subject to the control and subservient to the interest of a
haughty parent. You now have an interest of your own to augment
and defend – and a national character to establish and extend by your
wisdom and judgement' (Kohn 57). Nearly three decades later in 1815
periodical publisher Hezekiah Niles takes a similar stand when he declares that Americans have 'a NATIONAL CHARACTER' whose
virtues 'need no guarantee from the bloodstained and profligate
princes and powers of *Europe*' (Kohn 59).

7. In *The Essay Concerning Human Understanding* (1700) Locke notes that
it is the unconscious and habitual character of associationism that distinguishes it from rationally directed thought (with which he claimed
it interfered):

there is another connexion of ideas wholly owing to *chance or custom*: Ideas that in themselves are not at all of kin, come to be so united in some men's minds, that it is very hard to separate them; they always keep company, and the one no sooner at any time comes into the understanding, but its associate appears with it.

(Kallich 32)

However, by the time Irving published *The Sketch Book* popular aesthetic works had established associationism as more than an impediment to clear rational thought. They had demonstrated that associations, when propagated and controlled by art, could be made to contribute significantly to the production of consensus and cohesion in modern society. Aesthetician Archibald Alison may be counted among the foremost proponents of the belief that associationism provides a basis for national community of sensibility or taste. For example in 1790 he noted associationism's contribution to national sensibility and sentiment in his remarks on music:

There are other tunes of the same character, which, without any particular merit, yet always serve to please the people, whenever they are performed. The natives of any country, which possesses a national or characteristic music, need not be reminded, how strongly the performance of such airs brings back to them the imagery of their native land; and must often have had occasion to remark how inferior an emotion they excite in those who are strangers to such associations.

(24)

In addition Alison notes how the sentiments associated with given cultural productions link the individual to that sense of cultural and communal genealogy essential to nationalism:

There is no man in the least acquainted with the history of antiquity, who does not love to let his imagination loose on the prospect of its remains, and to whom they are not in some measure sacred, from the innumerable images they bring. Even the peasant, whose knowledge of former times extends but to a few generations, has yet in his village some monument of the deeds or virtues of his forefathers; and cherishes with a fond veneration the memorial of those good old times to which his imagination returns with delight, and of which he loves to recount the simple tales that tradition has brought him.

(28)

So too modern literary culture creates the 'traditional' tales that link its readers to a past and make the 'virtues' of the forefathers the cultural patrimony of the modern nation.

8.   In *Adrift in the Old World* Jeffrey Rubin-Dorsky argues that

Irving was preoccupied with the loss of the nation-as-home, a loss that was not yet viewed as permanent. Following Irving to Europe ... Americans sought along with him not only a release from the oppressive realities of a materialist culture but, as well, a source of continuity to replace the one that was fast becoming historically obsolete.

He concludes that 'Irving's fictional world' was 'a substitute for the political order of George Washington's republican vision' (xviii–xix). Although I agree that Irving's vision of patriarchal domesticity indeed served as a substitute for a lost Federalist order, I do not see it as a 'release' or escape from the problems of liberal democratic society. In fact Irving's nostalgic vision employs the press in a positive manner that contests liberal–democratic progressivism and makes of sentimental literature a basis for a more conservative American society. It is in this sense that Irving indeed uses literature to create a sense of continuity and construct the nation-as-home on the pages of *The Sketch Book.*

9. Rubin-Dorsky asserts that the patriarchal ruler of the English country home, the squire or yeoman farmer, represents

    the principal stabilizing force in his society, with no aristocratic yearnings, liberal, sensible, and, above all, virtuous, [he] is Irving's English version of the yeoman farmer championed by Thomas Jefferson and reclaimed by Andrew Jackson as the source and strength of an American agrarian republic.

    (141)

    Although he observes that, 'like these agrarian idealists, [Irving] believed that virtue resided in the country' (147), he recognizes that such a vision was 'anachronistic' in Irving's time and fashioned to appeal 'to a nation uneasy with its own progress and changing self-image' (146). In effect Irving 'retreated' from liberal–democratic reality 'to his imagination' where he created from elements of the English and American past the agrarian home he desired. Whereas Rubin-Dorsky locates the main tension in Irving's work between Jeffersonian agrarianism and an ascendant liberalism, I argue that that tension resides mainly between liberal–democratic progressivism and conservatism. Although Irving had abandoned the Federalist persuasion as a viable social and political ideology for modern America, he only did so in order to revive it in a conservative sensibility, not in order to celebrate the egalitarian idyll of Jeffersonian agrarianism.

WORKS CITED

Alison, Archibald, *Essay on the Nature and Principles of Taste*, Edinburgh, 1790: repr. Hildesheim, Germany: Georg Olms Verslagbuchhandlung, 1968.

Ames, Fisher, *Works of Fisher Ames*, Boston: T. B. Wait, 1809.

Anderson, Benedict, *Imagined Communities*, London: Verso, 1983.

Burke, Edmund, *Reflections of the Revolution in France*, New York: Penguin, 1969.

Elliot, Emory (ed.), *The Columbia History of the American Novel*, New York: Columbia University Press, 1991.

Fliegelman, Jay, *Prodigals and Pilgrims: the American Revolution Against Patriarchal Authority, 1750–1800*, Cambridge: Cambridge University Press, 1982.

Irving, Washington, *Salmagundi* in *The Complete Works of Washington Irving*, vol. 6, Boston: Twayne, 1977.

—— *The Sketch Book*, New York: G. P. Putnam, 1859.

Kallich, Martin, *The Association of Ideas and Critical Theory in Eighteenth-Century England*, The Hague: Mouton, 1970.

Kohn, Hans, *American Nationalism*, New York: Collier Books, 1961.

Kramnick, Isaac, *Republicanism and Bourgeois Radicalism*, Ithaca, NY: Cornell University Press, 1990.

Pocock, J. G. A., *Virtue, Commerce and History*, Cambridge: Cambridge University Press, 1985.

Reynolds, Larry, *James Kirke Paulding*, Boston: Twayne, 1984.

Rubin-Dorsky, Jeffrey, *Adrift in the Old World*, Chicago: Chicago University Press, 1988.

Silverman, Kaja, *The Subject of Semiotics*, Oxford: Oxford University Press, 1983.

Sundquist, Eric, *Home as Found*, Baltimore: Johns Hopkins University Press, 1977.

Warner, Michael, *The Letters of the Republic*, Cambridge, MA: Harvard University Press, 1990.

Williams, Stanley T., *The Life of Washington Irving*, Oxford: Oxford University Press, 1935.

4

The Birthing of the American Flag and the Invention of an American Founding Mother in the Image of Betsy Ross

JOANN MENEZES

On 12 October 1892 hundreds of schoolgirls in red, white and blue dresses marched out on the grounds of the Columbian Exposition in Chicago and formed a living flag. The girls, accompanied by millions of school children across the country, recited the 'Pledge of Allegiance to the Flag of the United States of America' for the first time in history. This performance was part of the dedication ceremony for one of the world's great fairs, and it was witnessed by over a hundred thousand people on what was to be the first Columbus Day. National sentiment soared as did the flag itself, and Americans reveled in their historical identity. In the Pennsylvania Building a painting was proudly displayed which linked that state with the nation's historic past. In 1895 Denton Snider described this painting and the experience he had upon viewing it:

> As we pass upstairs in the Pennsylvania House we look about and behold a significant picture. Another strong touch of national symbolism greets us; the picture portrays the Birth of the American Flag. Thus Pennsylvania again seeks to identify herself with the beginning of the Nation, in the present case with the origin of the national emblem itself. A woman is sewing its pieces together – three men are looking on, in the main helpless, yet making some remarks now and then, we may suppose. The woman is probably Betsy Ross, the deft needle woman of

The Birth of Our Nation's Flag, 1893, by Charles H. Weisgerber

Philadelphia, who is said to have first stitched together the Stars and Stripes, and also to have made elegant ruffled shirts for George Washington, such as were worn by gentlemen in those days. You and I, my reader, would like to have witnessed that scene in which the Father of his country gave specific directions to the cunning-handed seamstress about his wardrobe. Philadelphia still points out with pride the exact spot (239 Arch street) where the American Flag was born, born of a woman.

(200–1)

The painting, *The Birth of Our Nation's Flag*, by Charles H. Weisgerber, was a depiction of Betsy Ross displaying the original flag to George Washington, General George Ross and the Honorable Robert Morris, the flag committee. The subjects are portrayed in what we can assume to be the front room of the Ross house. The gentlemen occupy the left half of the composition while Betsy Ross and the flag occupy the right half. Washington is at far left, seated and shown in profile facing Betsy Ross. Washington looks directly at Betsy Ross, his right hand reaching towards her. He is in uniform with his sword in his lap and his tricorn hat on the floor, leaning against the leg of his chair. The hat leans so that the propped corner resembles an arrow pointing to the grandfather clock against the wall behind Washington. To Washington's left is General George Ross, also in uniform. He stands in front of the hearth and faces the viewer, looking directly out at us. His right hand rests on the back of the chair of the man sitting slightly to his left, the Honorable Robert Morris. Morris is seated, his chair turned toward the flag, but his head is turned back toward the viewer so he also looks out and meets our gaze.

Betsy Ross occupies the right half of the picture. The door separates her from the men. Depicted as a delicate young woman, she appears smaller than the gentlemen and is seated in a smaller chair. However, her chair is the same distance from the viewer as Morris's, and her head is level with Washington's head. She is posed in three-quarter profile, looking back at Washington and meeting his gaze. She is holding the flag with both hands, lifting it up off her lap and offering it to Washington's scrutinizing gaze. Directly behind her is a large open window with a small potted plant on the sill. The white curtains are parted and a pastoral landscape with fluffy white clouds can be seen outside the house. The sunlight streams in on her, creating a mystical aura. Betsy Ross, a

Quaker, is shown here in plain clothes wearing a white cap and shawl, which underscore her saintly appearance. At her left side is the sewing basket on a small stool. The scissors are prominently displayed on top of the cloth and thread that overflow the basket. Red, white and blue cloth cascades from the basket on to the floor where there are more scraps of cloth, discarded stars, and bits of color strewn about the floor encircling her. Under the window sill to her left there is a small table also laden with the seamstress's tools and more red, white and blue fabric. But prominently draped over these items is a sheet of paper with a drawing of a flag, the design of the flag that Ross now holds in her lap. This sketch represents the original design proposal brought to Ross by Washington, the design which became the finished flag – the flag she now holds on her lap and displays to the three men.

The Birth of Our Nation's Flag not only told the story of the origin of the national colors, it also introduced Betsy Ross to the American public. It was this image that propagated the story of the Philadelphia needlewoman and constructed the Betsy Ross myth in its own terms. In this image Betsy Ross is elevated to her position of national prominence as an historic figure – the mother of the new nation because this picture not only constructs an historic moment, it also creates an icon. Betsy Ross is not just the seamstress who assembled the original flag; in this painting she becomes the mother of the national emblem which is the sacred symbol of the United States of America.

The more official Betsy Ross story, however, is really quite different from the narrative constructed by Weisgerber in this painting. Betsy Ross first came to public attention in 1870, when her grandson William J. Canby read his paper on 'The Origin of the American Flag' before the Pennsylvania Historical Society. He claimed that the Congressional flag committee called on Ross in June of 1776 to request her services in the creation of the new flag. This was the story that he had heard from his grandmother Elizabeth (Betsy) Ross before her death in 1836. According to Ross's story General George Washington, accompanied by Robert Morris and George Ross (the uncle of her late husband, John Ross), came to her upholstery shop to ask if she could make a flag. Having never made a flag, she said that she 'didn't know' but 'would try'. General Washington showed her a preliminary design proposal, to which she suggested changes. One of her suggestions was that the stars should have five points instead of six. Presumably

Washington had proposed that the flag have six-pointed stars because he thought they would be easier to make than either five-pointed stars or the seven or eight-pointed stars which appeared on some local militia flags. She quickly showed him how, by folding a piece of paper and using 'only one snip of the scissors', she could easily make a five-pointed star. He agreed with her suggestions and modified the drawing himself at the table in her shop. The three men then left and later sent her a new design. This final design had been colored by William Barrett, a Philadelphia painter. From this design she made a sample flag and delivered it to the commander of the navy. It was later presented to Congress and adopted as the first flag of the United States.

Canby based his paper on the account he received from his grandmother and on the stories told by his aunts, Ross's daughters. The story was supported by the accounts of the women who had worked for Ross in the upholstery shop. Evidence in the form of letters, business correspondence, and affidavits was also submitted, along with the account of the Ross story as written in 1857, by Ross's daughter, Clarissa Claypoole Wilson. The Pennsylvania Historical Society accepted Canby's documentation, and Betsy Ross was written into history as the maker of the first flag.

Although Canby's story was accepted in 1870, it was not well known until the time of the Columbian Exposition. In the 1870s the nation was in turmoil, both economically and politically. Americans at the 1876 Centennial Exposition in Philadelphia wanted to look forward not backward, and although this fair commemorated the Revolution few colonial relics were exhibited. By 1893 the national sentiment had changed and Americans were reveling in their historical identity. There were historical pageants, the first commemorative coins and stamps were issued, and with this new nationalism a new ritual was added to everyday life. Francis J. Bellamy, the editor of *Youth's Companion*, devised the plan for the fair's dedication whereby school children across the country could participate in their own schools. Bellamy drafted 'The Pledge of Allegiance' and distributed copies to teachers nationwide, and it was on the quadricentennial of Columbus's arrival that American children first performed the ritual that would be repeated daily thereafter in the nation's public schools. That dedication day, 12 October 1892, also served to introduce Columbus Day as a national holiday. So it is not surprising that this fair provided the atmosphere necessary to elevate Betsy Ross to her position of glory.

It is clear with what pride and respect Americans in 1893 viewed their national heritage. Snider states that 'the affection with which the people regard the Exposition is profoundly significant, and shows that they still appreciate the heroic deed in whatever way it is done' (6). His description of the Liberty Bell, which was also displayed in the Pennsylvania Building, makes it apparent in what sphere these national symbols reside:

> A new emotion rises strongly within us. Pennsylvania salutes us with her most sacred relic – sacred, because of its connection with the Declaration of Independence. She wishes to associate herself with the birth of the Nation, and the first note inside her House is that of Patriotism. ... The Liberty Bell has become elevated, or transfigured into a symbol, ... the visible has become the mere sign of the invisible; the outer thing is marvelously transmuted into the inner spirit, ... its universal meaning; it still rings out the joy of the people at the Birth of the Nation ...; it is a ghostly symbolic bell which rings in the soul of the Nation, and will keep on ringing while nationality lasts. ... Such is the power of a symbol, when once made and adopted by the people: it stands for what is deepest and holiest in the man, and will stir the depths as nothing else can. ... [It is] their holy relic.
>
> (195–7)

The language is that of religious fervor, and such had been the rhetoric of the Revolution. The accounts of American settlement and Revolution constructed that movement as a sacred pilgrimage, the Revolution as a holy war, and the new nation as the promised land. George Bancroft, in his *History of the United States*, vividly exemplifies this tone when speaking of the Revolution:

> They were possessed by the truth, that man holds inherent and indefeasible rights; and as their religion had as its witness coeval and coextensive with intelligence, so in their political aspirations they deduced from universal principles a bill of rights, as old as creation and as wide as humanity. The idea of freedom had never been wholly unknown; it had always revealed itself at least to a few of the wise, whose prophetic instincts were quickened by love of their kind; its rising light flashed joy across the darkest centuries; and its growing energy can be traced in the tendency of the ages. ... For the first time it found a region and a race,

where it could be professed with the earnestness of an indwelling conviction, and be defended with the enthusiasm that heretofore had marked no wars but those for religion. ... A band of exiles, keeping watch by night, heard the glad tidings which promised the political regeneration of the world. A Revolution unexpected in the moment of its coming, but prepared by glorious forerunners, grew naturally and necessarily out of a series of past events by the formative principle of a living belief.

(22–3)

This holy war paradigm is also evidenced in the kind of images that were produced to memorialize and immortalize the heroes of the Revolutionary war. Fallen generals were often portrayed in compositions that are reminiscent of Lamentation scenes in which the generals are positioned so that they will be associated with the figure of Christ. Benjamin West's portrayal of the *Death of Wolfe*, 1770, is a particularly noteworthy example of this kind of composition.

In Weisgerber's painting Betsy Ross is placed in a compositional structure that is reminiscent of both an Annunciation and a Nativity scene. The condensation of time from annunciation to birth is even consistent within this composition because it reflects the condensation of the historical narrative that is portrayed in the image. The scene depicted in Weisgerber's *The Birth of Our Nation's Flag* is not one that was described by Canby in the story he presented to the Pennsylvania Historical society; rather it is a representation of a carefully constructed larger-than-life image of the entirety of that story. Weisgerber copied portraits of the three men to lend his painting authenticity. Because there were no existing portraits of Ross, he created a composite portrait of her daughters and granddaughters at the age Ross would have been to approximate her actual appearance. And yet the painting's narrative cannot possibly approach documentary status. Canby states that Washington and the committee approached Ross with a design, the design was modified and sent back to her, whereupon she made the sample flag and delivered it to the navy. In Weisgerber's construction all the story elements are compressed into a single moment.

Clearly the Betsy Ross story and its attendant representation in visual arts is bound up in the mythology which shapes cultural attitudes and behavior. In this image Betsy Ross is constructed as 'mother' of the new nation, but as she proudly displays her creation the image of the 'father' is also created or reinforced. The Revolution was often recounted in the language of filial rebellion, and thus there was a need to create a new familial relationship, to calm these rebellious sons in the parental care of a benevolent father. In this image Washington extends his hand towards Ross's wondrous gift. Although George Ross and Robert Morris are also present on this occasion and they too look pleased, they do not share the intimate moment with Betsy and George. As Betsy Ross and Washington look at each other they are completely absorbed in their exchange while the gentlemen of the committee look at the viewer. It is through these two men that the theatricality of the scene is acknowledged, and the viewer is made aware that the scene is a dramatization, a condensation of a series of events signified in this scene. Weisgerber depicts the presentation of the completed flag, the sewing basket and the remnants of her work, the paper star which exemplified Ross's unique skill, the design brought by Washington, as well as the three men who sought her out. Canby said that the men merely approached Ross to request her to make a sample flag, but Weisgerber refigures all the story's elements, relocates and reworks them so that they change what is signified.

A close reading of Weisgerber's painting reveals how 'proper' feminine subjectivity was naturalized by employing visual resonances that consign Ross to a traditional Christian mythological status of maternal saint. In Weisgerber's scene the committee is present as the flag is born. The subject of this painting is the mother, Betsy Ross, who has just given birth to her special creation, the sacred symbol of the nation. And this sacred birth, this 'nativity', is portrayed much like traditional nativity scenes. The mother holds her newborn on her lap and presents it to the adoring observers, to the three 'wise men'. The sun streams in through the window on to Ross as she sits serenely, her creation on her lap. She is bathed in angelic light. Her halo-like cap is echoed in the flag's circle of stars and, according to congressional resolution, 'the union [was to] be thirteen stars, white in a blue field, representing a new constellation'. If this union represented a new constellation, it meant more than just a new nation, or a bright new light, but rather a new star system, virtually a new universe, and definitely a divine creation. The circle symbolized the perpetuity of the union, also with divine resonance – just as God always was and always will be, so too was the spirit of America. Then the stars on the flag, the nation's sacred symbol, signaled the arrival of the new nation just as the star in the east signalled the arrival of Christ – and both were seen as saviors. Even the 'wise' men who sought out Ross were seeking the 'star', and she proved to be the woman uniquely capable of creating it. She produces what no man can – the five-pointed star – with feminine know-how and one snip of the scissors, just as a mother can produce what no man can, a child. Metaphorically she is sewing the seed that is the idea (or design) implanted by Washington. But Washington, without mortal children, is no mere man; he is rather the father of the country. From this god-like position his 'presentation' to Ross is a divine request. And when Ross agrees to this sacred mission, she sews the seed of this 'immaculate conception' and produces the offspring – the sacred flag, born of woman.

The symbol of divine motherhood may have been ideally suited to the ideology of the late nineteenth century, but it was precisely this holy myth that came under fire in 1942 in the writings of historian M. M. Quaife. Weisgerber's depiction of Ross attributes to her the spiritual and moral qualities of the Madonna, and it is these very qualities that Quaife discredits in his attempt to debunk the Ross myth. Quaife has written and collaborated on several volumes of historical accounts of the origin and evolution of the flag. In *The Flag of the United States* Quaife has a chapter called 'More Fictions and Myths'. Here he sets about discussing various stories surrounding possible origins of the early Stars and Stripes. Quaife is pleased to announce that he is the first to note the 'obvious fraudulent character' of a letter said to authenticate the *Bon Homme Richard* flag as the original Stars and Stripes, but when he turns to Ross his words have more sting:

> Of all the myths woven about the Stars and Stripes the one associated with Betsy Ross is the lustiest. At the opening of the Revolution, Betsy was a young Quaker of Philadelphia who had eloped with Ross, a non-Quaker, and who for this offense had been expelled from her church. The young husband was an upholsterer, and Betsy, apparently, labored with him in the conduct of the business, for when he was accidentally killed, while doing militia duty, on January 1, 1776, she continued to conduct the shop. On the day the Flag Resolution was adopted by Congress, June 14, 1777, she married Joseph Ashburn, a seaman engaged in

privateering ... he [was later imprisoned and] died, March 3, 1782. The news of his death was eventually carried to America by John Claypoole, a fellow prisoner, who on March 8, 1783, became Betsy's third husband. ... The fruit of Betsy's several marriages was seven daughters, whose descendants were numerous.

(183–4)

He attacks her personal morals and her character, using words like 'lusty', implying sexual promiscuity. He refers to her 'many husbands' and calls her first marriage an 'elopement' which caused her to be 'expelled' from her church, thus calling into question the legitimacy of her motherhood and the validity of her religious affiliations. He devalues the story by questioning her worthiness to be the mother of the flag. Quaife attacks Ross's purity and judges that she is not fit for such a sacred role. Quaife twists the facts (Mrs Ross was an equal partner in the business, having apprenticed alongside her husband before they married) and uses a derogatory tone while discussing Ross's personal life and morality for several pages before he even mentions the story of her making the flag. However at that point his attitude toward Ross remains condescending:

So we learn that in the presence of this poverty stricken young seamstress of Philadelphia such men as George Washington and Robert Morris became strangely submissive and childlike. The Committee, in fact, practically abdicated its function to Betsy, and General Washington at her behest obediently drew a picture of the flag as she conceived it. ... The naive conception, inherent in the entire story, that at a time when the life of the nation was hanging in the balance, men of the intellectual caliber and heavy responsibilities of George Washington and Robert Morris would fritter away an afternoon in familiar discussion with an indigent seamstress over the trifling detail of how the stars in a flag should be cut and arranged exceeds the reasonable bounds of human credulity.

(187–8)

When Quaife does point to the lack of what he considers 'real' evidence to substantiate Ross's story, it is significant to note what he considers 'real' evidence and the nature of 'true' historical documentation. He states that the Ross story is apocryphal because it is not documented. Although Canby presented letters documenting

Washington's whereabouts and showing that he was in the vicinity and therefore could have visited Ross, there is no written evidence of the meeting itself, that is, nothing written by Washington or a male contemporary. He dismisses Canby's apocryphal text because it is not properly authenticated by proper historians or witnesses (i.e. male). Although the Ross story is not actually contradicted by any real evidence or by Washington's word, neither is it confirmed in canonical writings – it is merely a woman's story. Quaife questions the validity of oral history as well as the particular veracity of a 'woman's word'.

Because the painting adds a religious level of significance to the myth, when Quaife debunks it he does so through the mediation of the religious implications the painting invokes. If Betsy Ross has been constructed as the Madonna, the mother of the sacred flag, then she can be dethroned if found morally unsuited to the position. His attacks on Ross are rooted in the rhetoric of the painting's narrative. For Quaife it is Ross herself who is apocryphal. It is Ross who is no virgin, and therefore no Virgin Mother to this sacred nation. It is not Canby's story that Quaife attacks, but Weisgerber's:

> An artist conveniently painted the 'Birth of Our Nation's Flag', showing the committee in conference with Mrs. Ross, and confounding the truth still further by exhibiting her in the act of displaying the finished flag to her callers. ... So the foolish hoax was perpetrated, and while today it is rejected by all reputable scholars it still remains firmly embedded in the minds of millions of American citizens.
>
> (188–9)

The virulence of Quaife's attack can only be understood in light of the powerful imagery with which Weisgerber originally set forth the myth, and attests to the lasting influence of Weisgerber's painting on American culture.

When the painting was exhibited in 1893, its image and narrative created such interest that it was reproduced as a chromolithograph by the newly-formed Betsy Ross Memorial Association and sold to over two million people from all over the country for a ten-cent subscription fee. The money raised was used to purchase and preserve the American Flag House, the building at 239 Arch Street,

Philadelphia, where Ross made that first flag. But Weisgerber's painting did not just preserve the house in which Ross sewed the flag, it preserved the household ideal as well. Although historical records indicate that Ross was a widowed business woman who ran an upholstery shop, Weisgerber's painting sets Ross at the side of a hearth in an obviously domestic setting. All signs of economic industry are erased and Ross's 'house' is transformed from a work-place into a 'home'. Ross the upholsterer is effectively removed from the labour force and contained within the proper frame of the domestic environment as Ross the seamstress. In this painting Weisgerber constructs Ross as the perfect heroic 'mother', shown presenting the offspring of her maternal labor. This domestic image was widely circulated as an example of female patriotism in Revolutionary America.

Chromolithographs of the Weisgerber painting were displayed in homes and public buildings all over the country; the image was also engraved and reproduced in standardized textbooks and viewed nationally as an historic document. The image and the per-sonality it suggests were embraced by the American people – Ross became a symbol for appropriate female action in the public sphere. The painting itself, however, has been lost to the public. It was ex-hibited for a short time at the American Flag House, but then was returned to the family of the artist when Ross's popularity waned. Weisgerber does not appear in any dictionary of American art. The painting does not appear in any catalogue of American paintings. This work, along with the Betsy Ross legend itself, has been erased from history; history textbooks and encyclopedias mention Ross only to refute the legend, if they mention her at all.

Nonetheless the legend has enjoyed periods of popularity as well as disfavor in the twentieth century. The popularity of this legend has apparently coincided with cultural climates in which the role of women in the public sphere has been particularly problematic. An exploration of these simultaneous occurrences may serve to demystify the way feminine service is constructed in the repre-sentation of historically important women. Deciphering the narra-tive of the painting and seeing that narrative as part of the ideological structure of the culture within which it was produced will give insight into the construction of myth, the construction of women's identity and women's power and its significance to American history.

POSTSCRIPT

In the course of my research on *The Birth of Our Nation's Flag*, I located the original painting, a 9' × 12' canvas which had been rolled up for nearly half a century. It is of course my thesis that it is in this painting that Charles H. Weisgerber not only created a portrait of Betsy Ross but constructed her image as it was carried through American cultural history. I am currently working to restore this painting to its proper place in American art history as well as American cultural history. With the support of the Michael C. Carlos Museum at Emory University along with a grant from the Mellon Foundation, the painting is being conserved and will be exhibited in conjunction with the publication of my work examining its cultural significance. The exhibition is scheduled to coincide with the 1996 Olympic games in Atlanta.

Although the image may be familiar to most of us, the painting itself has not been formally exhibited in nearly a century. Its last public display was in a department store window in Philadelphia. Even though the painting was exhibited at the Chicago World's Fair of 1934 and displayed alongside the Liberty Bell at war bond rallies during World War II, it remained in the possession of the Weisgerber family as Ross's popularity waned. Today the canvas is rolled up in a print shop in New Jersey, where it is stored.

I hope to exhume this painting from the oblivion to which it is now consigned and resurrect it as an important cultural relic. This image was fundamental in the construction of Betsy Ross as an historical figure and as a cultural phenomenon; and Betsy Ross, cultural icon, became a significant figure in the construction of American identity. She remains a singular female patriotic role model in our cultural knowledge of Revolutionary history. This painting deserves a place alongside images of American male historical figures sanctified through artistic representation. The flag remains a sacred object and a re-viewing of this image may illustrate the cultural grounding of this American belief-system as well as give insight into the contemporaneous cultural attitudes that in part produced this image. While the current trinity may be 'Mom, Flag, and Apple Pie' (with dessert firmly placed in the position of holy spirit), Weisgerber's clear construction of the trinity of the holy family in his 1893 portrayal of Betsy Ross has continued to induce accounts of her story to be written either with saintly reverence or with blasphemous contempt.

WORKS CITED

Bancroft, George, *History of the United States from the Discovery of the American Continent, The American Revolution*, 12th ed., vol. 1, Boston: Little, Brown, and Co., 1875.

Snider, Denton J., *World's Fair Studies*, Chicago: Sigma, 1895.

Quaife, Milo Milton, *The Flag of the United States*, New York: Grosset and Dunlap, 1942.

5

Mother India Through the Ages: the Dilemma of Conflicting Subjectivities

SABINA SAWHNEY

'The scriptures tell us,' persisted Gora, 'that Woman is deserving of worship because she gives light to the home, – the honour which is given her by English custom, because she sets fire to the hearts of men, had better not be termed worship.'

'Would you contemptuously dismiss a great idea because it occasionally gets clouded over?' asked Binoy.

'Binu,' answered Gora impatiently. 'Now that you have clearly lost your own power of judgement you ought to be guided by me. I affirm that all the exaggerated language about women that you find in English books has at bottom merely desire. The altar at which Woman may be truly worshipped is her place as Mother, the seat of the pure, right-minded Lady of the House.'

(Tagore, *Gora*, 9)

This conversation between Gora, the eponymous protagonist of Tagore's novel, and Binoy, Gora's closest friend, presents in a nutshell the two issues that animate the concerns of postcoloniality today. One, how do we negotiate the passage from being subjects of colonialism to becoming citizens of independent nation-states in the so-called 'family of nations'? In other words what cultural influences, colonial or indigenous, do we accept or reject? And two, what will be the status and role of women in this new family?

Neither issue allows for an easy resolution. We are after all concerning ourselves with nothing less than a definition of 'decolonization' and with the identity of the members of the decolonized states. Does the accession to a new identity necessarily involve a wholesale rejection of the cultural and political dominance of the colonizing power and if so, is it possible after centuries of colonialism to shrug off this influence like an ill-fitting garment? And if it were possible to do this, what should we enthrone in its stead? What sort of guidelines should the recently independent nations adopt that would help to usher them into the new era? How shall we surmount the split between the traditionalist demand for a stable system of reference and the articulation of new cultural demands in the political present?[1]

Initially for Gora the answers to these questions seemed simple and easily available. He recognized his primary imperative as a refusal to 'allow our country to stand at the bar of a foreign court and be judged according to a foreign law. Our ideas of shame and glory must not depend on minute comparisons at every step with a foreign standard' (23). India must acknowledge that her greatest strength lay in her traditional virtues and Gora exerted himself to 'get together arguments from reason and scripture to prove the blameless excellence of Hindu religion and society' (23). The evocation of 'traditional' truths as revealed in the scriptures thus provides a space from which the development of the new nation can proceed. Recourse to these traditional values, however, is based on a denial: the desire to disregard the historical fact of colonialism itself, to pretend that it is possible to forget the violent interruption of colonialism and carry on in the present by denying the recent past.

The invocation of traditional values was attractive not only because they provided a stable and simple answer to some of the most vexing questions of identity-formation, but also because the heaviest burden of carrying these values fell on women. Gora and Binoy, in their argument about the differing positions accorded to women in the English and the orthodox Indian cultures, unknowingly manage to articulate the problems of the postcolonial woman. For connected to these points of departure and return promised by the traditional values stands the figure of woman, determined by these beliefs but not a part of them. She is still seen, not as an independent entity in her own right, participating as an equal in the debate about the course of the country, but merely as one of the subjects of such debate. Her position in the nation has to be defined anew, no longer by the colonizers but by the men of the nation who are now in power. And the problem of her position is the same as that of the nation: what sort of identity will the two of them be granted, such that the transition to independence and modernity is not adulterated by the value-systems of the Western colonizers?

The call by Gora for a nationalist regeneration by using slogans of cultural and religious revival is immensely ironic. Gora's unyielding and fervent belief in the greatness of Hindu orthodoxy suffers a series of shocks as he encounters the miseries that ensue from an unquestioning acceptance of outmoded rituals and mores. But the hardest blow to his beliefs is delivered by the facts about his birth – available to the reader early in the text but revealed to Gora only at the end of the novel, which implies that he never noticed that the literal meaning of his name is 'white man'. Born to an Irish-English couple, Gora was orphaned as an infant during the rebellion of 1857. He had been adopted into a Hindu family, who hid the nature of Gora's birth from him as well as everybody else.[2] The fact that he had no right to consider himself a Hindu, since one can only be born into the religion and there are no opportunities for conversion to Hinduism, forces him to radically reconsider his position. Instead of asserting the primacy of the Hindu religion as the foundation of an Indian identity, Gora is eventually willing to reconsider the whole issue of the constitution of national identity.

In this essay I propose to read Gora as a brilliant demonstration by Tagore of the predicament of postcolonial nations. *Gora* delineates the attempt of the people to determine a new identity for themselves and the nation to which they belong. Rejecting the solutions based either on traditional orthodoxy or on a complete assimilation to the Western ideals, Tagore proposes instead a concept of dynamic interaction, one that will evolve in order to deal with the internal contradictions of decolonization.[3] Remapping the boundaries of national identity through the character and education of Gora such that there exist no eternal verities that will facilitate the emergence of a new nationalism, Tagore focuses on the complexities of cultural authority. It is the very authority of culture as it is formulated in the process of enunciating its supremacy – as the repository of referential truths – that becomes the issue in this novel.

However this radical questioning of cultural authority in the name of religion, class and caste-based discriminations turns mute when it encounters the name of woman. The complex dynamic exchange that Tagore envisions for the people of India is based on a determinate exclusion of women from the process. This exclusion is not incidental, brought about in a fit of absent-minded forgetfulness; the woman *has* to figure as the bearer of traditional values which will animate and stabilize this exchange. That is to say, the interplay between tradition and modernity Tagore proposes is underpinned by the role of the woman; she underwrites the process of evolution and change by becoming the still point authorizing the movement towards progress.

I

If the ambivalent figure of the nation is a problem of its transitional history, its conceptual indeterminacy, its wavering between vocabularies, then what effect does this have on narratives and discourses that signify a sense of nationness?

(Bhabha *Nation* 2)

Before I return to *Gora* and the novel's responses to the conflicting demands of decolonization, I think it will be useful to summarize the pitfalls and difficulties that lie in the field of postcolonial studies as scholars deal with some of the concerns mentioned above.[4] The foregrounding of (post)coloniality and its relation to the Western formulations of modernity and postmodernism has so far been largely accomplished in two ways. First, an investigation into the ways in which knowledge of cultural differences has been repressed or distorted within Western culture. The critique of Western culture thus takes into account the ways in which the West is represented, at the expense of the Other, as progressive and civilized. Second, archival research and engagement with texts from decolonized nations, which seek to disprove the stereotypical conceptions imposed on cultures other than European or North American.

Both these methods, however, are liable to fall prey to the problems they attempt to uncover and undermine. If the analysis of the Western production of culture remains at the level of excoriation of the West for its racist and supremacist approaches towards dealing with difference, it does not advance the understanding of the reasons that initially produced these approaches and made them necessary. The condemnation may certainly be apt, especially in light of the fact that the declarations of intent which preceded and justified colonization were rarely adhered to during the process. That is to say, the ideas of civility and ethics that partly comprise the image of Western civilization were almost completely turned on their head or ignored when it came to dealing with cultures other than the European. The brutal exploitation and oppression maintained in the cause of civilizing savages surely gave the lie to the concept of Western civilization, and pointing this out may certainly be very satisfying. However so long as the analysis remains at this level and does not question the modes of construction which maintained the supremacy of the European subject, it merely sets up a binary opposition between the colonizer and the colonized. This opposition now functions in the same way as the one promulgated by a Eurocentric tradition, except that there is a simple reversal of the identificatory value-judgements placed on the two terms. Instead of the civilizing and progressive colonizers who were engaged in the process of helping the benighted savages, we are now subjected to portraits of vicious and cruel Europeans ruthlessly conquering and appropriating the resources of innocent Africans and Asians.[5] Both these viewpoints subscribe to the notion of the colonized as being without agency, as passive subjects existing merely to record the acts of the colonizers. The image of the colonized as innocent and passive is actually an aspect of the colonial discourse itself: an obverse of the colonial coin.[6]

The scholars in the field of postcoloniality who take the once-colonized cultures as the main area of their research have to deal with a different set of problems. In order to deny that the colonized cultures were primitive or savage, the practitioners of the second mode may try to demonstrate that these cultures are as civilized as the Western cultures by which they have been tested and found wanting: the desire for a homogeneity which conceives of culture and civilization as synonymous with Westernization gives rise to studies which attempt to deny the difference between the Western and non-Western societies in order to prove that the non-Western societies were always engaged in the production of a culture similar to that of the West.[7] According to this reading, the labelling of non-Western societies as barbaric or primitive was a mistake, since any substantive analysis of their culture would have proved these labels false. However the assertion 'we are as cultured as you' merely mimics Western notions of civilization and culture without questioning either their formation or value.[8]

The more rigorous studies in the same mode which pay attention to the diverse facets of Western culture recognize that the desire to inscribe differences between self and other, such that the other is always viewed in negative terms, reflects a problem within

Western culture. In this case a wholehearted consumption of Western standards becomes thoroughly problematic. In order to deal with this difficulty the studies then attempt to reconstitute the Other tradition, one which is as different from the West as possible.[9] While the production of an Other tradition with different codes of behavior and philosophy may maintain a 'separate but equal' theme, a sort of liberal multicultural pluralism, this production too falls prey to the same problems it had initially set out to oppose. The constitution of a tradition, after all, does not take place in a neutral zone where all the various silenced and neglected elements of a society finally discover their true value and manage to articulate an identity of self-affirmation. Just as the deliberate marginalization of the colonized cultures was an essential attribute of the European colonial culture at the metropolis and was structurally necessary for the very terms of its production, similarly the reconstitution of an African or an Asian tradition becomes radically dependent on the peripheralization of certain groups within Asia or Africa.[10]

The need to develop a self-affirming tradition was particularly urgent in light of the centuries of subjection to humiliation and of being considered second-rate solely because of one's status as a non-European. As Frantz Fanon states, the 'passionate search for a national culture which existed before the colonial era finds its legitimate reason in the anxiety shared by native intellectuals to shrink away from that Western culture in which they all risk being swamped' (209). The demand for a recovery of cultural values with which one could identify without feeling ashamed, however, colored the search and the expression of such values. I am not arguing that had there been no such demand, a pristine, pure and authentic tradition could have been recovered. Any search for a cultural history and the consequent management of its expression arise out of, and are influenced by, the material conditions which necessitate this search. So, without denying the desire for inspirational models from the past, it needs to be emphasized that just what will be seen as inspirational depends on the climate in which this need arises.

The quest for a regenerating self-definition in postcolonial studies thus inevitably proceeded in the direction most favorable to those engaged in this quest. The formulation and regulation of certain nationalist traditions arising out of the decolonized societies were managed by the people who had the resources to engage in these pursuits as well as the accessibility to modes of mass dissemination. Hence there was a selective retrieval of those traditions which confirmed the values and principles of a certain class, religion, ethnicity or gender, and those values gained the dominant voice in this reproduction of the past.

The other problem that faces those who are engaged in postcolonial studies concerns the notion of the postcolonial subject. The discourse of national affiliation is based on assumptions of identity and subjectivity that must be exposed to a critical analysis.[11] An unproblematic acceptance of the unity of a precolonial with the postcolonial subject depends heavily on a discourse that censors those elements which indicate a threat to this seamless identity. This threat comes into existence through those discourses that depend on nostalgia to produce a naturalized national subject: inevitably male, middle or upper class, and belonging to the dominant ethnic and religious group: 'Once upon a time we were all princes ...'. The radical exclusion of others from this essentialized national subject produces a gap between the identity and the people to whom it refers. The studies that assume an unproblematic notion of the postcolonial subject, one whose national affiliation and national identity have been finally resolved, reify the subject such that any modification is seen as a threat to national unity. In other words, once independence has been achieved, the subject of that independent nation has now no more negotiations to manage, no more issues of identity to resolve, has in fact foreclosed all possibilities of doubt and confusion. If doubt and confusion still exist, if people still articulate their dissatisfaction with the existing order of things, it is because the attack on the 'indigenous elites' is motivated by the lingering influence of colonial ideologies.

Thus these ultra-nationalist studies posit an existing identity which constitutes the subjectivity of the postcolonial. However 'postcolonial' does not refer to a common identity under which all the differences are calmly subsumed: rather the differing effects of the colonial moment facilitate the constitution of specific postcolonialities. The denial of the specificity of the colonial subject leads to its isolation from all the other axes of power relations constituting identity. 'Postcolonial' does not function as a stable signifier to which everyone from a former colony can uncritically assent. Furthermore in these studies the legitimacy and justification for a postcolonial subject depend on its unity with the precolonial self – one which has apparently retained its essential attributes un-

touched by the experience of colonization and may now be recuperated for representation.

What I propose instead is an analysis that notes the predicament
inherent in the post of the postcoloniality (by analogy with the post
of poststructuralism) in focusing upon two forms of the troubling
of identity. On the one hand there is the clash of divergent indigenous traditions in the postcolonial situation: Muslim, Sikh and
Hindu in India, Kikuyu and Kalenjin in Kenya, Tutsi and Hutu in
Rwanda, etc., along with the more familiar class and gender differences. On the other hand there is a focus upon the fact of cultural métissage which is the legacy of colonialism. During the
colonial period 'colonized' was the only identity available to the
people of the colonies, an identity which functioned in terms of a
binary opposition to the colonizers. After decolonization,
however, the binding confines of this generic identity were
removed, so that various specific identities now burst on the
scene. The departure of the colonizers did not automatically mean
a departure of all the prohibitions which had hedged the colonial
society: the fracturing of 'colonized' led to the creation of boundaries around the new identities that had arisen. These troublings
of identity must be considered in any account of the postcolonial
situation.

II

'When the whole world has forsaken India and heaps insults
upon her, I for my part wish to share her seat of dishonour – this
caste-ridden, this superstitious, this idolatrous India of mine!'

(*Gora* 267)

Depicting the conflict between the two modes of tradition–
constitution – the one imitating the West, and the other asserting its
radical difference from the West – *Gora* concerns itself with nothing
less than the identity of the nation of India and its peoples. In *Gora*
Tagore analyzes the significance of Indian nationalism as it relates
to the clash between old and new, between rigid orthodoxy and
free inquiry.

Considered by many to be Tagore's finest novel, *Gora*[12] is set in
pre-independence Bengal, a state in north-east India. Ostensibly
about the friendship of two men, Gora and Binoy, as they struggle
through their youth, the novel's main theme foregrounds the con-

tested issues of racial, religious and national identities in the context of colonialism. The responses of the various factions of Indian society to the presence of English colonialists are represented in terms of a rigid opposition: either a total rejection of Western values or a total acceptance. Gora is a firm adherent to the policy of complete repudiation. In his view any adoption of Western values could only attack the foundations of the Hindu society such that there may be no recovery of its inherent strength thereafter. Haran Babu is the spokesperson for the people who view the English as the epitome of perfection; he is among those who have been so cowed by their conquest that their only hope seems to lie in a blind imitation of the English. Talking to a British magistrate after Gora made an impassioned plea for an investigation into the exploitation of villagers, Haran attempts to allay the magistrate's displeasure by asserting that Gora's fervent demand reflected a failure of his education:

> 'There is no spiritual and moral teaching at all. These fellows have not been able to assimilate the best in English culture. It is only because they have only learnt their lessons by rote, and not had any moral training, that these ingrates will not acknowledge British rule in India to be a dispensation of Providence.'
>
> (141)

Thus Tagore represents the two extremes – excessive mortification at racial humiliation and excessive gratification at occasional approval by the English – which characterized the Indian response to the colonial situation. The tension was heightened by inverted pride seeking compensation in a glorious past. Gora represents that section of society which engaged in an increasingly chauvinistic defence of Hindu customs and institutions. While the end of the novel attempts to overcome the strongly Hindu flavor of an Indian patriotic emotion, through most of the text Tagore's sympathies clearly lie with Gora. Gora's statement to Sucharita, the woman he eventually comes to love and marry, that any imitation of the English would only result in the production of a counterfeit culture resonates strongly:

> 'If we have the mistaken notion that because the English are strong we can never become strong unless we become exactly like them, then that impossibility will never be achieved, for by

mere imitation we shall eventually be neither one thing nor the other.'

(102)

But Gora's views, while striking a chord in the readers, are obviously suspect. Ardently nationalist, he envisions an India of myths and legends – a recourse to nostalgia which is all too pervasive in a colonial situation. Through his character the novel explores the ramifications of a determination to oppose the imposition of negative stereotypes on the colonized subjects through a blind acceptance of a mythic greatness.

The seduction of Gora's vision is countered in the novel not only by the views of the rather ineffectual Haran Babu but also by the original ideals and principles of the Brahmo Samaj. Founded in 1828 by Raja Rammohun Roy,[13] the Brahmo Samaj was initially conceived as a reformist movement against some of the particularly opprobrious superstitions and taboos of Hinduism. More important, Rammohun's basic idea that all major religions had similar traditions in spite of their diversity of form became the universalist credo of the Samaj. Inspired by the Unitarians and by the writings of Locke, Bentham and Montesquieu, the Samaj had a decidedly Western bias, and was to a certain extent directed towards the West. The 'Brahmos', as the members were called, challenged all forms of obscurantism and ritual as well as the oppression of women associated with orthodox beliefs.

In the course of time however the Brahmo Samaj acquired a rigid anti-Hindu bias. The Hindu revivalist upsurge was in part a response to the attacks of the Brahmo Samajists who joined with the Christian missionaries to denigrate Hindu practices, especially idol worship. All of these issues provide the social and cultural backdrop to the action of *Gora*. The original ideal and the contemporary practice – the two strands in the Brahmo Samaj – are represented through the figures of Paresh Babu and Haran Babu. Paresh Babu, the adoptive father of Sucharita, is the main proponent of the ideals of Brahmo Samaj. Responding to Gora's argument that the truth of 'religion is revealed through the laws of society' and any attempt to change these laws is motivated by a mistaken understanding of the laws, Paresh Babu insists:

'Truth cannot be tested except by opposition and obstacles ... the testing of truth has not been carried out once and for all by a group of learned men in some past age; truth has to be discovered anew through the blows and oppositions it encounters from the people of every age.'

(344–5)

Paresh Babu articulates Tagore's ideal mode of being – the refusal to depend on 'revealed truths', whether the revelation came from ancient scriptures or from the Western traditions – as a pedagogical imperative for Indian society. The pedagogical imperative becomes especially conspicuous as Paresh Babu invariably couches his teachings in the manner of a rather distant schoolmaster. The ideal however becomes a performative in the actions of Anandmoyi, Gora's adoptive mother, who disdains the injunctions of her society in her love for the orphaned infant. The position of Paresh Babu – an outcast in the Brahmo Samaj for his espousal of non-discrimination against the Hindus – is paralleled by Anandmoyi in the Hindu society. Both of them occupy a similar niche with regard to their respective societies – Brahmo and Hindu – believing in the ideals but gently rebelling against the orthodoxies. This leads to a special role for both of them since neither can be considered as belonging wholly inside or outside of their particular culture.

But it is Anandmoyi's act in adopting the European boy as her own, an act that according to the rules of orthodox Hinduism exposed her to constant contact with an outcast, an unclean member of the society, that fully incorporates Tagore's vision of an independent India. Anandmoyi's courage in defying the rules of a religion that is strongly bound by notions of pollution and committed to rituals of cleanliness is almost unbelievable. Ironically it is Gora himself who berates his mother for her lackadaisical attitudes towards the finer points of Hindu rituals. And it is Gora who in response to the regulations of Hinduism develops a strong obsession with pollution and becomes most punctilious about these rituals. He regularly bathes in the Ganges, performs ceremonial worship morning and evening and takes particualr care of what he touches and eats. He even stops accepting water in his mother's room as she employs a Christian maid. The horror of an unclean touch persuades him to forbid Binoy to eat in Anandmoyi's room.

Of course all of this comes to naught when the secret of Gora's birth is finally revealed to him.[14] The disclousure itself acts as the final denouement of the text and is set up with pomp and circumstance. Some of Gora's friends and protegés plan a huge religious ceremony to bestow upon Gora the title of 'The Light of the Hindu Religion':

> Several Sanskrit slokas were to be printed in letters of gold on a parchment which was to be signed by all the Brahmin pandits and would then be presented to Gora in a box of sandalwood. After that a fine edition of Max Muller's book on the Rig Veda, bound in the most expensive morocco cover, would be offered to him by the oldest and most honoured of the learned men present as a token of the blessings of India herself. In this way would be beautifully expressed the appreciation they felt for Gora, who in the present fallen state of Hinduism had done so much to preserve the ancient forms of the Vedic religion.
>
> (347)

It is of course doubly ironic that the celebrations for the 'light of the Hindu religion' include the presentation of a book on the Rig Veda by a European – Max Mueller[15] – to another European, Gora. The prominent role envisaged for the Mueller book irretrievably compromises the very principles of cultural and religious purity that the occasion was meant to commemorate. The almost gratuitous introduction of this incidental fact brings into stark relief the utter impossibility of erecting boundaries around national and religious ideologies. A cultural tradition which may form the basis of a national society cannot exist or be maintained in isolation from all the influences that may not be indigenous to the country.

The same ironic paradigm is replayed when Gora, amidst all the festivities, learns of his father's illness and hastens to his bedside in time to hear the truth about his birth. The ceremonies are necessarily suspended and Gora tries to come to terms with the fact that all that he had held valid for so long had been based on a misapprehension:

> The foundations upon which, from childhood, all his life had been raised had suddenly crumbled into dust, and he was unable to understand who he was and where he stood … . He had no mother, no father, no country, no nationality, no lineage, no God even. Only one thing was left to him and that was a vast negation.'
>
> (402)

It is out of this 'vast negation' that Tagore finally creates his desired image of a true Indian – one who refuses to accept any barriers between himself and the rest of humanity, whether the barriers be related to religion, caste, or even 'foreign' birth. Gora articulates this vision when he announces to Paresh Babu that now 'I am really an Indian! In me there is no longer any opposition between Hindu, Mussalman, and Christian. To-day every caste in India is my caste, the food of all is my food!' (406). The shifting margins of cultural displacement experienced by Gora finally confound any hermetic or authentic sense of a 'national' culture. The dislocation of Gora from the positions in which he had entrenched himself makes a profound statement about the cultural and historical hybridity of the postcolonial world.[16]

This would seem an ideal place to stop were it not for the fact that the profundity of Tagore's statement about the hybrid identity of the postcolonial is negated by his refusal to allow women to participate in the formation of such identity. This complex dynamic, this imbrication of foreign and domestic, English and Indian, this hybridity which refuses to be slotted into any pre-set categories is possible only at the expense of postcolonial women.

III

'The mother whom I have been wandering about in search of was all the time sitting in my room at home. You have no castes, you make no distinctions, and have no hatred – you are only the image of our welfare! It is you who are India!'

(*Gora* 407)

Gora ends with this invocation to the mother, an invocation that collapses the difference between the nation and the mother such that both become objects of worship. What, one might wonder, is the cause for any dissatisfaction with the identification of the woman with the nation in which both are set on a pedestal and regarded with devout reverence? However this seeming improvement in the status of women functions more like a 'kick upstairs' would function in today's corporate world. Set on a pedestal or 'sitting in my room at home', the woman as mother is effectively immobilized. Agency of being and doing is conveniently retained by men. The only role that this image vouchsafes to women is that of a caretaker. Looking after the welfare of all, i.e. all the men, she is also responsible for the upkeep of the desired image of 'Mother India' which will presumably inspire her sons in the performance of their national duties. The possibility of movement among different modes of being that *Gora* holds forth as an ideal is granted only to the men of the postcolonial nations.

The reference to the condition of postcoloniality is deliberate; I am not making an argument about universal patriarchy which confines women to the private sphere of home and domesticity while retaining the public arena as the natural habitat for men. The inner/outer distinction in a nationalist framework becomes particularly urgent under the impact of colonialism. Reactions to the event of colonialism may take different forms, as I have suggested earlier, but most oppositional strategies do share a common element. The attack on colonialism goes hand-in-hand with the attempt to raise the self-esteem of the colonized. In other words almost all anticolonial struggles must try to combat the enervating effects of conquest by appealing to the innate dignity and worth of those who have been laid low by colonialism. Partha Chatterjee's essays perform one of the most useful analyses of this aspect of anticolonialism:

> The world was where the European powers had challenged the non-European peoples, and by virtue of its superior material culture, had subjugated them. But it had failed to colonize the inner, essential, identity of the East which lay in its distinctive, and superior, spiritual culture. … No encroachments by the colonizer must be allowed in that inner sanctum. In the world, imitation of and adaptation to the western norms was a necessity; at home they were tantamount to annihilation of one's very identity.[17]
>
> (*Nationalist Resolution* 239)

Determined by the terms of this dichotomous formulation, the colonized woman is made to represent the inner identity of the colonized nation. The anticolonial struggle, fought on the cultural and political terrain of the colonizers, is sanctioned by the image of woman that remains uncontaminated by this struggle. Thus upon the constructs of a generic patriarchy which restricts women to the private sphere, another constraint is fabricated.

In reference to *Gora* however the ideal women figures do not seem to fall neatly within this formulation. Both Anandmoyi, Gora's mother, and Sucharita, Gora's beloved, owe part of their virtue to their contact with Gora – a European. It is in fact Anandmoyi's loving adoption of the little Irish baby as her own that grants her an exemplary stature; her refusal to heed the orthodox prohibitions enables Gora to revise his nationalist vision in accordance with Tagore's principles. Does it mean then that just as Tagore's novel opposes the anticolonial stance on its rhetoric of pure and traditional nationalism, *Gora* also counters the anticolonial point of view with regard to the symbolic position imposed upon women? Unfortunately the answer must be 'not really'. The seeming contradictions between the analysis delineated above and the novel vanish when we subject both to a closer look.

While both Anandmoyi and Sucharita are admirable because of their warm-hearted welcome of Gora, this welcoming in itself does not constitute any serious rejection of the prevalent discourse. Both adhere to the notion that women must embody a pure spirituality, uncontaminated by the material struggle around them. Contact with Gora does not translate into association with the material, Western world. In fact, Gora can be held as a representative of the West only if we assume that nationality is a condition of blood and biology and not culture. Gora's absorption into Indian culture, and particularly into its Brahmanical Hindu aspect, is almost absolute. Hence the precepts that enjoin women not to draw near the corrupting influences of the Western culture remain unquestioned by both Anandmoyi and Sucharita when they take Gora to their hearts.

What is perhaps even more disturbing is that Gora's accession to a new and revitalizing sense of self and the nation to which he belongs is generated by his belated recognition that 'Mother India' would not exist without the sacrifices of the maternal figures that have nurtured him since his birth.[18] Gora's glorification of such sacrifice ensures that the role-models for women in the new nation will be virtually identical to those celebrated in the myths and legends of India's past. Indian girls have been reared on stories of all-sacrificing women – the exemplars of Sati, Savitri, and Sita[19] are constantly invoked in order to silence any dissatisfaction felt by Indian women about the narrow confines of their activity.

Anandmoyi explains her philosophy of calm resignation and sacrifice, admitting that her son and other members of the family occasionally scorned her since she did not observe all of the rituals against pollution. 'I remain in that society, and in that house, accepting all the abuse they like to give me – but I don't find that such a great hindrance' (*Gora* 256). The theme of sacrifice and self-abnegation for women is reinforced by Sucharita's responses to Gora: 'Today Sucharita had humbled herself [to Gora] and had even rejoiced in her humiliation, because she felt that by sacrificing herself she had gained greatly' (317).

In effect *Gora* delineates a very static portrayal of women in an otherwise dynamic postcolonial society. While the changes that animate the novel and its hero run the gamut from religion, society, politics and ritual, the role of women remains distressingly at odds with all this activity. The opinions of Gora about the status of women, stated in his argument with Binoy near the beginning of the book, endure to the end: 'The altar at which Woman may be truly worshipped is her place as Mother, the seat of the pure, right-minded Lady of the House' (9). While Gora learns to appreciate the *importance* of the role of women in his version of a postcolonial society, there is no reference to changing the parameters of the role itself.

NOTES

1. The demand for a stable system of reference is linked to unease at the changes brought about by decolonization. The desire for a known tradition and a stable community must be negotiated with the knowledge that both must be modified in response to the changing present. Hence a necessary loss of certitude accompanies the articulation of new political realities.
2. The bald facts about the plot necessarily draw comparisons with Rudyard Kipling's *Kim*; a comparison that Tagore apparently did not consider a compliment. See Lago.
3. In 'Nationalism' Tagore stated that neither 'the colorless vagueness of cosmopolitanism, nor the fierce self-idolatry of nation worship is the goal of human history' (199).
4. One should note that the novelty of interest in the field of postcoloniality is a Western phenomenon. The scholarship and the interest are new only for North American and European institutions, not in Asia, Africa or South America where they have been pursued for a considerable length of time.
5. Amilcar Cabral in *Revolution in Guinea* suggests that 'the essential characteristic of imperialist domination remains the same: the negation of the historical process of the dominated people by means of violent usurpation of the freedom of development of the national productive forces' (San Juan 149). Cabral's narrow definition of historical process denies any agency to the colonized and depends on a simple binary opposition between the oppressors and the oppressed, thus occluding the complexities of the colonial situation.

6. There is of course another way of dealing with the West through a postcolonial perspective: one that interrogates the construction of the colonial subject in Western ideology such that the elements which participate in such construction are identified and analyzed – that is, an internal critique of the interpretive frames of Western culture so as to produce an oppositional mode of reading which intervenes radically in the ideation of Western civilization.

7. Sumit Sarkar shows that a number of Indian intellectuals in interpreting the evolution of Indian thought in terms of a conflict between 'Westernization' and 'traditionalism' had completely accepted Westernism as the historically progressive trend.

8. Naipaul's *The Mimic Men* delineates the problems inherent in such mimicry, parodying the colonized as they attempt to talk and speak like the European rulers.

9. The best example of this is the négritude movement. The term 'négritude' came into being sometime around 1935, and the leaders of this movement, Léopold Senghor and Aimé Césaire, are both associated with the anticolonial struggle against France in West Africa. According to Senghor in 'Rapport sur la doctrine et le programme du parti' given at the Constitutive Congress of the African Assembly Party in 1959, the colonizers 'deemed we had invented nothing, created nothing, written, sculpted, painted, and sung nothing. ... [W]e had to assert our essential being, namely our négritude.' Senghor defines négritude as the 'total of black Africa's cultural values' (Kesteloot 102).

   Conceived as a response to Western declarations of superiority, négritude affirmed the cultural values of black Africa. However, as Soyinka points out, the re-entrenchment of black values was not only based on 'the dialectical structure of European ideological confrontations but borrowed from the very components of its racist syllogism' (127).

   The négritude movement did not challenge the Western claims to superiority based on its presumed highly developed analytic thought and reason. Instead négritude asserted its pre-eminence in the field of emotive and intuitive understanding, thus leaving the basic framework of divisions intact. Sartre could thus conveniently label négritude as the antithesis to the thesis of white supremacy and foretell its end in the synthesis of a raceless society.

   Furthermore négritude, while making these vast claims on behalf of black Africa, was a creation by and for a small elite. The search for a racial identity was undertaken by a minority of uprooted individuals – a property of the bourgeois–intellectual elite. The vast population of colonial Africa remained largely untouched by this phenomenon.

10. A number of scholars saw the history of India in the late nineteenth and twentieth centuries as a conflict between reactionary and progressive forces. The opinions and beliefs of the indigenous elite intellectuals were identified as the agents of progress trying to overcome the anti-modern and conservative notions which impeded India's progress. See for instance R. P. Dutt, S. C. Sarkar, and A. R. Desai.

11. According to Homi Bhabha the 'question of identification is never the affirmation of a pre-given identity, never a self-fulfilling prophecy – it is always the production of an image of identity and the transformation of the subject in assuming that image. ... The "atmosphere of certain uncertainty" that surrounds the body certifies its existence and threatens its dismemberment' ('Interrogating Identity' 188).
12. See G. V. Raj, Sisirkumar Ghose and Niharranjan Ray.
13. Raja Rammohun Roy (1772–1833) was influenced by Western liberal thought and had attempted to reform and revitalize Hinduism. He championed women's rights on four issues: sati, polygamy, women's education and women's property rights. Considered by many to be the 'Father of the Bengal Renaissance' Roy attempted to counter the attacks and criticisms of the British by advocating a re-interpretation of the Vedas along with a selective appropriation of Western ideas.
14. A number of critics have expressed dissatisfaction at the way the plot of *Gora* is finally resolved. B. C. Chakravorty regards it as an 'artificial solution' (108); Nirad C. Choudhary sees it as 'a victory for liberal cosmopolitanism [which] is pulled off only by means of a deus ex machina' (15).
15. Max Mueller, probably one of the best-known Orientalists, was partly responsible for popularizing the racist Aryan myth of a Hindu golden age that influenced a number of Indian thinkers.
16. Homi Bhabha's notion of 'hybridity' is important to consider. See especially 'The Commitment to Theory'.
17. See also Chatterjee's essays on women and nation in *The Nation and its Fragments*.
18. Both Anandmoyi and Lachmi, the Christian maid employed by Anandmoyi, have been Gora's adoptive mothers. It was only after Gora decided to take up the cause of orthodox Hinduism that he refused to deal with Lachmi anymore.
19. Sita, Savitri and Sati are the heroines of various mythological stories and ancient Indian epics whose devotion compels them to sacrifice everything for the well-being of their husbands.

WORKS CITED

Bhabha, Homi K., 'The Commitment to Theory', in Jim Pines and Paul Willeman (eds), *Questions of Third Cinema*, London: British Film Institute, 1989.

—— 'Interrogating Identity: The Post Colonial Prerogative', in David Goldberg (ed.), *The Anatomy of Racism*, Minneapolis: Minnesota UP, 1990a.

—— (ed.), *Nation and Narration*, London: Routledge, 1990b.

Chakravorty, B. C., *Rabindranath Tagore: His Mind and Art*, New Delhi: Young India Publications, 1971.

Chatterjee, Partha, *The Nation and its Fragments*, Princeton: Princeton University Press, 1993.

—— 'The Nationalist Resolution of the Women's Question', in Kum Kum Sangari and Sadesh Vaid (eds), *Recasting Women*, New Brunswick: Rutgers University Press, 1989.

Choudhary, Nirad C., 'Tagore and the Nobel Prize', *The Illustrated Weekly of India*, 11 March 1973.

Desai, A. R., *Social Background of Indian Nationalism*, Bombay: Popular Book Depot, 1948.

Dutt, R. P., *India Today*, Bombay: People's Publishing House, 1949.

Fanon, Frantz, *The Wretched of the Earth*, trans. Constance Farrington, New York: Grove Press, 1963.

Ghose, Sisirkumar, *Rabindranath Tagore*, New Delhi: Sahitya Akademi, 1986.

Kesteloot, Lilyan, *Black Writers in French*, Washington, DC: Howard University Press, 1991.

Lago, Mary, *Rabindranath Tagore*, Boston: Twayne, 1976.

Raj, G. V., *Tagore the Novelist*, New Delhi: Sterling Publishers, 1983.

Ray, Niharranjan, 'Three Novels of Tagore', *Indian Literature* 4 (1961).

San Juan, E., 'Art Against Imperialism', in N. Rudich (ed.), *Weapons of Criticism*, Palo Alto, CA: Ramparts Press, 1976.

Sarkar, S. C., *Bengal Renaissance and Other Essays*, New Delhi: People's Publishing House, 1970.

Sarkar, Sumit, 'Rammohun Roy and the Break with the Past', in V. C. Joshi (ed.), *Rammohun Roy and the Process of Modernization in India*, Delhi: Vikas, 1975.

Soyinka, Wole, *Myth, Literature and the African World*, Cambridge: Cambridge University Press, 1976.

Tagore, Rabindranath, *Gora*, trans. by author, Madras: Macmillan India, 1924.

—— 'Nationalism', in Amiya Chakravarty (ed.), *A Tagore Reader*, New York: Macmillan, 1961.

Naipaul, V. S., *The Mimic Men*, New York: Macmillan, 1967.

6

Willa Cather's *My Ántonia* and the Politics of Modernist Classicism

JOHN N. SWIFT

Almost all of Willa Cather's writing involves inheritance: both the legal passing on of property and, more important, the transmission and replication across generations of traditions, of culture itself. As a result her protagonists look back to their own pasts or to history in general, anxiously framing two questions: Who are my legitimate ancestors, biological or metaphorical? And what is the nature of their bequest to me? This thematic insistence has two consequences in her great mid-career novels of the late 1910s and 1920s. First, since culture is always *read* as a relationship of signs, one prominent concern of Cather's fiction is education, which literally allows the present to read and thus receive the past's cryptic legacy. Second, her heroes often confront an apparent *choice* of familial or cultural origins, and in response construct or act out some version of what Freud called the 'family romance', the childhood fantasy in which real pasts and parents are repudiated in favor of a more glamorous symbolic lineage. Thus for example Tom Outland in *The Professor's House* (1925) emotionally replaces his dead 'mover people' parents with the vanished Anasazi Indians; *A Lost Lady's* Niel Herbert (1923) similarly chooses Captain and Marian Forester over a biological family marked by 'failure and defeat' (30); and Claude Wheeler of *One of Ours* (1922) rejects his stifling small-town past for the defense of an idealized France – and trades his Nebraska parents for the courtly, childless Jouberts.

I want in the following essay to consider both of these effects – the centricity of education and the family romance structure – in the semi-autobiographical *My Ántonia* (1918), whose preoccupation with the 'old country' makes it at once perhaps the clearest and the

107

most ambivalent of Cather's explorations of ancestry and inheritance. I will argue that the orphaned narrator Jim Burden's academic education and discovery of high 'classical' culture constitute an attempted re-choosing of origins, and that this process of choice simultaneously allegorizes both Cather's own struggles with personal identity and a dominant anxiety of her historical moment, a moment when a perplexing, pressing cultural question – who shall inherit America? – could find expression in inverted, retrospective form: from whom shall America be inherited? Like the other great modernists of the 1920s, Cather looked frequently and fondly back toward an uncorrupted, regularized and essentially *masculine* classical past, the serenely womanless world imagined (and briefly inhabited) by henpecked Godfrey St. Peter in *The Professor's House*. But against such a nostalgia her fiction developed a strong countercurrent, an attention to the present (and future), the irregular and the feminine: and in *My Ántonia* the two impulses co-exist in an uneasy equilibrium.

I

When at the novel's midpoint Jim Burden – roughly following Cather's own 1890 path – leaves his grandparents' home in rural Black Hawk for the University of Nebraska, he falls under the spell of the passionate young classicist Gaston Cleric, whom he later follows to Harvard. In this new relationship's intensity, his discovery of classical literature seems radically transformative, a 'mental awakening' (257): 'Cleric introduced me to the world of ideas; when one first enters that world everything else fades for a time, and all that went before is as if it had not been' (257–8). And this transformation's central characteristic is Jim's alignment of *himself* with literary classicism's world, his assumption of a position and identity in a regressive structure of mentoring texts, at whose origin he hears the ancestral voice of Virgil. 'I can hear [Cleric] now', he recalls, 'speaking the lines of the poet Statius, who spoke for Dante: "I was famous on earth with the name which endures longest and honours most. The seeds of my ardour were the sparks from that divine flame whereby more than a thousand have kindled; I speak of the *Aeneid*, mother to me and nurse to me in poetry"' (261–2). Such a self-conscious gesture of filial allegiance to classical (and specifically Virgilian) genius, represented here biparentally in Dante's metaphor as the potent but maternal *Aeneid*, had already provided Cather with the crisis of her 1907 short story 'The Namesake' (whose protagonist discovers 'the pull of race and blood and kindred' (179) while contemplating an American flag scribbled on the flyleaf of his dead uncle's *Aeneid*). It was to become an important mechanism for her novels of the 1920s, the signal for a particular kind of maturation in her protagonists. Thus in *One of Ours* Claude escapes suffocating, feminized Nebraska via the troop ship *Anchises*; in *The Professor's House* Tom Outland imaginatively fuses the *Aeneid* and the Blue Mesa's redemptive landscape at the 'high tide' of his experience. In *A Lost Lady* Montaigne and Ovid play a related though somewhat different role in Niel's first attempted repudiation of Marian Forester and his move from Sweet Water to Cambridge. But nowhere in Cather's work is the association of the classical world and self-discovery clearer or more fully elaborated than in *My Ántonia*.

The enthusiastic affiliation with Virgilian classicism marking Jim's transition from 'parish' to 'world' (the terms by which Sarah Orne Jewett famously defined the poles of Cather's own early work) has two immediate narrative effects on the novel. First, classicism provides the rich organizing structure of literary allusion, particularly to Virgil's *Georgics*, that John Murphy has recently charted in *My Ántonia: The Road Home*. In this framework Jim's own perceptual style imitates Virgil's famous elegiac mode, producing *My Ántonia's* characteristic narrative nostalgia by severing the mundane present from a strong lost past. The novel's epigraph from *Georgics* III – '*optima dies ... prima fugit*' ('the best days are the first to flee', in Jim's translation) – is also a formula for retrospective valorization: that which is gone, Jim learns, is the best, in part paradoxically because only what's gone can be stably and fully repossessed *as epitaphic text*, as valued representation. (This 'textualizing' function of Jim's nostalgia – what Murphy calls his 'penchant to view the past aesthetically' (85) – is clearest in his eventual adult repossession of Ántonia as '*My Ántonia*', his memory and his manuscript.) Thus Virgil's elegiac language of images and values abstracts, re-frames and vitalizes Jim's pre-University experience:

In the very act of yearning toward the new forms that Cleric brought up before me, my mind plunged away from me, and I suddenly found myself thinking of the places and people of my own infinitesimal past. They stood out strengthened and simplified now, like the image of the plough against the sun. ...

Whenever my consciousness was quickened, all those early friends were quickened within it. ... *They were so much alive in me that I scarcely stopped to wonder whether they were alive anywhere else, or how.*

(My Ántonia 262, italics mine)

Second, the re-vision of the historical past, mediated by another textual world, has a specifically *sanitizing*, sexually repressive function. Blanche Gelfant has shown (150–2) how Jim's pre-college dream of Lena Lingard, for example, is suffused with anxious sexuality: 'Lena Lingard came across the stubble barefoot, in a short skirt, with a curved reaping-hook in her hand, and she was flushed like the dawn, with a kind of luminous rosiness all about her. She sat down beside me, turned to me with a soft sigh, and said, "Now they are all gone, and I can kiss you as much as I like"' (225–6). But a year later the influences of Jim's new life permit the dream's transformation into a general emblem of pastoral nostalgia – while denying Lena the specific qualities of sexual temptation and threat that marked her earlier characterizations (and incidentally denying also the active sexualization of Jim's and Lena's friendship). Virgil's words literally replace both kiss and reaping-hook in Jim's reconstruction of the dream:

As I sat down to my book at last [after a visit from Lena], my old dream about Lena coming across the harvest field in her short skirt seemed to me like the memory of an actual experience. It floated before me on the page like a picture, and underneath it stood the mournful line: *'Optima dies ... prima fugit'.*

(270–1)

The epigraph's placement is deeply, symptomatically ironic, suggesting Cather's awareness of the repressive acrobatics that Jim performs since, as Gelfant has also pointed out, this particular line occurs as part of Virgil's discourse on cattle-breeding, and is immediately preceded by a bald injunction to sexual intercourse and reproduction: 'Let loose the males; be first to send your cattle to mate, and supply stock after stock by breeding' (Gelfant 153; Virgil 159). The irony typifies Jim's generally partial and idealized reading of the classics: the *Georgics* themselves are anything but effete or sanitized. But the rigorous exclusion of sex from his personal history seems essential to Jim's maturation-as-escape. His final pre-

University Black Hawk experience is a beating and near-rape at the hands of Wick Cutter, an assault he blames on Ántonia and her tempting sexuality. 'I hated [Ántonia]', he says, 'almost as much as I hated Cutter. She had let me in for all this disgustingness' (250). The monastic, cleanly cerebral pleasures of bachelor life with Gaston Cleric and Virgil are thus a welcome relief for him and a clear narrative defense against the lurid sensual extravagance that's preceded them.

Jim's assumption of a classical tradition and heritage, with these corollary effects of nostalgic textualization and sexual repression, resolves (or attempts to resolve) one of *My Ántonia's* major thematic ambivalences: his childhood love-hate relationship with Ántonia, her family, and the European 'old country' they represent. In the novel's first two sections, 'The Shimerdas' and 'The Hired Girls', Jim's attraction to Ántonia (and to some extent to the other immigrant hired girls) is tempered by a physical fear of all that's 'foreign'. His first meeting with Ántonia is deferred by his guardian Jake's warning that 'you were likely to get diseases from foreigners' (5); he consistently describes the Shimerdas as living like dirty animals; the various rumored memories and embedded anecdotes of the 'old country', most strikingly Pavel and Peter's fantastic story of the bride and groom thrown to the wolves by their best man, repeatedly involve death, sexual betrayal, illegitimacy. Gaston Cleric's idealized classicism thus does more than simply refine Jim's response to Lena. It potentially rewrites the myth of the 'old country', offering him an alternative set of origin narratives (or, to return to the vocabulary of the Freudian family romance, a new exemplary parentage): the noble literary passions of Greece and Rome, the 'drama of antique life' (262) to replace the modern immigrants' squalid real past.

In short, Jim's encounter with the classics can be read as quite specific developmental allegory, defining a process of conceptual *regularization* or socialization in the moment of passage from childhood to maturity. 'Real' childhood in this scheme (whether Jim's literal pre-college history or the symbolic glimpses of the 'old country') appears a time of vaguely threatening sexuality, betrayal, and foreignness, while the maturity into which he emerges – as embodied in the person of Gaston Cleric, for example – is abstract, asexual, spiritualized. In fact, in constructing this allegory Cather deploys quite precisely the cultural American stereotypes attached connotatively to the terms 'Bohemian' and 'Classical'; and Jim's self-imposed maturational task, to some extent like Cather's in her own unruly life, is to subdue his bohemianism to his classical idealism, to foresake the barbarous forests of northern Europe for Golden Age Athens or Virgil's orderly Rome.

II

This last observation invokes a larger political context in which Cather's and Jim's insistent dualism can be understood. What appears in *My Ántonia* as an individual's choice, a decision for the ideal over the real, the refined over the sensual, reason over desire, was also a cultural choice for the United States, a nation seeking the means of modern identity. Precisely *My Ántonia's* two complemental categories of experience – the Classical and the Bohemian – were the focuses of American cultural discussion in the 1910s and 1920s, though in generally separate arenas: the relation of classicism to national character became, appropriately, a theme for the professoriat, while what to do with modern Bohemians (and Poles, Russians, and Greeks, among others) was a volatile public issue ultimately decided in Congress.

In these decades American universities experienced an energetic last-ditch defense and revival of the beleaguered classical curriculum in a sometimes acrimonious debate over the purpose of university education in a progressive, growing democracy. In June of 1917, for example (as Cather took time off from writing *My Ántonia* to receive an honorary degree from the University of Nebraska), Princeton University hosted a conference to consider what the graduate Dean called 'the latest assault on mental training': the challenging of Greek and Latin studies' centrality, the suggestion that they might be in the twentieth century merely 'fretting hindrances to intellectual progress' (West 7–8). Unsurprisingly the professors and their guests – like hundreds of other commentators in journals and at similar gatherings – uniformly upheld not only the aesthetic but also the practical value of classical education. And they did so often with a vocabulary echoing Jim Burden's insistence on the epistemological value of classicism's universal 'new forms', on the interdependence of the classical and the contemporary or personal, as in the welcoming address by John Grier Hibben, Princeton's President:

> In coming in contact with the original language we come in contact with those original forms of thought that have made our

civilization possible. ... These forms of thought, in the very language of Greece and of Rome, have a universal significance; they do not apply to any age; they have no geographical limitations; they are the forms that we are following (unconsciously it may be to ourselves) in every thoughtful enterprise in which we are engaged.

(40)

For Hibben as for Jim Burden, classicism is a privileged *language* in the very specific sense, developed by Ferdinand de Saussure in the preceding decade (and in obedience to similar universalizing impulses), of a 'collection of necessary conventions that have been adopted by a social body to permit individuals to exercise [speech] ... a self-contained whole and a principle of classification' (9). Hibben's classicism offered the student the transhistorical *langue* of Western culture and of thought itself, and thus provided a matrix in which modern individual life might become coherent and meaningful.

Furthermore, as Walter Benn Michaels has convincingly argued with reference to Cather, the study of the classics could be – and was – linked directly to the immediate *political* aim of creating a uniquely American character, with Greece and Rome the imaginative progenitors of American society. 'Ours is the civilization', said Hibben, 'that has come directly from that original civilization of Greece and Rome' (39). Calvin Coolidge argued a few years later to the American Classical League that 'the great and unfailing source of [America's] power and ... ideals has been the influence of the classics of Greece and Rome. Those who believe in America, in her language, her arts, her literature, and in her science, will seek to perpetuate them by perpetuating the education which has produced them' (67). Jim's adopted classicism in part simply indicates Cather's alignment with what Michaels describes as a national project, the construction of an abstract 'American', defined not so much by ethnic origin as by *cultural* 'inheritance' (230) – one aspect of which was the apparently democratic 'common language' of the classics.

But like Jim's choice of Virgil, the classical revival had an exclusionary side: although it could frame and even ennoble some features of American political experience – participatory democracy, informed citizenship, patriotism – others eluded its terms. In particular, the historical realities of late nineteenth- and early twentieth-century immigration worked to produce a heterogeneous population in some ways resistant to the abstract 'acquired inheritance' of classical culture. In 1911 the University of Michigan scholar Francis Kelsey acknowledged this difficulty in the way of a philosophically Graeco-Roman national identity, conceding that foreign immigration, despite its contributions to American life,

> has nevertheless introduced into our urban life ideals of citizenship and education different from those which were the inheritance of the present generation of American born and bred. ... The existence of a tradition or ideal of literary culture [among immigrants] is much more rare than in American homes. ... The majority of boys and girls from homes without an atmosphere of culture may, influenced by the advice of teachers and the general spirit of the schools, be led to study Latin; Greek seems to them very remote.
>
> (11–12)

In fact Kelsey was optimistic: the great task faced by the American educational system in the East and Midwest was vocational education, the teaching of functional English, not Latin or Greek, to three generations of working-class Europeans; it was borne not by the universities but by states and municipalities (Abbott 549–80).

Academicians and politicians following the turn of the century shared the ideal of a citizenry steeped in a Graeco-Roman literary and philosophical tradition. Reality, however, brought them a flood of immigrants – the non-Saxon 'new immigration' of 1890 and after – whose educational needs were necessarily practical and vocational. Academic classicism thus paradoxically (and generally unconsciously) lent implicit support to the exclusionary nativist voices in the political scene, direct descendants of the 'Know-Nothings' of the 1850s: voices boosting Americanism but fearful of a polyethnic future asking, in the words of Coolidge's Labor Secretary James J. Davis, 'What sort of qualities are we allowing other nations to pour into our national blood stream through immigrants and the descendants of immigrants[?]' (44). Nativism expressed its fears in exactly *My Ántonia*'s terms, mythologizing immigrants as degenerate, diseased, irresponsible, immoral – and hypersexualized, threatening to dilute the old 'American stock' with impure blood. In its overtly racist manifestation, nativism led to the reflorescence of the Ku Klux Klan or the Nordic eugenics of Madison Grant and Lothrop Stoddard; in mainstream politics, it allowed the scholarly patrician Henry Cabot Lodge very consciously to link classicism, repression and good citizenship in his long Senate struggle for immigration restriction. In an 1896 speech supporting literacy tests for immigrants Lodge admiringly quoted Gustave Le Bon, identifying the significant similarity of Roman and Anglo-American cultures:

> It is only in proportion as they have mastered their instincts – that is to say, as they have acquired strength of will and consequently empire over themselves – that nations have been able to understand the importance of discipline, the necessity of sacrificing themselves to an ideal and lifting themselves up to civilization. *If it were necessary to determine by a single test the social level of races in history, I would take willingly as a standard the aptitude displayed by each in controlling their impulses. The Romans in antiquity, the Anglo-Americans in modern times, represent the people who have possessed this quality in the highest degree.*
>
> (263, italics mine)

Eventually sentiments like these produced the two Immigration Acts of 1921 and 1924, which, as Michaels has pointed out, ironically and radically curtailed the immigration of Greeks and Italians, among others – even while the universities sought to reappropriate Athens and Rome as the essence of 'Americanism' (230).[1]

III

Simultaneously *bildungsroman* and social history, *My Ántonia* thus straddles private and public worlds, tracing in parallel Cather's explorations of individual identity (through Jim) and her society's larger anxiety. It sketches a Freudian 'family romance' for both worlds, a rechoosing of origins: in favor of abstraction and idealism, against history and material reality; in favor of the austere male world of Gaston Cleric, against the Shimerda household's fecund confusion; in short, as I've said, in favor of Greece and Rome, against Bohemia. And, in ways significant for the development of her fiction in the 1920s, this choice involved Cather in an attempted general repudiation of femininity. Her family romance reproduces the sexual asymmetries of Freud's, which was more than a simple heroic aggrandizement of parental figures; at its core, Freud insisted, was the child's discovery of 'secret infidelity' (239) in the exalted mother-figure (a discovery that was itself a distorted expression of unacknowledged Oedipal desire). As a result maternal femininity reveals itself as essentially flawed, corrupt, while purity is only available to the masculine. A misogynist differential something like this was at work in Cather. It gave her the plot of *A Lost Lady* five years after she wrote *My Ántonia*; more generally, it sketched a loose set of equations fundamental to her thinking (and to that of her culture), according to which masculinity, purity, intellection, 'American-ness', and celibacy or self-restraint could be associated with one another and in contrast to an opposing constellation of femininity, corruption, irrationality, foreignness and fertility. Thus Stoddard in *The Rising Tide of Color* could extoll '*clean, virile, genius-bearing* blood, streaming down the ages through the unerring action of heredity, which ... will multiply itself, solve our problems, and sweep us on to higher and nobler destinies' (305, italics mine); thus Cather herself, in her 1912 short story 'Behind the Singer Tower' (one of her few works directly concerned with urban immigration), imagined the Italian laborer Caesarino as one of 'the swarms of eager, panting animals ... with such a curiously hot spark of life in them' (284): simultaneously impulsively childlike, devoted to a mother in the old country, and strangely feminized, 'like a girl in love' (286), in relation to the masculine narrator.

The revisionist family romance, along with its complicated array of beliefs and loyalties, performed parallel stabilizing functions in both cultural and individual realms. For the United States the choice of classical origins responded to a compelling political need: to maintain the mythology of the melting pot, to manage the population and its means of self-representation so as to preserve the idea of a uniquely homogeneous 'American' culture (even if this meant replacing real origins with invented classical ones). For Cather herself the decision for classical origin (and her identification through Jim with Virgil) had to do in part with the formation of a coherent *literary* identity. As Randolph Bourne put it in his 1918 *Dial* review, *My Ántonia* lifted Cather 'out of the rank of provincial writers' and into the company of 'modern art the world over' (557). It marked her full transition from regionalism to modernism, aligning her with Eliot's ideal 'tradition' and shaping the great next decade of her career, whose typical fiction was increasingly elegiac, stylized, spiritualized, and – as Deborah Lambert has argued (122) – masculine and misogynist in its orientation. Probably the repudiation of sexuality implicit in Cather's classicism had a specific personal function as well, as a way of putting behind her the 1915 loss (to marriage) of her close friend Isabelle McClung, or of stabilizing the uncertainties of gender, the swings of identification, that had marked her private life from the 1890s.

A distinctively modernist classicism thus became the characteristic, the signature of the great novels of the 1920s: *A Lost Lady, The Professor's House, Death Comes for the Archbishop*, and others. More interesting finally is the extent to which the domination of the classical ideal *failed* or was at least incomplete or unconvincing in *My Ántonia* and its successors. In the first place, fully identifying Jim's classicism with Cather is risky. One effect of the framing 'Introduction', with its genderless, nameless 'I', is to make possible an *authorial* relation to Ántonia different from (and corrective of) Jim's nostalgic efforts at recapture. This narrative doubleness marks the instability in Cather's own 'classical choice', insisting on her distance from Jim's civilized but sterile adulthood. Furthermore, through most of Jim's post-Black Hawk experience Ántonia alone among his childhood experiences escapes subjection to (or rewriting in the language of) the Virgilian code. Unlike Jake, Otto, the hired girls, and Lena Lingard, who can all be recalled and revivified through the forms of the classical pastoral (and thus, in Lena's case, desexed), Ántonia – the novel's center and the object of Jim's desire – resists idealized representation or memorialization, and in effect vanishes from Jim's memories and attention.

Nor does she return to Jim, exactly, at his narrative's end: more remarkably, he is returned to her in a reversal of nostalgia's typical strategy of evocative repossession. In this encounter Cather identifies Ántonia specifically, in precise terms reminiscent both of President Hibben and of Jim's first revelation of Virgil's power, as a creative source of meaning herself, a matrix of 'forms' and an explicit *rival* to Virgil's educative authority:

Ántonia had always been one to leave images in the mind that did not fade – that grew stronger with time. In my memory there was a succession of such pictures, fixed there like the old woodcuts of one's first primer. ... She lent herself to immemorial human attitudes which we recognize by instinct as universal and true. ... She was a battered woman now, not a lovely girl; but she still had that something which fires the imagination, could still stop one's breath for a moment by a look or a gesture that

somehow revealed the meaning in common things. She had only
to stand in the orchard, to put her hand on a little crab tree and
look up at the apples, to make you feel the goodness of planting
and tending and harvesting at last. All the strong things of her
heart came out of her body, that had been so tireless in serving
generous emotions. ... She was a rich mine of life, like the
founders of early races.

(352–3)

In the closing metaphor she re-offers Jim a cultural parentage to set
against Greece and Rome: her bohemianism, now for the first time
deliberately understood as a primary language, as the shaping
structure of 'common things'. Where Lena had earlier reacquired
meaning for Jim in embodying, fleshing out, a Virgilian epigraph,
here Ántonia *herself* provides the gestures and paradigms that
confer meaning on experience. And unlike the austere vocabulary
that Jim takes from Virgil, the language that Ántonia teaches is of
the body, of the material world, of labor, production and reproduction, and sexuality.

Cather gives and takes away. Jim and his narrative beat an
anxious retreat from this vision of an overwhelming physical and
cultural fertility: first into the anti-creative parable of Wick Cutter's
grotesque end, then to Cuzak's asexual cosmopolitan companion-
ship. He leaves the novel looking forward to the peculiarly ambivalent promise of future masculine adventures, 'trips I meant to take
with the Cuzak boys, in the Bad Lands and up on the Stinking
Water. There were enough Cuzaks to play with for a long while
yet' (370). Here he anticipates, at least in outline, a pattern of heroic
comradeship for his idealistic, misogynous successors: Claude
Wheeler and David Gerhardt, Tom and Roddy (or Tom and
St. Peter), Latour and Vaillant. This withdrawal into the company
of men, art and ideas looks like a final farewell to messy material
Bohemia, a victory for classical repression and the choice of bodi-
less origins, and it's not surprising that Cather's next novel, *One of
Ours*, combined masculinism, patriotism and a literal return to the
highest of European culture. Nonetheless the ambiguous power invested in the female body and sexuality in Ántonia's last appearance continued to haunt Cather's novels through the 1920s, often as
a shadowy, unsatisfied or betrayed maternal presence – Marian
Forester, Mother Eve, Magdalena – to reappear triumphantly in
Sapphira and the Slave Girl's slave matriarch Jezebel: as though

Cather, having read early from Ántonia's 'first primer', could not in fact forget that lexicon and grammar of creation.

NOTES

1. These Acts offer a compelling instance of nostalgia's realization as backward-looking policy. Both depended on census analyses of national origin. The 1921 Act set annual immigration quotas for most nations at 3 per cent of those countries' 'American' population shares according to the census of 1910, despite minority protests that 'no logical reason can be urged why ... the 1920 statistics of population in the United States of the nationals of the particular countries should not be adopted as the basis of calculation' (Abbott 243). Its 1924 successor, however, went still further in turning back the American ethnic clock, reducing the quota to 2 per cent and making the 1890 census the basis for computation. Taken together, the Acts sought to undo the consequences of the 'new immigration' between 1890 and 1920.

WORKS CITED

Abbott, Edith (ed.), *Immigration: Select Documents and Case Records*, Chicago: Chicago University Press, 1924.
Bourne, Randolph, 'Morals and Art from the West', *The Dial* LXV 779 (14 December 1918), 556–7.
Cather, Willa, *A Lost Lady*, 1923, New York: Random House, 1972.
—— One of Ours, 1922, New York: Random House, 1991.
—— 'The Namesake', 1907, in Sharon O'Brien (ed.), *Willa Cather: 24 Stories*, New York: New American Library, 1987.
—— 'Behind the Singer Tower', 1912, in Sharon O'Brien (ed.), *Willa Cather: 24 Stories*, New York: New American Library, 1987.
—— *My Ántonia*, Boston: Houghton Mifflin, 1918.
—— *The Professor's House*, 1925, repr. New York: Random House, 1973.
Coolidge, Calvin, *The Price of Freedom*, New York: Charles Scribner's Sons, 1924.
Davis, James J., *Selective Immigration*, St Paul, MN: Scott-Mitchell Publishing Company, 1925.
de Saussure, Ferdinand, *Course in General Linguistics*, 1915, reprinted eds Bally and Sechehaye, New York: McGraw-Hill, 1959.
Freud, Sigmund, 'Family Romances', 1909, *Standard Edition of the Complete Psychological Works of Sigmund Freud*, vol. 9, London: Hogarth Press, 1958.
Gelfant, Blanche, 'The Forgotten Reaping-Hook: Sex in *My Ántonia*', 1971, in John J. Murphy (ed.), *Critical Essays on Willa Cather*, Boston: G. K. Hall, 1984.

Hibben, John Grier, 'Welcoming Address', in Andrew F. West (ed.), *The Value of the Classics*, Princeton: Princeton University Press, 1917.

Kelsey, Francis (ed.), *Latin and Greek in American Education*, New York: Macmillan, 1927.

Lambert, Deborah, 'Autonomy and Sexuality in *My Ántonia*', in Harold Bloom (ed.), *Willa Cather's My Ántonia*, New York: Chelsea House, 1987.

Lodge, Henry Cabot, 'The Restriction of Immigration' (Senate Speech, 16 March 1896), *Speeches and Addresses 1884–1909*, Boston: Houghton Mifflin, 1909.

Michaels, Walter Benn, 'The Vanishing American', *American Literary History* 2:2 (1990), 221–41.

Murphy, John J., *My Ántonia: The Road Home*, Boston: G. K. Hall, 1989.

Stoddard, Lothrop, *The Rising Tide of Color against White World-Supremacy*, New York: Scribners, 1921.

Virgil (Publius Vergilius Maro), *Georgics*, in H. Rushton Fairclough (trans.), *Virgil*, 2 vols, London: William Heinemann, 1986.

West, Andrew F., 'The Present Outlook', in Andrew F. West (ed.), *The Value of the Classics*, Princeton: Princeton University Press, 1917.

7

Scripting Woman into the Discourse of Nostalgia: Gender and the Nation State

HEMA CHARI

Of all the evils for which man has made himself responsible, none is so degrading, so shocking or so brutal as his abuse of the better half of humanity – to me, the female sex, not the weaker sex.

(Mahatma Gandhi, *Young India*, 21 July 1921)

In the anticolonial conflicts during India's independence movement the woman's struggle was tied in with the political cause of nationalism and nation-building. Women actively participated in all stages of the non-violent movement (*ahimsa*) inspired by Mahatma Gandhi, who openly acknowledged the significant role of women within the nationalist movement. He consistently supported what at that time was a revolutionary proposal: the coeval participation of women in the emancipatory struggle against British rule. In Gandhi's view, 'If non-violence is the law of our being, the future is with women' (*All Men Are Brothers* 148).

The contribution of women during the anticolonial struggle cannot be overestimated. Women engaged in various nationalist activities and assumed different roles – as activists and as symbols – both within and outside the home. At home they participated in the ideology of self-reliance (*atmashakti*) as emphasized by the Gandhian movement, spun on the *charka* or spinning wheel, participated in women's literacy programs, and contributed articles, essays, poems and anticolonial pieces of writing.[1] Women provided shelter and nursing care to nationalists who were fleeing British authorities. In addition women organized public meetings attended by women from all classes, castes and religions. Commenting on the public role women played during the Indian nationalist movement, Kumari Jayawardena suggests that '[i]t was in the political struggle against imperialism that Indian women (both Hindu and Muslim) began actively to participate in life outside the home; and in doing so, they had the support of many nationalist political leaders' (93). Women participated in non-violent demonstrations or *satyagrahas*, picketed toddy shops, instigated boycotts of stores that sold foreign goods – especially textiles – and suffered imprisonment. In these and other activities Mahatma Gandhi's movement notably encouraged women to participate in the public sphere of politics and nation-building and strove to organize a solidarity among women. Thus in pursuing its political agenda, the nationalist movement had the additional consequences of raising the consciousness of women's positions and of interrogating the social roles of women in Indian society. However the social role of woman was never an explicit ideological objective within the nationalist movement, and in fact the woman's issue was subsumed by the nationalist cause.

The development of the nationalist movement and of women's role in it forms the backdrop for Narayan's novel *Waiting for the Mahatma*. The novel traces Gandhi's leadership of the Indian nationalist movement, particularly emphasizing his relationship with two young nationalists, Bharati and Sriram. In Bharati, Narayan portrays the ideal nationalist woman who fulfilled the nationalist expectations of woman's role in the movement. Narayan uses Sriram to show the young man's gradual initiation into the nationalist cause, and in this initiation it is Bharati's responsibility to indoctrinate Sriram with the Gandhian philosophy. While developing the relationship between Gandhi, Bharati and Sriram, Narayan reveals a crucial blindness within the nationalist movement: how, even as it appropriated women for the nationalist cause, it failed to address the question of their subjectivity. In Bharati's narrative the novel provides the experience of colonialism but, in accordance with the nationalist agenda, does not reinforce colonial displacement as problematic for women.

The trajectory of the Indian nationalist movement and women's contribution to Gandhi's anticolonial struggle are traced in Narayan's depiction of the development of Bharati's and Gandhi's relationship as that between a father and daughter (58–9). During one of Bharati's early conversations with Sriram she discloses to him that Gandhi, the Father of the Nation, had given her a name that means the 'Daughter of India'. This raises Bharati to the privileged status of being the daughter of the nation and reinforces her role as a nationalist. Adopted by Gandhi, Bharati becomes a *sevika* or server of the country in Gandhi's ashram. She travels from village to village organizing public meetings.

Bharati's evolutionary narrative as a nationalist under Gandhi's tutelage replicates the historical contradictions inherent in the nationalist involvement of women for the nationalist cause. Bharati's portrayal demonstrates the contradictions that arose from the nationalist movement's demands that Indian women should fulfill their roles as both political activists and as preservers of the traditional concepts of femininity. In assigning this dual role to women the nationalist movement betrays a slippage in terms of women's identity, which was constantly split as both subject and object. Women's subjectivity is contradictorily represented in the nationalist movement and in Bharati's narrative as both a semiotic object (representing the traditional prescriptions of Indian womanhood) and a speaking subject (representing the modern woman). In several ways the novel indicates how the nationalist movement was both emancipatory and enslaving to women, as the consciousness of women's identity was obliterated in terms of historical agency and subjectivity even as women's political consciousness was raised. The agenda of the 'politics' of the woman's cause was inconsistent with the 'politics' of nationalism largely due to the fact that the nationalist construction of the 'new' woman was still framed within the traditional roles assigned to women and was still dominated by traditional expectations of womanhood, especially in terms of suffering, silence and sacrifice. Consequently woman's subjectivity was kept confined within the private sphere and their material and sexual power relations within the society remained unchallenged. The nationalist construction of the 'new' woman was used to confront colonial domination but not to question the historical and materialistic basis of women's oppression.

Nonetheless it is extremely important to locate the historiography of the woman's question in nineteenth century India within the site of the cultural, political and ideological confrontation of England and India (Chakravarti 27–87). During the early and mid-nineteenth century, the nationalist movement was confronted with the extremely problematic issue in terms of the cultural identity of

India: wasn't the very concept of India a cultural construction challenged by British ethnocentrism? To a large extent the British rulers justified their colonial rule over India to themselves and to their colonized subjects on the grounds that it was their mission to civilize and enlighten the natives, even with regards to the woman's question (Mani 352–3).

In this justification several cultural issues were raised. Because the British held the 'native' culture to be degenerate, they imposed an Orientalist and colonialist interpretation of Indian culture as being morally, culturally, psychologically, socially and intellectually inferior and weak. Moreover by representing 'native' men as primitives who allowed barbaric customs to be practiced against their women, the rhetoric of the colonizers was carefully crafted to argue that the colonizers were protecting the 'native' women from their own oppressive men and culture (Mani 319–56). In addition the colonizers justified their ruling discourses on the grounds that the Indian men were not manly enough to rule themselves. Ashis Nandy argues that the 'effeminacy' of the Indian men was considered as the fundamental reason for colonization because the colonizers postulated that the femininity of the Indian men incapacitated them from ruling themselves (4–16).

The political nationalism of the Indian independence movement in its mission to establish its own identity and self-respect in terms of both the material and spiritual aspects of the Indian culture reinstated the traditional values attributed to Indian womanhood. Unable to forge an alternative identity for women, while also realizing that there was no autonomous prototype of womanhood, the nationalist movement traced the infrastructure for the nation's identity back to past culture, history and the scriptures (Chakravarti 32–55). However in this process of retrieving the golden past to construct a cultural identity of nationalism, the nationalist construction of womanhood was split. On one hand the image of womanhood significantly upheld those aspects of femininity that projected positive and strong moral qualities, which in turn demanded that the 'modern' woman endorse the traditional images and roles of women. On the other hand the new woman had to move out into the public sphere to participate in the decolonization movements, and this in turn demanded that she question the social and political roles of women which were derived from the 'golden age'. However, despite having created this split in the construction of women as political subject and traditional object, the nationalist movement still placed the burden of constructing the rejuvenated and positive Indian identity on a gendered subaltern that was inherently dichotomous.

A nationalist woman like Bharati was required to propagate those ideas of inner strength and spiritual integrity that would eventually empower the nationalist culture to overcome colonial domination. Bharati reflects these very qualities, and it is her strength and will power that first attracts Sriram to her. To Sriram, Bharati continues to retain her privileged status of the consciousness-raising and politically active nationalist. She becomes the cultural icon of the revolutionary and modern woman even as she retains her double-coded identity, which fragments her as a revolutionist and as a woman. In Sriram's mind Bharati stands as the icon of nationalism reflecting the apostolic tradition even more forcefully than Gandhi its leader. She always wears *khadi* or homespun *saris* and Sriram is aware not just of the cultural symbols of nationalism that are embodied in her, but more significantly of her lifestyle and character which are those of a true server of the nation (a *satyagrahi* or *desh sevika*). He is equally aware of her moral strength, and her portrayal goes back to the nationalist tradition where women were the guardians of morality and spirituality.

The double-coded role for women within the nationalist movement exemplified in Bharati's relationship to Gandhi and later to Sriram, crucially depends upon distinctions of private and public space in terms of gender roles. As Partha Chatterjee has observed, the nationalist construct of woman associated the inviolable inner sanctity and purity of Indian identity with concepts associated with home and spirituality as symbolized by the Indian woman:

> The home was the principal site for expressing the spiritual quality of the national culture, and women must take the main responsibility of protecting and nurturing this quality.
>
> (238).[2]

In consequence women became fixed as cultural markers destined to be represented and understood as caretakers and preservers of spirituality, strength and sacrifice. The cultural identity of woman was ambivalently split between the 'home' and the 'world' as the nationalist movement struggled to establish its subjectivity in the process of decolonization and nation-building. Chatterjee also suggests that the nationalist movement elided the subjectivity of woman when its discourse resorted to the representation of woman within these inner/outer, home/world, material/spiritual dichotomies: 'Now apply the inner/outer distinction to the matter of concrete day-to-day living and you get a separation of the social space into *ghar* and *bahir*, the home and the world' (239). Chatterjee concludes that the social roles of men and women were separated in accordance with the divisions of the social space into the home and the world (12). Within the context of nationalism, therefore, the nationalist issue overtook the woman's question by presenting it within the nationalist movement's own epistemological predicament of subjectivity and nation-building, thus preventing women from articulating their own politics and identities. The predicament of woman in nationalism exemplifies the claim made by Gayatri Spivak when she exposes the contradictions inherent in positions of any speaking subject. Referring to the significance Marx assigns to class in his analysis of the Eighteenth Brumaire, Spivak broadens Marx's thesis to include colonized, gendered identities. Extending Marx's analysis of the contradictions inherent in the discursive aspects of 'vertreten' and 'darstellen', or of the discrepancy innate to the notion of speaking subject and spoken-for object, Spivak concludes that the gendered subaltern is already spoken for or spoken at, so that in consequence she cannot speak for herself (594–617). The nationalist movement enacts just such an ambivalence with reference to women's subjectivity. The nationalist agenda politicized the woman's movement with its own patronage and ideology by implicating women in this self-defeating discourse.

This paradox within nationalism of obliterating the interests of the women it claimed to speak for was matched with another: that the nationalist movement was itself feminized. Gandhi's nationalist movement was aware of the disintegrating politics of nationalism, of the historical and cultural specificity of the nationalist agenda. Gandhi was no less aware of the impediments of conservative traditionalism, especially with reference to women. To Gandhi the goal of the nationalist movement was not merely political independence in terms of governmental self-rule but also personal self-confidence and self-reliance, and it was in pursuit of these endeavours that he critiqued the ideology of the scriptures with regard to the woman's question:

it is sad to think that the *Smritis* contain texts which can command no respect from men who cherish the liberty of woman. ... I have ... suggested ... all that is printed in the name of scriptures need not be taken as ... the inspired word.

(quoted in Chatterjee 244)

In its endeavour to achieve an ethics of self-reliance and self-sufficiency, the nationalist subject within the Gandhian movement strove to dissolve binary oppositions of masculine/feminine, inner/outer, home/world, family/state, doing so not just as a political strategy against colonization but as an ethical imperative for an emerging nation.[3] The nationalist movement in its epistemological exigency for cultural self-reliance and subjectivity discursively placed itself within the subject/object split of the speaking subject and the spoken-for object through Gandhi's strategy of active/passive resistance.[4] The Gandhian movement of *ahimsa* required male nationalists like Sriram to adopt the traditional female forms of passivity, self-sacrifice and non-violence.

Narayan's novel seizes that historically and materialistically determined, and culturally specific moment of nationalism when the politics of nationalism apprehends the ambivalences of establishing a gendered identity, in terms of a political (speaking subject) and semiotic (spoken-for/spoken-at object) representation. The ambivalences that are part of the nationalistic discourse are dominant not only because of the epistemological quest of cultural self-identity but also because the nationalist movement hesitates to take into consideration the political aspects of the woman's subjectivity in its efforts to solve the epistemological crisis. Narayan's novel registers the contradictions of the political processes of such a representation within the nationalist movement. In other words the nationalist project of subject formation for a gendered identity has to be epistemological, historiographic and political. As this often remains a utopian and nostalgic desire for the gendered identity in the nationalist narration, the nationalist movement fails to represent the diversity of its 'imagined community'. As a result, nationalism as a representation of an 'imagined community' is forced to disintegrate and dissolve.

Tracing the Indian nationalist movement through the love story of Sriram and Bharati, *Waiting for the Mahatma* captures this dislocated and discursive subject/object position in Bharati's narrative. Bharati's orphaned subjectivity pushes her identity away from the bourgeois determinations of the family causing her to migrate from the 'home' to the 'world' of the nationalist arena. As the daughter of the father of the nation, Bharati is carefully groomed to fulfill the requirements of the political needs of a shackled country. Sriram's first glimpse of Bharati is in the market-place when she is collecting money for the nationalist movement. Sriram is struck by her beauty and intelligence, but he registers the fact that she is out of the domain of the domestic and in the public sphere:

> 'What a dangerous thing for such a beauty to be about!' ... 'She has something to do with Mahatma Gandhi and is collecting a fund. You know the Mahatma is coming.'
>
> (22, 24)

In the very beginning of the novel Bharati transgresses the social roles of gender and crosses over from the traditional confines of the home to the outside world.[5] During Sriram's first encounter with her at the market-place, traditional gender roles and expectations are traversed. By publicly carrying out her role as a nationalist Bharati retains her subject-position as a modern woman, and it is Sriram who expresses the traditional and societal expectations of her gender.

The novel does not dissipate the subject/object split but situates the crisis and the ambivalence within Bharati's gendered body. By manipulating simultaneously her identity and subjectivity within this subject/object split under Gandhi's guidance and by discursively placing herself as both the subject and object with a divided subjectivity, Bharati empowers her position as a woman in the nationalist struggle for independence and nation-building. In her interactions with Gandhi and Sriram, she enacts her role as a nationalist and as a single woman whom Sriram notices in the market-place. In this instance, her identity is double-coded: as daughter of the nation she is the 'new' woman, the revolutionary nationalist, but as an ordinary, normal single woman she is expected to fulfill the traditional obligation of marriage that Sriram would prefer her to assume. In spite of this double-coding and in spite of Sriram's expectations of her gendering she succeeds in retaining her subject-position. The discursive aspect of Bharati's subjectivity can be historically traced back to the epistemological predicament of the nationalist movement, where the expectations of a woman's role was divided.

Even though she is the subaltern gendered-identity Bharati continues to appropriate agency when she becomes the dominant nationalist and, by bringing Sriram to Gandhi's public meeting at Malgudi, serves as the chief catalyst initiating him into nationalism. But Bharati is not literally a catalyst, for she herself is affected by her contact with Sriram, as the novel later explores. The encounter with Gandhi at Malgudi becomes an epiphanic moment for Sriram and marks a whole cultural, personal and political upheaval in his life: 'Sriram suddenly awoke from an age-old somnolence to the fact that Malgudi was about to have the honour of receiving Mahatma Gandhi' (24). The meeting brings Sriram not only an awareness of Gandhi's pivotal anticolonial movement but also of the question of woman's roles and identity. In the early stages of the novel, Sriram is instantly attracted to Bharati's self-assuredness and confidence, and he is in awe of her modern ways. At this point, he is able to draw a distinction between the 'modern' and the traditional woman, but he is ambivalent toward and confused by Bharati's strong self-identity. He is sure only of his attraction to her, although he is charmed by her strong personality and political acumen. Despite his admiration he is not always comfortable with her strong-willed personality and confidence.

A conflation of motives – boredom at home, curiosity about the movement, and attraction to Bharati – pushes Sriram from the comfort and protection of his grandmother and her home to the outside world of the nationalists. He follows Bharati and desires to be in her company. But to be able to achieve that, he has to be aware of the political situation of India. He has to be initiated into the Gandhian movement of *satyagraha*. Inspired by Gandhi and his message, he realizes that he is on the threshold of a very significant turn of events in his life, of falling in love with a nationalist woman – Bharati – and of falling in love with his own country. He realizes that the two are intertwined. His school-teacher intensifies the significance of the moment by applauding his decision to join the nationalists: 'Join the Congress, work for your country, you will go far, God bless you …' (35–6). The weight of his teacher's counsel to serve his country is further intensified when he meets Bharati. She continues to retain her high stature in his consciousness. He is envious and proud of her close association with Gandhi, and he feels that just by being in her company he can become a member of the privileged nationalist group.

It is, however, during their first face-to-face encounter that Sriram becomes completely aware of Bharati's force of character and ability to have complete control of the situation, even in front

of strangers. She draws upon Gandhi for her moral strength and
demeanor, and as far as her interaction with Gandhi is concerned
she is the subservient disciple and the obedient daughter: she slips
into her object-position. But she appropriates the inspiration she receives from her interaction with Gandhi to retain her subject-
position when interacting with others in her role as a nationalist.
Take, for example, the initial meeting of Bharati and Sriram after
Gandhi's speech in Malgudi when Bharati notices Sriram hanging
around Gandhi's hut:

> 'You will have to go now,' and Sriram sprang up and found
> himself outside the hut. ... 'Of course, I knew it. I was only
> waiting for you to come out.' 'Who are you? I don't think I have
> seen you before.' ... 'What are you doing here?' she asked.
>
> (53–4)

The mood and tone of their initial interaction seem to set the pace
of their relationship as it develops. She is very much in control
when she is with him.

To Sriram, Bharati continues to retain her privileged status as
the consciousness-raising and politically active nationalist. She
becomes the cultural icon of the revolutionary modern woman
even as she retains her double-coded identity, which fragments her
as a revolutionist and as a woman. Bharati always wears homespun
saris, and Sriram is aware that her nationalist ensemble separates
the two of them and sets her apart as the privileged and politically
conscious nationalist who is sensitive to the needs of her country.
Part of Gandhi's insistence on wearing homespun clothes was to
encourage self-reliance and independence from British-owned
mills. Sriram realizes that even his clothing divides him from
Bharati. She would never approve of what he is wearing: a 'half-
arm shirt and *mull dhoti*, probably products of the hated mills' (34).
Even as far as assuming the appropriate garb and posture of a
nationalist, Sriram has to surrender to Bharati.

Thus Bharati retains control over her subjectivity because of her
higher status in the nationalist movement. Nonetheless she willingly surrenders her agency to Gandhi's guidance. Her double-
coded identity with Sriram and with Gandhi replicates again the
nationalist problem with the woman's question. Her dichotomous
identity is further reinforced when she patiently teaches Sriram the
use of the spinning wheel, a feminine activity. In this instance she is

the master weaver and he is her disciple. Gandhi is aware of Bharati's subject-position in their relationship when he comments: 'Be happy. Bharati will look after you'; Gandhi added: "'Remember that she is your Guru, and think of her with reverence and respect, and you will be alright and she will be alright"' (93). However, even as she assumes her privileged role of the 'guru' and political revolutionist, she simultaneously registers and accepts the Indian cultural code of servitude in her roles of single woman and daughter. Before leaving for Mempi Hills where later he was jailed, Gandhi reminds Bharati of her responsibilities as his daughter: 'You will of course keep up your programme and write to me often.' 'Yes, of course, Bapu.' 'Be prepared for any sacrifice' (94). Bharati never lets her cultural position and responsibility as the daughter and single woman slide.

Sriram on the other hand is not always comfortable and accepting of her role as his guru. He wants to claim his cultural and patriarchal agency; he wants to claim her as his wife and to bring her back into the domain of the domestic. While she is entrenched in political work, especially during the period of Gandhi's imprisonment in 1942, Sriram resents her role as the subject in their relationship. His doubts are particularly prevalent during one of their meetings, and in the course of their conversation Sriram reflects on the artificiality of their roles, with her in command and him as the follower:

'She ought to be my wife and come to my arms.' … Absurd to think that she was just his 'guru' …! Absurd that a comely young woman should be set to educate a man!

(100–1)

Sriram very soon realizes that Bharati is a determined and committed nationalist and that the only way in which he could hope to earn her respect and affections is by becoming a nationalist himself. Consequently, tutored by Bharati, Sriram participates in the various nationalist activities: in the different villages he tours he spreads Gandhi's message and ideology, and he pickets shops that sell British goods and toddy. He burns his mill-manufactured clothes and aggressively joins the 'Quit India' movement.

Throughout all these political activities as he is becoming a revolutionist his love and passion for Bharati increase. He is more in touch with his feelings for her than she is willing to acknowledge.

Here Narayan taps into the Gandhian philosophy that women more than men are the preservers of morality and spirituality and that they should not acknowledge their sexuality. Further, as Ketu Katrak convincingly argues, Gandhi believed that female sexuality should be channeled for national service ('Indian Nationalism' 399; 'Decolonizing Culture' 167).[6] Nonetheless in the instance of their passion for each other Bharati again resorts to her discursive identity and ambiguously moves between the subject and object positions. For example, whenever Bharati receives a letter from Gandhi she shares it with Sriram and pays him a visit. On one such occasion Sriram throws himself on her and expresses his desire to marry her. He takes the situation completely under control by overpowering her, to some extent anticipating her reciprocal feelings:

> 'You will only write to him that we are married.' It was an assault conducted without any premeditation, and it nearly overwhelmed her. ... 'No, this can't be, Sriram.' Sriram muttered, 'Yes, this can be. No one can stop me and you from marrying now.' ... She wriggled in his grasp ... and at the same time seemed to respond to his caresses.
>
> (132)

She loses her hierarchical superiority to Sriram and thus control over her subjectivity every time he confronts her with his passion, largely because she does not want to acknowledge her own passion for him.

Instead she commits herself to the core of the nationalist culture, which is to safeguard the spiritual essence of Indian womanhood and thus to deny her sexuality.[7] In her object-position here she establishes the essential femininity of woman not in terms of her sexuality but within the nationalistic dictates of culturally visible spiritual and patriotic qualities for women. She finds herself committed to her role as a nationalist, and her service to the nation takes prominence. She regains her subject-position with Sriram, however, by merging with her object-position as daughter. She surrenders to her familial position as daughter, retains her political position as nationalist to gain access to her subject-position as a single-woman nationalist. She insists she will marry Sriram only if Gandhi approves. Reiterating her cultural position as the obedient daughter she uses her role to subvert Sriram's male position in their relationship. She resumes her subject-position by saying, 'I won't marry if he doesn't sanction it. I can't do it' (134).

Hiding behind the word of the Father she retains her nationalist and single woman's identity, postponing the identity of a married woman. Her subjection to obedience allows her to move from one kind of patriarchal discourse to another and in the process she stabilizes her subject-position. In a letter Gandhi responds to her request for permission to marry Sriram, 'I want you to give yourself up at the nearest police station. Take your disciple along too' (136). She decides to surrender to the British authorities and to her role as Gandhi's daughter. As a true nationalist she prepares herself for the political imprisonment that her revolutionary role demands. Even here she is guided by Gandhi who advises her of her duties in prison: 'take your *charka* along. I would like to hear that you are spinning your quota in jail' (138).

Dissolving the cultural and societal expectations of a single woman, Bharati, finally out of prison, acquires the role of surrogate mother to refugee children. In the meantime Sriram is indoctrinated into the cultural basis of community living when he joins Bharati at Delhi. In this camp, Bharati informs him, gender-specific roles and power structures have been dismantled to practice the ethics of self-sufficiency and self-reliance. Nonetheless he hands her a bundle of laundry:

> She snatched the bundle from his hand and went out. He reflected, 'She is almost my wife, she is doing what a wife would do. ...' She returned in a moment saying, '... Here in this camp everyone is expected to wash his or her own clothes and not employ others to do the job, but you are new and I have got a *dhobi* to wash for you as an exception'.
>
> (240)

Sriram is still a disciple as long as his expectations of Bharati are gender specific in terms of her identity as a woman. He is also not completely indoctrinated into Gandhi's philosophy of self-reliance and self-sufficiency.

Bharati's surrender of her role as daughter coincides with Ghandi's ultimate approval of her marriage to Sriram. However in this instance, although on one level she retains her object-position as the obedient daughter, by the time she commits herself to her conjugal rights she has established her personality and identity with Sriram. He continues to be impressed: 'She spoke English, Tamil, Hindi, Urdu. ... She spoke with great ease to men, women, young boys, and old men of all nationalities' (247). Sriram realizes at this point that she belongs to the world and to the people.

For his part Gandhi is extremely apologetic for being what he terms a negligent father and approves of their decision to marry. While still a dutiful daughter Bharati accepts Gandhi's decision to marry her to Sriram. However, just before he leaves for the prayer meeting, he expresses doubts about his ability to be present for her wedding. In the end he makes her promise that she will marry Sriram. A few seconds after Gandhi receives her promise he is assassinated. Bharati loses her semiotic object-position as a daughter but has to keep her obligation to her Father and marry Sriram, which is also her desire.

The love story of Bharati and Sriram is finally realized when the nationalist narrative attains its goal of independence from the British. Narayan's novel traces the issue of gender to that cultural and historical moment within the nationalist movement when the role of woman was specified for the very definite purpose of securing nationalistic objectives. Through her training in the nationalist movement, Bharati succeeds in strategically manipulating her different gender-coded roles to attain her own identity. She is also able to maintain her individuality in her relationship with Sriram. Further if one takes into consideration Gandhi's vision for the nationalist movement – to empower *all* the people in such a manner that it would enable them to rule themselves self-reliantly – then the nationalistic goal was achieved in the case of Bharati and Sriram. Gandhi believed that the nationalist movement should be historically determined and should eventually dissolve. For Gandhi the subject of nationalism was complicated and eclectic. His reconstitution of the nationalist subjectivity he envisioned as the 'people' was in many ways a divided subject. It was not a subject/object split and a mere gendered binary of male/female, nor an autonomous subject, but a heterogeneous one composed of contradictory identities: cultural/nationalist, male/female, imaginary/symbolic, colonizer/colonized and historical/ideological. From this perspective, by discursively placing herself as subject and as object in the nationalist discourse, Bharati retains her subject-position. The nationalist subject for Gandhi was a historical agent within a limited context and for a definite purpose.

The novel's ending with Gandhi's death signifies how the nationalistic narrative cannot continue beyond a certain historical, materialistic and culturally specific moment. For Bharati and Sriram participation in the nationalist movement was an epistemological quest, an education in the significance of the intersubjectivity of social roles and positions. Gandhi consistently believed in the model of a society where social roles such as that of teachers, leaders and disciples are interchangeable, where the cultural choices of subject/object positions are discursive.[8] In this sense then the nationalist movement within its own historical location did raise the issue of women. However since the nation is an 'imagined community' and since, as it cannot represent the diversity of the population, the subject of nationalism is a myth, the nationalist narrative is doomed to be nostalgic and utopian. It is destined to deconstruct itself.

NOTES

I would like to thank John Holland and Jack Blum (both of the Freshman Writing Program, University of Southern California) and Sharon Bassett (California State University, Los Angeles) for reading various drafts of this paper and for their suggestions.

1. For a selection of literary and political output by women during the nationalist movement see Tharu and Lalitha; Talwar.
2. For further discussion of the ways in which the woman's issue is spoken for by the Indian nationalist agenda, see Sangari and Vaid (1–8). See also Radhakrishnan (85).
3. I am indebted to Radhakrishnan for his analysis of what he calls the 'ethico-political' project of nationalism. In its endeavour to signify the culture, nation and people of India, the nationalist movement realized that such an attempt would necessitate the inclusion of a variety of other positions and social identities (87–9).
4. For an analysis of the complexity of subject-positions in colonial and postcolonial contexts I am indebted to Spivak (594–617), Bhabha, 'Of Mimicry and Man' (71–80), Sharpe (137–55), Parry (27–58), Mohanty (51–80), Rajan (196–222). In my own essay I move away from Rajan's article to show that the nationalist movement strategically used the feminine mode for an epistemological and political representation and articulation of nationalist consciousness. I argue that the Indian nationalist movement itself under Mahatma Gandhi's leadership was discursively split as subject/object. This double articulation of the nationalist movement, I assert, is part of the historical foundation of the nationalist movement in its efforts to establish its own subjectivity.

5. For a detailed analysis of the complicated way in which these two domains of the 'home' and the 'world' are portrayed in colonial, national and postcolonial writings in India, see Rajan (71–92).
6. On the other hand, other writers on the Gandhian movement consider the Gandhian movement as feminist in several ways. For example Kishwar argues that the Gandhian movement did not interrogate the ideological basis of the women's question but sought ethical and personal changes for women which empower women as a whole (1698).
7. Here Katrak's analysis is useful:

    > Male power and male sexuality are legitimate; female sexuality, understood as female power, must be controlled and bounded through social custom, primarily within marriage. … When sexuality and spirituality merge, women are socialized into subsuming sexuality within a spiritual realm, leaving behind the realms of the physical, of desire, of pleasure.
    >
    > ('Indian Nationalism' 398–9)

    I argue, however, that Bharati deflects her sexuality to access another subject-position by retaining her familial role as daughter by surrendering her cultural expectations of marriage.
8. See also Radhakrishnan's views on these issues (89). For a discussion of the heterogeneous narrative of nationalism see Bhabha.

WORKS CITED

Bhabha, Homi, 'Of Mimicry and Man: The Ambivalence of Colonial Discourse', *October* 28 (1984).

—— (ed.), *Nation and Narration*, London: Routledge, 1990.

Chakravarti, Uma, 'Whatever Happened to the Vedic *Dasi*? Orientalism, Nationalism and a Script for the Past', in Sangari and Vaid 27–87.

Chatterjee, Partha, 'The Nationalist Resolution of the Woman's Question', in Sangari and Vaid 233–53.

Gandhi, M. K., *All Men Are Brothers: Autobiographical Reflections*, New York: Continuum, 1990.

Jayawardena, Kumari, *Feminism and Nationalism in the Third World*, London: Zed Books Ltd, 1986.

Katrak, Ketu, 'Indian Nationalism, Gandhian 'Satyagraha', and Representations of Female Sexuality', in Parker *et al.* 1992: 395–406.

—— 'Decolonizing Culture: Toward a Theory of Post Colonial Women's Texts', *Modern Fiction Studies* 35 (Spring 1989): 167–82.

Kishwar, Madhu, 'Women in Gandhi', *Economic and Political Weekly* 20 (1985): 1691–702.

Mani, Lata, 'Contentious Traditions: The Debate on Sati in Colonial India', in Abdul R. JanMohammad and David Lloyd (eds), *The Nature and Context of Minority Discourse*, New York: Oxford University Press, 1990.

Mohanty, Chandra Talpade, 'Under Western Eyes: Feminist Scholarship and Colonial Discourse', in Chandra Mohanty, Ann Russo and Lourdes Torres (eds), *Third World Women and the Politics of Feminism*, Bloomington: Indiana University Press, 1991.

Nandy, Ashis, *The Intimate Enemy: Loss and Recovery of Self Under Colonialism*, Delhi: Oxford University Press, 1983.

Narayan, R. K., *Waiting for the Mahatma*, Chicago: University of Chicago Press, 1955.

Parker, Andrew, Mary Russo, Doris Sommer and Patricia Yaeger (eds), *Nationalisms and Sexualities*, New York: Routledge, 1992.

Parry, Benita, 'Problems in Current Theories of Colonial Discourse', *Oxford Literary Review* 9 (1987): 27–58.

Radhakrishnan, R., 'Nationalism, Gender, and the Narrative of Identity', in Parker *et al.* 1992: 77–95.

Rajan, Gita, 'Subversive–Subaltern identity: Indira Gandhi as the Speaking Subject', in Sidonie Smith and Julia Watson (eds), *De/Colonizing the Subject: The Politics of Gender in Women's Autobiography*, Minneapolis: University of Minnesota Press, 1992.

Rajan, Rajeswari Sunder, 'The Feminist Plot and the Nationalist Allegory: Home and the World in Two Indian Women's Novels in English', *Modern Fiction Studies* 39, 1 (1993): 71–92.

Sangari, Kum Kum and Sadesh Vaid (eds), *Recasting Women: Essays in Indian Colonial History*, New Brunswick, NJ: Rutgers University Press, 1990.

Sharpe, Jenny, 'Figures in Colonial Discourse', *Modern Fiction Studies* 35, 1 (1989): 137–55.

Spivak, Gayatri Chakravarti, 'Can the Subaltern Speak?' in Cary Nelson and Lawrence Grossberg (eds), *Marxism and the Interpretation of Culture*, Urbana, IL: University of Illinois Press, 1988.

Talwar, Vir Bharat, 'Feminist Consciousness in Women's Journals in Hindi, 1910–20', in Sangari and Vaid 204–32.

Tharu, Susie and K. Lalitha (eds), *Women Writing in India: 600 B.C. to the Present*, New York: The Feminist Press, 1991.

8

Female Sacrifice: Gender and Nostalgic Nationalism in Rebecca West's *Black Lamb and Grey Falcon*

LORETTA STEC

Near the end of *Black Lamb and Grey Falcon*, her sprawling, compelling, encyclopedic account of traveling through Yugoslavia in the late 1930s, Rebecca West describes a spectacle she and her husband witnessed. As they sat at a hotel cafe in Prishtina, with elbows 'on a tablecloth stained brown and puce' eating 'chicken drumsticks … meagre as sparrow bones', a Serbian couple walked towards them, clearly having traveled a great distance. The woman had 'the better part of a plough' tied to her back while the man 'went free'. As the man conversed with the hotel-keeper, the woman stood nearby, unable to sit down, with 'a blue shadow of fatigue' on her face. Although West did not converse with the couple, she felt able to sum up their situation and explain the condition of the cafe's repast by drawing on Balkan history (894–5). West reads this incident as emblematic of the effects of imperial oppression by the Turks, the Austrians, the Italians, the Russians, and the Hungarians over centuries in the Balkans. Imperialism, she argues, had created the material and spiritual squalor, and what she interpreted as the distorted gender roles, of some communities in Yugoslavia. West describes finding these mean conditions in her travels interspersed with remnants of the admirable peasant cultures of the Balkan peoples. West anachronistically associates these cultures with 'nations'.[1] She opposes them to the cultures of the imperialist rulers which, she believed, infiltrated and debased the arts and social arrangements of the Slavs. West finds 'disgusting' the sight of the woman carrying the plough, not so much because of

138

the effect on her but because of the 'nullification' of the husband who loses his masculinity and is no longer able to defend the nation or community against imperialists and intruders (895). *Black Lamb* suggests that West wished to mitigate the subjection of the woman to the man but not abolish it. Rather she argues that the woman needs to stop carrying the plough in order to protect her womb, an 'instrument of the race', or nation; she nostalgically argues for a return to essentialist definitions and roles of gender that subordinate women in sex–gender systems more subtle than the one this episode implies (895). West concludes in *Black Lamb* that women must heroically submit to male domination for the sake of national security while nations must actively and heroically resist domination by other powers.

In writing *Black Lamb and Grey Falcon* on the brink of World War II, West created an argument for strong British and Yugoslav nationalism in the face of fascist imperialist desires.[2] Throughout most of *Black Lamb* West creates an opposition between imperialism as villain[3] and nationalism as defensive hero. In defining nationalism as the defensive ideology that will save Europe from fascist domination, and in imagining a method through which this nationalism will be stable, West participates in a nostalgic logic of gender domination.

Nationalism has been mobilized in numerous historical situations for numerous purposes, from the struggle to free a people from colonial domination to the repression of a minority group within national boundaries: nationalist ideologies have the power both to liberate and to oppress. At its most negative extreme, nationalism becomes a 'dynamic of domination – where groups battle for control over geographic territory, and justify violence and aggression in the name of national security' (Bunch 339). West's response to the historical moment in which she was writing led her to elide in *Black Lamb and Grey Falcon* the potential contradictions in the definitions and uses of nationalism. West suppressed the fact that nationalism could be used as an ideological rationale for aggressive as well as defensive behavior, emphasizing instead the need for defensive national security which she believed could be bolstered through a strong imaginative identification with one's nation. Literature and myth are two significant constituents of imaginative nationalism, and West presented a strong and persuasive case for the 'nation' – both Yugoslavia and England – in her widely read travelogue *Black Lamb and Grey Falcon*.

While suppressing the potentially contradictory uses of national-ist ideologies, West imagines the intersection of nationalism and gender in profoundly contradictory ways in this work. Women have been differently placed in relation to nationalism, at times benefitting from its uses and embracing it, and, more often, it seems, having their identities constructed for, and agendas subordi-nated to, the needs of the 'nation'.[4] West's logic of submission for women in the name of the nation is a common and oppressive aspect of numerous nationalisms in this century, for example in the 'Black Power' movement in the United States[5] and in the current war in the former Yugoslavia. West's conclusion stands in contra-diction to the feminist stance in her former work and in some pas-sages of *Black Lamb and Grey Falcon*, as well as to the authority she claims for herself as a writer in producing this enormous generic hybrid of a book.

The text of *Black Lamb and Grey Falcon* runs to 1150 pages, includ-ing a bibliography and maps. The generic mix of the text has been seen as its strength by a number of critics (Glendinning 164). This travel narrative takes the reader on a journey through the bloody history of the Balkans as well as through the many regions and 'na-tional' enclaves of Yugoslavia in the late 1930s. West joins a very au-thoritative intellectual, political and social history of the region with impressions and personal revelations, fusing her 'masculine' author-ity with 'feminine' details of domesticity, aesthetic appreciation, and human interaction. The success with which West was able to combine traditionally masculine and feminine modes of writing in this book is not replicated in its gendered content and arguments.

West's ability to reach the conclusion that women should submit to men for the sake of national security is a function of, and a con-stituent of, the nostalgia that undergirds *Black Lamb and Grey Falcon*. Throughout the text the reader is confronted with a series of nostal-gic rhetorical moves that work to construct West's argument about nationalism and imperialism, and that constitute her demand for fixed gender roles. The nostalgic elements in the text are complex and interrelated; I separate them into four modes merely to identify them. First, West claims that her interest in the Balkan lands derives from images from her dreams and daydreams. She claims that 'from childhood' 'Macedonia is the country I have always seen between sleeping and waking' (1088). West creates in her text a Yugoslavia in the image of her childhood imaginings, with a nostalgic glow of glory. This element of personal nostalgia tinges her representation of the country.

Despite the hardship and the results of oppression she encounters in her travels, West's portrait of Yugoslavia in *Black Lamb* is that of a land with all the glories Western Europe lacks, full of the best and purest sentiments, art and heroism, a veritable Eden. In this way West participates in the mode of nostalgia Raymond Williams analyzes in *The Country and The City*, that of longing for the 'organic community' which is an imaginative substitution for Eden (9–12). The crossing of national boundaries bolsters West's nostalgic argument by veiling its idealization of the past. The implication is that if an organic and heroic society exists somewhere in the late 1930s, it can exist in England also, despite the historical differences between the two nations.

West's idealized representation of Yugoslavia inscribes another, or third, mode of nostalgia, as a result of the historical circumstances surrounding the book's publication. By 1941 when *Black Lamb* was published, Yugoslavia had been occupied by the Germans, 'bombed and abolished, and Rebecca West found that she had been a visitor to a now lost world' (Wolff 28). West feared destruction as severe as that in the Balkans for the rest of Europe, and her text includes a kind of anticipatory nostalgia for all the lands and peoples about to be destroyed by the fascists.

In the interest of defense from hostile powers West was a strong proponent of the multi-ethnic nation of Yugoslavia. The conspicuously artificial joining of many ethnic and linguistic groups into the 'nation' of Yugoslavia at the end of World War I is opposed to West's naturalizing of 'nation' and 'nationalism' in *Black Lamb* (Singleton 68–70). West defines nationalism as 'the determination of a people to cultivate its own soul, to follow the customs bequeathed to it by its ancestors, to develop its traditions according to its own instincts' (1101). The terms 'soul' and 'instincts' remove the national idea from the realm of history, and contradict the time-bound terms 'customs' and 'traditions'. In invoking the 'soul' and 'instincts' of a national people, West suggests that the 'nation' is a natural entity, fused with the essential natures of its subjects. This tendency in West to appeal to an essential nature, a fixed identity – in this case for the people of a nation – is a fourth mode of nostalgia that marks her text. It is a nostalgia for fixity, for categories of identity and social relations that do not shift.[6]

This mode of nostalgia is very prominent in *Black Lamb and Grey Falcon*, and it exerts itself most strongly in West's thoughts on gender. The desire for fixed gender roles as a component of fixed national identity brings the root meaning of the word 'nostalgia' into play: a longing for 'nostos', or home. West's text was part of a widespread attempt before and during World War II to constitute the English nation as a stable homeland. Many demands for a strong and stable English nation were couched in the terms 'homeland' and 'home front' during World War II. The 'home front' stood in contrast to the combat zone, the alien territories of ally and enemy who did not share one's national identity (Lant 44). The term 'home front' also resonated with gendered meanings. World War II impelled the largest mobilization of women into war work in England's history, which reversed the employment trends of the interwar years. After the large-scale participation of women in World War I the British government, aided by the media, the trade unions and the medical establishment, dictated a return of women to the home and the roles of wife and mother.[7] Women were assigned the tasks of replenishing the population of the British Empire, buying and consuming Empire-made goods, protecting the private property that helped to define national identity and defending the 'home' against socialism (Campbell 51–60).

When a second war with Germany began to look inevitable, the British government acknowledged that it would need women's help, and it instituted conscription for women in war work in December 1941. The Conservative government, however, tended to abandon traditional definitions of women's roles reluctantly, and instituted measures that bolstered the ideology of separate spheres, and women's 'natural' place as caretakers of children (Braybon and Summerfield 161–2).

As is clear from these struggles surrounding women's mobilization, an ideological battle was in full swing as World War II began over the relationship between gender roles and national identity and security. As Penny Summerfield puts it, 'production' and 'patriarchy' were in conflict. West contradicted the feminist stance she took earlier in her career and even in certain passages of *Black Lamb and Grey Falcon* by joining the debate on the side of 'patriarchy'. West participates in the nostalgia for a lost national identity and at the same time exhibits a longing for the place of the woman in that stable nation – the literal 'home' of the patriarchal nuclear family. This conservative desire for a stable home and role is somewhat understandable in the face of fascist threats to destroy all recognizable civilization. It is disturbingly ironic, however, that West's nostalgia echoes a major element in both Italian fascist and Nazi social organization – the confining of women to their roles in the home and in the sexual division of labour (De Grazia, Koonz).

Through her use of the nostalgic rhetorical strategies outlined above, West constructed analogies between Yugoslav history and myth and the European crisis of World War II to comprise an argument for both strong national security and strictly defined gender roles. In one of these analogies West interpreted Neville Chamberlain's policy of appeasement as a repetition of the mistake of the Slav Prince Lazar who sacrificed his men to the invading Turks in 1389. In the Slav myth the prophet Elijah is transformed into a grey falcon. He flies from Jerusalem to Tsar Lazar and offers him a choice between an earthly kingdom and a heavenly kingdom. The falcon explains to him the result of his choosing a heavenly kingdom:

> all your soldiers will be destroyed,
> And you, prince, shall be destroyed with them.
>
> (910)

Despite this certainty Lazar chooses the heavenly kingdom. The historical result of this mythical choice was that the Turks conquered the Slavs and, as West put it, 'night fell for four centuries' on these Balkan lands (840).[8]

West interprets the myth of Lazar as a manifestation of masochism, the desire for self-sacrifice she believes she has witnessed among her friends in the political opposition. West believed that those on the Left, particularly pacifists, had a deep desire to be defeated: 'They want to be right, not to do right' (913). The difficulty she raises here is that of being able to defend one's principles and one's nation without becoming cruel and oppressive. This was a poignant dilemma for a writer who had lived through one world war and was about to live through another, who was simultaneously fascinated and disgusted by the power of monarchs, empires, and men. The question of masochism thus became crucial to West's reconsideration of gender roles in the face of fascism and the need for strong national identity.

West locates the root of the masochistic approach to politics in religious belief, and explains it through the other symbol of the book's title, the black lamb. West had attended a fertility ritual in Macedonia at a large rock in the middle of 'Sheep's Field'. She was thoroughly revolted by the spectacle:

> Women do not get children by adding to the normal act of copulation the slaughter of a lamb, the breaking of a jar, the decapitation of a cock ... . If there was a woman whose womb could be unsealed by witnessing a petty and pointless act of violence ... her fertility would be the reverse of motherhood, she would have children for the purpose of hating them.

(826)

This act of sacrificing the lamb is the sadistic analogue to the masochistic desires of those who wish to be sacrificed. The human imagination, West argues, is disgusted by the cruelty of sacrifice as she was disgusted by the fertility rite at the Sheep's Field; in response human beings imaginatively 'exchange the role of priest for the role of lamb', the sacrificer for the sacrificed, the sadist for the masochist, out of fear of becoming cruel. West believes this causes us to fail to defend actively our beliefs and our nations (915).

The psychic structure of sacrifice that West outlined – the masochistic desire to be sacrificed rather than perform the sadistic act of sacrificing – had profound political ramifications for her. With the rise of fascism, as at so many other times in European history, Jews were condemned for the 'sacrifice' of Christ and became those literally 'sacrificed' by the Nazis in the name of creating a purer and better Europe. Those in the position to defend the Jews, the gypsies and the Slavs against the brutality of the sacrificial myth had also become its victims, psychologically rather than physically. West believed the liberals of Western Europe had undergone an imaginative transformation that led them to become proponents of appeasement.[9] England had moved from a position as a dominant imperial power in the late nineteenth century to that of an appeaser of another power, and a weak defender of its own national integrity. For West the masochistic response was entirely inadequate for coping with the great cruelty of Nazism which had the potential to turn the whole of Europe into a 'Sheep's Field'.

Within the text of *Black Lamb* West illustrates this dynamic between the psychology of sacrifice and its political manifestations through the literary use of characters, in particular Constantine, the

Jewish Serbian poet who serves as the official travel guide for West through Yugoslavia, and his German wife, Gerda.[10] Gerda is the consummate figure of imperialism and fascism; she is an extreme and exaggerated representation of the qualities of empire, and West uses her to illustrate the contempt for other races that fascism fostered.[11] Gerda plagues their every traveling step with intolerance, peevishness, and bad taste. In one of her most offensive moments she remarks of a Macedonian cemetery full of French soldiers who fought the invading Germans, 'think of all these people dying for a lot of Slavs' (766). Henry concludes that she is 'finally and exclusively, a threat to existence' (800). Constantine, on the other hand, is an open, insightful, loquacious guide through centuries of Balkan history and disparate geographical zones. He is an irrepressible lover of life, of poetry, of art, of politics, even of Gerda, in spite of her childlike contempt for him. Constantine is the great-hearted lion in West's narrative, who guides his friends through city and country with the stereotypical magnanimity of the Slav soul.

Gerda is the figure of the sadist in the text; Constantine, despite his love of life, is the masochist who has willingly submitted to Gerda's domination: 'He had bared his throat to Gerda's knife, he had offered his loving heart to the service of hate, in order that he might be defeated and innocent' (916). West sympathizes with Constantine and his increasing depression in the narrative, diagnosing him as 'dying of being a Jew' in a world increasingly threatening to Jews (991). Eventually, however, West makes his submission, his masochism, symbolically as great a sin as Gerda's sadism.

The extreme reaction West records to what she interprets as Constantine's masochism is in part due to her Manichean imagination struggling in *Black Lamb and Grey Falcon* to extricate itself from the binary options of masochism and sadism, in both psychological and political terms. West believed the citizens of Britain, of Yugoslavia, of all anti-fascist nations, must overcome masochism, and risk the temptation to cruelty to defend themselves and others. By arguing against masochism in response to fascist violence, a masochism which she associates with women or effeminate men of the peace movement in Europe, West sets up strict and nostalgic definitions of gender as the categories of stable goodness Western Europe must defensively fight to protect – and as a way to mobilize that defensive fighting.

Disgusted by the ineffectual British men she regarded as masochistic, West compared them to the virile, heroic men of Yugoslavia she describes throughout *Black Lamb and Grey Falcon*.[12] These 'virile' men are heroic in being neither sadistic nor masochistic, but merely defensive against imperialists and invaders. For example she provides the following impressions of three Slav men she saw in a shipyard:

> They were all three beautiful, with thick, straight, fair hair and bronze skins and high cheekbones pulling the flesh up from their large mouths, with broad chests and long legs springing from arched feet. These were men, they could beget children on women, they could shape certain kinds of materials for purposes that made them masters of their worlds.
>
> (208)

These beautiful and virile men are the Adams of the Balkans whom West idealizes throughout her travels. Her description joins the Edenic, organic formation of the men, their 'long legs springing from arched feet', as if the arched feet had just sprung from the earth, with their positions as creators in a pre-industrial economy. West claims they could 'shape materials for purposes that made them masters of their worlds', a nostalgic claim that contradicts her chronicle of the many imperialists who had ruled Dalmatia over the centuries, and others who were vying for domination over these very men and their worlds.

West contrasts this portrait of creative, virile, essential manhood with 'two kinds of men that the West produces':

> the cityish kind who wears spectacles without shame, as if they were the sign of quality and not a defect, who is overweight and puffy, who can drive a car but knows no other mastery over material, who presses buttons and turns switches without comprehending the result, who makes money when the market goes up, and loses it when the market goes down; the high-nosed young man, who is somebody's secretary or is in the Foreign Office, who has a peevishly amusing voice, and is very delicate, who knows a great deal, but far from all there is to be known about French pictures. I understand why we cannot build, why we cannot govern, why we bear ourselves without pride in our international rela-

tions. It is not that all Englishmen are like that, but that too many of them are like that in our most favoured classes.

It is strange, it is heartrending, to stray into a world where men are men, and women are still women.[13]

(208)

The first portrait figures the alienation of the urban man from his own body as well as from an organic community. He is defective, lacking the power to see his surroundings. He lacks even knowledge of his pitiable state, having lost all values or standards by which to judge; he 'wears his spectacles without shame'. He is completely subordinated to his environment. Such a man is no man, West suggests; he could not have any power to stop fascism.

The second description in the passage above snidely offers a portrait of a stereotypically homosexual man. He is 'high-nosed' and high-voiced, concerned with the arts, 'delicate', subordinate to another man. Because of definitions of the nation that are bound up with 'home' and family, homosexuals, like Jews, are not considered capable of true patriotism. The homophobic remarks throughout *Black Lamb* indicate West's discomfort with the slightest gender confusion. West's nostalgia for fixed categories of gender condemns what she perceives as the effeminacy of men in the educated classes. This tendency becomes more emphatic as she tries to conceive of gender categories so stably linked to nation and home that they will resist the growing threat of fascism, even as they echo some of the constructions of nation and gender found in the fascism she wished to fight.

In an attempt to reinforce the male heroic role, West idealizes Yugoslav men as able to master their worlds and suggests that they do not need to practice cruelty to do so. West reserves her greatest praise for the most 'manly' Serbs, those who fought the Turks for five centuries to defend their lands and families and cultures. These she finds in a little village on the Black Mountain of Macedonia, the Skopska Tserna Gora. West's traveling companion Constantine says of the inhabitants of this village: 'They [are] magnificent people ... . Never were the Turks able to settle here ... . These men of the Skopska Tserna Gora, they could not be conquered' (677). These men and this society are the fulfillment of West's nostalgic vision. In her representation they have kept up the traditions of the past and successfully defended their society and land through a system of strict gender roles and definitions of ethnic identity. West thus finds the ideal past dwelling in the present in this village and values it as a model for the rest of Europe. The sex–gender system maintained by these Macedonian Serbs is at once admirable to West in its effect of allowing the community to survive but disturbing and damnable in its effects on the women. In her use of this Macedonian village as a model she runs up against a contradiction between her feminism and what she perceives as necessary to cope with Europe's imminent future.

West begins the chapter that unfolds the Macedonian social system by describing a traditional dance, the kolo. The men's part is marked by extreme liveliness, but the women's part is composed of steps reminiscent of the dead. The women wear elaborate and excessively heavy costumes and headdresses. These clothes, coupled with the Slav ideal of femininity – 'the stiff and stylized Virgin of the icons' – force the women to dance without lifting their feet off the ground, in slow and morbid rhythms. These Macedonian women were asked to do much more than wear heavy clothing. They 'were treated as if courage or cunning on their part was inconceivable, as if they were lucky to be used as beasts of burden' – an idea consonant with the image of the woman carrying the plough tied to her back (677). West finds that 'it is impossible for women to be happy in such a society' and that they are 'victims' of gender-based 'social persecution' (674). However in this case West justifies the society modeled on the inferiority of women as necessary for the defense of that community. Men have ample reason to declare their 'universal superiority' based on their 'physical superiority':

> If the community is threatened by any real danger, and only a few fortunate communities are not, women will be fools if they do not accept that declaration without dispute. For the physical superiority of men and their freedom from maternity make them the natural defenders of the community, and if they can derive strength from belief in the inferiority of women, it is better to let them have it.
>
> (679)

Two main ideas mark her conclusions in this passage as conservative: the insistence on the 'natural' division of labor – maternity versus defense – based on an essential, biological definition of gender, and the advice that women freely submit to men's dominance in order to obtain protection against other men.[14] West rationalizes this 'persecution' as what 'at one and the same time makes life possible and intolerable for women' (678).

These propositions radically contradict West's feminist stance in her earlier work. For example, in an article in *The Clarion* of 1913 entitled 'The Sin of Self-Sacrifice', West argued against both separate spheres and the submission of women to men by advocating work for wages. Here her argument went beyond the right to economic self-sufficiency, however; she rejected the very ideology of nationalism and race survival that *Black Lamb and Grey Falcon* later perpetuates, asserting that

> sacrificing the individual to the race never works. ... If half the individuals agree to remain weak and undeveloped, half the race is weak and undeveloped. ... Every nation that has contained a slave class has fallen to dust and ashes.
>
> ('Sin', 237)

In *Black Lamb and Grey Falcon*, written in 1940, however, West maintains that women in Macedonia must suffer the humiliation of being defined as inferior, and sacrifice themselves by submitting to the material practices that are the consequence of such a definition. West's definition of nationalism as the 'equivalent of the individual's determination not to be a slave' (1101) is given a new twist here; her argument in *Black Lamb* is that half of the individuals in a community should consent to be virtual slaves for the sake of that community, or the imagined community – the nation.

The tension between these differing ideas about gender systems causes West to continue her rationale with increasingly convoluted prose. West tries to modulate her suggestion that men are indeed naturally superior in some ways. She believes that when a society reaches a time of peace, men and women both 'use their full capacities of mind' and something rather astonishing happens:

> There has been drained from him the strength which his forefathers derived from the subjection of women; and the woman is amazed because tradition has taught her that to be a man is to be strong. There is no known remedy for this disharmony. As yet it seems that no present she can make him out of her liberty can compensate him for his loss of what he gained from her slavery.
>
> (679)

The syntactic difficulties of that last sentence suggest West's own discomfort with the implications of her argument. She concludes that unless a condition of world peace exists, 'there never can be a society where men are men and women are women' (679). Significantly this conclusion contradicts what she says hundreds of pages earlier in the text, namely that Yugoslavia is one of the only societies in which 'men are men and women are still women' (208). Her nostalgia inevitably clashes with her feminism, and the conditions of a threatened war impel her argument that women must submit to men. She reaches her conclusion with grim resignation: the most we can do in response to the situation is to 'rejoice when a boy is born and ... weep for a girl' (680).

The women of the community, then, become its sacrificial lambs in the perpetuation of hostilities and rivalries among men. West confounds her analysis of sacrifice in *Black Lamb and Grey Falcon* by arguing for women's self-sacrifice of their 'full capacities of mind and body' to shore up men's fragile sense of their own power. This can of course be interpreted as masochism, but West chooses to avoid that term when speaking of the necessary submission of women. In spite of her understanding of its inherent contradictions and probable ineffectiveness (678–80), West proposes the subordination of women to men as part of a solution to imperialist threats.

West transforms her resignation about the possibility of change into a determined optimism in her conclusion to *Black Lamb and Grey Falcon*, an epilogue written as London was being bombed nightly, and the suffering of the Slavs was increasing at the hands of the Nazis. As West tells it, the Yugoslavs under the regent Prince Paul had been forced to sign a pact with Hitler making Yugoslavia subservient to the Nazi will;[15] soon after in 1941 a coup overthrew Paul and installed the young Peter Karageorgevitch II as king. His government refused to cooperate with the Nazis, preferring to consider itself 'neutral' (Taylor 525). The Yugoslavs prepared to resist Hitler with their small and inadequate but determined forces with full knowledge that they would be defeated. During this time, West claims, the Yugoslavs often repeated the poem of the Tsar Lazar and the grey falcon, which she saw as celebrating an 'appetite for sacrificial self-immolation'. West posits that this was an inappropriate source for them to quote, and then transforms her interpretation of the poem to make it appropriate:

It was their resistance, not their defeat, which appeared to them as the sacred element in their ordeal. ... The poem of the Tsar Lazar and the grey falcon tells a story which celebrates the death-wish; but its hidden meaning pulses with life.

(1145)

Just as the Slavs resisted the Turks in the full knowledge of defeat, the Yugoslavs would resist the Nazis. West reinterprets the poem by emphasizing resistance rather than defeat in order to put forth the determination of the Yugoslavs as a model for the rest of Europe. By reinterpreting the poem to fit the circumstances West turns a cautionary tale into an exemplary one and infuses it with an almost desperate longing for action in the face of oppression.

West does not, however, reinterpret her analysis that women should submit to male oppression in order to be safe. She does not consider the possibility that women might rather band together in the face of a common enemy and resist. She never explicitly returns to her arguments about gender in this epilogue, as if gender relations were not important to a reconsideration of Europe's relation to fascism and war. Rather her text leaves her nostalgic definitions and arguments for the submission of women intact, implying that the submission of women to men is a precondition to the resistance of one nation or people to the invasion, colonization or oppression of another.

Black Lamb and Grey Falcon promotes the submission of women to men as necessary for a strong nation, and in this way participates in the nostalgic and resistant arguments of the British government, many servicemen, and many women themselves against the mobilization of women for war. Contrary to all their nostalgic propositions, as the threat of fascism grew it became clear that the mobilization of women was a necessary condition for national defense. Thus both West and the British government had to channel their nostalgia in other directions until the war was over and women were again relegated to the home, as they were after World War I.

During the war West demonstrated that what she advocated for other women she had no intention of performing herself. She retreated to her house in the country for most of the war, and performed traditionally female domestic duties (Glendinning 182). At the same time, however, she continued to revise *Black Lamb and*

Grey Falcon for publication in 1941 and began to write 'regularly, brilliantly, and profitably' for *The New Yorker* (Glendinning 165). By actively pursuing her career in this way West made evident that she was by no means content to sacrifice her 'full capacities of mind and body' to bolster the masculinity of the British men she found ineffectual or those who were fighting fascism on the continent.

While West pursued her boldly feminist path as a writer she wrote her nostalgia for fixed gender roles into the structure of *Black Lamb and Grey Falcon* as well as in its arguments. West refers continually to 'my husband' throughout the text, never once in 1150 pages naming him as Henry Andrews. She presents the voice of her 'husband' to give opinions and provide facts about significant issues in their travels. Through this rhetorical strategy West seems to be suppressing her authority in favor of that of a virile male. Some critics, most notably Mary Ellmann (114–15), have read this strategy as a detriment to West's authority as a writer, as a kind of literary submission on the order of that more radical submission she suggests for the women of Yugoslavia. I believe, however, that this literary strategy is an unconvincing charade. The illusion is so transparent that although the voice of the 'husband' is presented without irony in the text, the reader's judgement of his authority is qualified by the surrounding thousand pages of West's narration. And those thousand pages contain enough remarkable writing to refute the claims of male superiority to which West counsels women to submit for the sake of national security.

* * *

West does not suggest in *Black Lamb and Grey Falcon* that women might actively take part in defending a homeland or a nation against imperialists or other invaders. She ignores this possibility not only in relation to England but also to Yugoslavia. Barbara Jancar-Webster has documented the participation of Yugoslav women in resisting the Nazis and in supporting the Partisans during World War II. She asserts, 'In no other country in the world have women played such a decisive part in the achievement of victory over an occupying enemy and the realization of a communist state' (1). For Jancar-Webster, the actions of the women in the front lines as medical personnel and in the rear as support staff led to a 'rapid transformation, achieving in five years of war what they had been unable to accomplish during twenty-odd years of interwar peace – the right of entry into society on male terms' (4). The women of Yugoslavia have never been the passive pack-horses West imagines them to have been in parts of her travelogue.

Yugoslav women's 'entry into society on male terms', and particularly their achievement of equal status as members of the nation, however, has hardly been as successful as Jancar-Webster claims. Although Yugoslavia had achieved a 'formal legal equation of genders' under communism, 'women remained segregated and subordinated in all walks of life' (Milic 111). A feminist movement began in 1978 to respond to that subordination and had made important but limited inroads into public opinion before the war began in Croatia and Slovenia in 1991 (Drakulic, 'Women' 127).[16] During these tragic recent years women in the former Yugoslavia have adopted and embodied widely differing attitudes toward their nation and national identity. Some women identify strongly with their nation and participate in the nationalist fervor of the moment. Others find the categories of national identity confining: as Slavenka Drakulic explains in one of her many moving essays, 'the war is ... reducing us to one dimension: the Nation' ('Overcome' 51). Still others actively protest the actions taken by governments in the name of the nation, such as the women from Serbia, Croatia and Slovenia who demanded the return of their sons from the federal army in 1991. These women might have changed the course of the war if they had not divided amongst themselves into groupings based on ethnic/national identity (Drakulic, 'Women' 128–9). Women's responses to nationalism, then, have ranged from active resistance to enthusiasm, clearly demonstrating that women are agents in nationalist struggles, not simply subordinate figures who help men to feel superior.

Women's participation in national life, however, is circumscribed by the limited vision of those who hold the most power in the former Yugoslavia. This is a vision that shares characteristics with West's in *Black Lamb and Grey Falcon*. Throughout the region post-communist states are enacting or attempting to enact pronatalist policies to encourage women to have ethnically pure children for the nation.[17] Analogous policies are overturning the universal access to abortion that women had under communism. Franjo Tudjman, leader of Catholic Croatia, even blessed an empty cradle representing 'the nation's unborn children' at his inauguration (Benderly 26). With these pronatalist policies and the restructuring of the Eastern European economies, women are encouraged to take up the maternal role as their primary function,[18] indicating the expected limits of women's participation in the new 'democratic' societies.[19] This restructuring effectively subordinates women to men by making them economically dependent and reinforcing the ideology of patriarchal power through the 'family wage'.

Reaching the goal of pronatalist policies, ethnically pure children, is clearly as impracticable as creating states whose borders encompass only people of one ethnicity, religion and language. The idea of a 'nation' in this sense is very much an imagined community that trades on nostalgic images; it is a pure fiction that never could have existed when we consider the complications of intermarriage, migration, religious conversion and previous ethnic tolerance. This pure fiction, however, has severe political ramifications for those in the former Yugoslavia, including the formation of state policies that place women in limited and often subordinate roles for the sake of the nation.

Even the most irrationally brutal acts are being justified in the name of the nation in the former Yugoslavia. Thousands of women[20] have been raped in the war in Bosnia in the past two years, mostly Muslim women raped by Serb soldiers. Some of these rapes were the product of wartime policy – the Serb soldiers are told they 'can do with the women what [they] like' as long as they kill them afterwards (Burns, 'Serbian' A12). Some of the rapists, however, have explained their actions to their victims by saying that 'It is better to give birth to Chetniks [Serbs] than to Muslim filth.' These women have been imprisoned to keep them from having abortions (Burns, '150 Muslims'). The illogic of this rationale is obvious; if the mother is Muslim, she may be the descendent of a Slav family who converted but she may well have Turkish blood in her family, which would interfere with the 'purity' of the Serbian 'Chetniks' about to be born. But, as one Bosnian woman suggested, the use of this wartime policy and rationale is a cost-effective way to terrorize and destroy physically and psychologically a large sector of the population without investing in weapons or training for the soldiers, except the ideological training of nationalism.

The nation is 'conceived as a deep, horizontal comradeship ... that makes it possible, over the past two centuries, for so many millions of people, not so much to kill, as willingly to die for such limited imaginings', says Benedict Anderson (7). I would add that this comradeship is imagined in relation to an other who does not belong to it, and that this makes possible the willingness to kill and

rape and maim in the name of 'nation' we have witnessed throughout the twentieth century and in the current war in the former
Yugoslavia in particular. The nostalgic narratives invoked to build
up nationhood can be used for the purposes Rebecca West enumer-
ates, to create a defensive front against imperialists and invaders;
they can also be used to justify terror, murder and rape. The
dangers of narratives that nostalgically link the subordination of
women with definitions of nationhood are dramatically displayed
in the violent transformation of the former Yugoslavia. Women, of
course, are not the only ones affected by this terror – all citizens are
subject to the horrifying 'dynamic of domination' that is one consequence of nostalgic nationalism.

NOTES

1. E. J. Hobsbawm explains that although the word 'nation' is indigenous to Romance languages it did not take on the meaning that joined
   people, state, and territory until the late eighteenth century (19).
2. See Colquitt and Tillinghast.
3. In the epilogue to *Black Lamb and Grey Falcon* West argues most thoroughly the pros and cons of imperialism, and admits her own
   conflicted position as a daughter of the British Empire (1089).
4. For examples of the varying relations between women and nation, see
   Jeyawardena, Funk and Mueller, 'Feminism and Nationalism', the
   May 1992 special issue of the *Journal of Gender Studies*, and Yuval-
   Davis and Anthias.
5. See Combahee River Collective.
6. I am drawing here on the definition of nostalgia Janice Doane and
   Devon Hodges put forth in *Nostalgia and Sexual Difference: The
   Resistance to Contemporary Feminism*. Their work is significant to this
   essay in equating nostalgia with fixity and rigid definitions of gender
   through the desire for stable linguistic referents. Doane and Hodges
   find that nostalgic writers long for an Eden of pre/poststructuralist
   linguistic certainty as well as a set of rigid social or political
   categories.
7. See Beddoe.
8. West's attitude toward the victory of the Turks is not simply an anti-
   imperialist position but is also an anti-Muslim position. Anti-Muslim
   attitudes have taken on a new shape in the current war in the former
   Yugoslavia; Muslims seem to be bearing the greatest burden of 'ethnic
   cleansing'.
9. The reasons Neville Chamberlain and his government, and many citizens of Britain, supported an appeasement policy are numerous and
   complex. See Taylor (414–17) and Benny Morris.
10. See Colquitt.

11. Gloria Fromm argues that *Black Lamb and Grey Falcon* 'suffers from extremist characteristics' including 'portraits that seem almost like caricatures' (51). I find that the complexity of West's representations offset the exaggerated proportions of some of her characters.
12. Larry Wolff remarks on the 'many good-looking men in *Black Lamb and Grey Falcon*' and interprets West's attention to and praise of their physiognomy as 'in strange and defiant counterpoint to contemporary anthropology in Nazi Germany ... [which] was studied as racial science, and construed to establish the inferiority of Jews and Slavs in Eastern Europe' (29).
13. Victoria Glendinning remarks, 'There is an uncomfortable echo in this sentiment of the words of the British Fascist leader Sir Oswald Mosley, who in his manifesto *The Greater Britain* (1932) had written that "we want men who are men and women who are women" – with women consigned to the domestic role' (166).
14. See Campbell and Dworkin.
15. A debate about the loyalties of Prince Paul continued through the 1980s. West portrays him in *Black Lamb* as sympathetic to the Nazis, although she was writing the epilogue in England with limited access to information about what was happening in Yugoslavia. Defenders of Paul have tried to correct what they see as West's uniformed characterization of him, claiming he was most in sympathy with Britain and was merely carrying out a policy of appeasement similar to Britain's in his negotiations with Hitler (Glendinning 171).
16. In July of 1991, a gathering of feminists from throughout Europe and North America took place in Dubrovnik, one of the cities that has been almost entirely destroyed by shelling in the war.
17. See Milic (113) and Molyneux (72).
18. Some Eastern European women are enthusiastic about the opportunity to be full-time caretakers of children; many are disgusted by the discourse of 'equal rights' spoken by the communists but never delivered. They see this social transformation as a way to avoid the 'double shift'. See Wolchik, Antic (152) on the Slovenian Constitution's conflation of 'woman' with 'mother'.
19. See Einhorn (148–81) on the decline of women's participation in electoral politics and representation in governmental bodies in Eastern Europe since 1989.
20. The *New York Times* reported in January of 1993 that 20,000 women had been raped in the Bosnian war thus far. The figure was based on an estimate by European Community investigators. See Burns, 'ISO Muslims', and Riding.

WORKS CITED

Anderson, Benedict, *Imagined Communities*, London: Verso, 1983.
Antic, Milica G., 'Democracy Between Tyranny and Liberty: Women in Post-"Socialist" Slovenia', *Feminist Review* 39 (1991): 149–54.

Beddoe, Deirdre, *Back to Home and Duty: Women Between the Wars, 1918–1939*, London: Pandora, 1989.

Benderly, Jill, '"We Don't Want a Country of Invalids and Fresh Graves": Yugoslav Women Against War', *On the Issues* 21 (Winter 1991): 25–7.

Braybon, Gail, and Penny Summerfield, *Out of the Cage: Women's Experiences in Two World Wars*, London and New York: Pandora, 1987.

Bunch, Charlotte, *Passionate Politics*, New York: St. Martin's Press, 1987.

Burns, John F., '150 Muslims Say Serbs Raped Them in Bosnia', *The New York Times*, 3 October (1992): 5.

—— 'A Serbian Fighter's Trail of Brutality', *The New York Times*, 27 November (1992): A1, A12.

Campbell, Beatrix, *The Iron Ladies: Why Do Women Vote Tory?*, London: Virago Press, 1987.

Colquitt, Clare, 'A Call to Arms: Rebecca West's Assault on the Limits of "Gerda's Empire" in *Black Lamb and Grey Falcon*', *South Atlantic Review* 51:2 (May 1986): 77–91.

Combahee River Collective, 'Combahee River Collective Statement', repr. in Barbara Balliet (ed.), *Women, Culture, and Society: A Reader*, Dubuque: Kendall/Hunt Publishing, 1992.

De Grazia, Victoria, *How Fascism Ruled Women: Italy, 1922–1945*, Berkeley: University of California Press, 1992.

Doane, Janice, and Devon Hodges, *Nostalgia and Sexual Difference: Resistance to Contemporary Feminism*, New York and London: Methuen, 1987.

Drakulic, Slavenka, 'Overcome By Nationhood', in Slavenka Drakulic (ed.), *The Balkan Express: Fragments from the Other Side of War*, New York and London: W. W. Norton, 1993, 123–30.

—— 'Women and the New Democracy in the Former Yugoslavia', in Nanette Funk and Magda Mueller (eds), *Gender Politics and Post-Communism*, New York and London: Routledge, 1993.

Dworkin, Andrea, *Right-Wing Women: The Politics of Domesticated Females*, New York: Perigee Books, 1983.

Einhorn, Barbara, *Cinderella Goes to Market: Citizenship, Gender, and Women's Movements in East Central Europe*, London and New York: Verso, 1993.

Ellmann, Mary, *Thinking About Women*, New York: Harcourt, Brace and World, 1968.

'Feminism and Nationalism', special issue, *Journal of Gender Studies* May 1992: 408–17.

Fromm, Gloria, 'Rebecca West: The Fictions of Fact, and the Facts of Fiction', *The New Criterion* (January 1991): 44–53.

Funk, Nanette and Magda Mueller (eds), *Gender Politics and Post-Communism*, New York and London: Routledge, 1993.

Glendinning, Victoria, *Rebecca West: A Life*, New York: Alfred A. Knopf, 1987.

Hobsbawm, E. J., *Nations and Nationalism Since 1780: Programme, Myth, Reality*, Cambridge: Cambridge University Press, 1990.

Jancar-Webster, Barbara, *Women and Revolution in Yugoslavia: 1941–1945*, Denver: Arden Press, 1990.

Jayawardena, Kumari, *Feminism and Nationalism in the Third World*, London and New Jersey: Zed Books, 1986.

Koonz, Claudia, *Mothers in the Fatherland*, New York: St. Martin's Press, 1987.

Lant, Antonia, *Blackout: Reinventing Women for Wartime British Cinema*, Princeton: Princeton University Press, 1991.

Milic, Andjelka, 'Women and Nationalism in the Former Yugoslavia', in Nanette Funk and Magda Mueller (eds), *Gender Politics and Post-Communism*, New York and London: Routledge, 1993: 109–22.

Molyneux, Maxine, 'The "Woman Question" in the Age of Perestroika', in Maxine Molyneux (ed.), *After the Fall: The Failure of Communism and the Future of Socialism*, London: Verso, 1991.

Morris, Benny, *The Roots of Appeasement*, London: Frank Cass, 1991.

Riding, Alan, 'European Inquiry Says Serbs' Forces Have Raped 20,000', *The New York Times*, 9 January (1993): 1, 4.

Singleton, Fred, *Twentieth-Century Yugoslavia*, London: Macmillan Press, 1976.

Taylor, A. J. P., *English History: 1914–1945*, New York and Oxford: Oxford University Press, 1965.

Tillinghast, Richard, 'Rebecca West and Yugoslavia', *The New Criterion* 10:10 (June 1992): 12–22.

West, Rebecca, *Black Lamb and Grey Falcon* (1st ed. 1941), New York: Viking Press, 1943.

—— 'The Sin of Self-Sacrifice', *The Clarion*, 12 December (1913), repr. in Jane Marcus (ed.), *The Young Rebecca*, Bloomington: Indiana University Press, 1982: 235–8.

Williams, Raymond, *The Country and the City*, New York: Oxford University Press, 1973.

Wolchik, Sharon, 'Women in Eastern Europe', *The World and I* 6 (September 1991): 556–67.

Wolff, Larry, 'Rebecca West: This Time, Let's Listen', *The New York Times Book Review*, 10 February (1991): 1, 28–30.

Yuval-Davis, Nira and Floya Anthias (eds), *Woman–Nation–State*, London: Macmillan, 1989.

9

Where Are the Missing Contents? (Post)Modernism, Gender, and the Canon

ELLEN G. FRIEDMAN

In *The Postmodern Condition*, Jean-François Lyotard writes about 'missing contents' and the 'unpresentable' in the literature of modernity.[1] What are missing and unpresentable, and what this literature expresses nostalgia for, according to Lyotard, are the master narratives that sustained Western civilization in the past and that have now been delegitimated. By calling into question the Western paternal narratives of philosophy, religion, and history, as well as the great quest and goal narratives, modernity has provoked a 'crisis in narrative' resulting in a literature that can present the sense of loss but not what is lost (78–81). Fredric Jameson, in his introduction to the English translation of Lyotard's book, observes that these master narratives have not disappeared. Rather, they have gone underground, protected in the culture's unconscious, a site from which they still wield power (xii).

Indeed, the yearning for fathers, for past authority and sure knowledge that can no longer be supported, permeates male texts of modernity. A clear example of this condition is Donald Barthelme's novel *The Dead Father*. The plot follows a brother and sister's journey to bury their reluctantly dead father. The size of a Titan, this father is introduced as '[d]ead, but still with us, still with us, but dead' (3). On the way to the burial site, the daughter asks, 'Tell me ... did you ever want to paint or draw or etch?' The dead father answers, 'It was not necessary ... because I am the Father. All lines my lines. All figure and all ground mine, out of my head. All colors mine. You take my meaning' (18, 19). The narrative ends

159

with the dead father speaking 'resonantly' and 'grandly' from his hole in the ground even as the bulldozers approach. Although he is buried, he is not silenced.

The missing father as irresistible presence is even more striking in Thomas Pynchon's new work, *Vineland*, since it begins as a daughter's quest for her mother. The mother, Frenesi, who was a sixties radical, abandons her infant daughter, Prarie, as well as her husband, Zoyd, the man Prarie presumes is her father. Frenesi leaves her husband and child to run away with Brock Vond, a powerful member of the FBI. As Prarie searches for her mother, evidence mounts that Brock is also looking for Frenesi. In fact, as Brock's presence in the narrative increases, the importance of the quest for the mother diminishes. Indeed, the final meeting between mother and daughter is anticlimactic. The narrative focus, by this time, has moved to Brock. Although he is an elusive, rarely glimpsed figure, he is also an inescapable, controlling presence, with an insidious power and a talent for locating his victims' vulnerabilities. His colleagues call him 'Death from Slightly Above'. For Pynchon, Brock is an avatar of the paranoic systems that drive American culture, but he is more than that. Ten pages from the end of the book, he appears to Prarie and tells her, 'I'm your father. ... Your real Dad' (375, 376).

With these words, Brock presents himself, in Lyotard's terms, as the missing contents. Hearing these words, Prarie finds her world destabilized. Zoyd, the man who claimed her as his daughter and raised her, may not be her father. As a result, her focus shifts, significantly, from a quest for her mother to a quest for her father. When the FBI suddenly relieves Brock of his funds and other resources, he loses his source of power but not the force he represents, which persists in Prarie's yearning for him. Pynchon emphasizes the nature of this father figure by replacing Zoyd – a local joke who argues the state into supporting him by an annual leap through a plate glass window – with the imperious and relentless Brock. Thus *Vineland* follows Lyotard's paradigm of modernity, in which master narratives are yearned for but cannot be raised. As soon as Brock tells Prarie that he is her father, a statement that may or may not be true, he disappears from her life, leaving her at the end of the novel – as the texts of modernity are left – in a condition of loss. In this state, she focuses on her past, frozen in the oedipal backward glance. As Pynchon turns away from the quest for the mother, he suggests that the longing for the

lost father is inevitable, because the father's order is the only one
that Pynchon can imagine.

The emphatic reign of Oedipus in current explanatory cultural
narratives is honored even in philosophical works that propose alternatives. In *Anti-Oedipus: Capitalism and Schizophrenia*, a work
provocatively resisting oedipal determinism, Gilles Deleuze and
Félix Guattari sum up a position taken by cultural and orthodox
psychoanalysts: 'They all agree that, in our patriarchal and capitalist society at least, Oedipus is a sure thing. ... They all agree that
our society is the stronghold of Oedipus. ...' Moreover, as Deleuze
and Guattari concede, Oedipus is not an invention of these ana-
lysts; rather, he 'is demanded, and demanded again and again ...'
(174–5). The oedipal preoccupation with fathers – missing, lost, or
otherwise inaccessible – is a compulsive theme in male modernism.
It is the great theme of William Faulkner's *Absalom, Absalom!* and
Light in August. The missing father is the link to the past that, for
the protagonists, determines identity. That sons are refused their
fathers renders these narratives tragedies.

A variation on the search for the father is the profoundly nostalgic conviction that the past has explanatory or redemptive powers.
This belief is expressed as the futile desire to stop time or to understand, recoup, or re-create the past, summoning it into the present.
Such a desire, of course, informs Gatsby's obsession with Daisy and
illuminates the narrative voice in T. S. Eliot's *Four Quartets*. The
object of the longing in the poem's final lines is clear: 'And the end
of all our exploring / Will be to arrive where we started and know
the place for the first time' (208). This futile desire underlies Ernest
Hemingway's portrait of Jake's impotence in *The Sun Also Rises*. For
Jake, who has lost the tie between past and present in the conflagra-
tion of the war, meaning evaporates or degenerates into the sentimentalism of Cohn or the ersatz religions of bullfighting and
fishing. In the rituals that mark these sports, Jake attempts to locate
meaning, but the inadequacy of such attempts to replace the
missing contents is emphatically represented in Jake's impotence.
He never acquires the father's power; he remains forever the yearning son. Similarly, the center of Ezra Pound's directive to 'make it
new' is *it*, signifying past texts, past ideologies, the determining
word of the father that controls all narratives. James Joyce's final
work is about the 'wake' of Finnegan – the mythic, protean father
who never stays quite dead but reasserts himself repeatedly in
multitudinous reincarnations.

Women's works of modernity, however, show little nostalgia for the old paternal order, little regret for the no longer presentable. The master narratives are not buried in the unconscious of these texts, nor do they create a vacuum that longs to be filled. Although all the texts of modernity express a yearning for the unpresentable, female texts often evoke this unpresentable as the not yet presented. As Lillian Robinson wisely observes, patriarchal myths and traditions are 'essentially external to any central female project' (29). Thus the lack of nostalgia for them in women's narratives seems natural. In fact, reading the texts of modernity through the lens of gender reveals how gender inflects the missing contents and how this inflected unpresentable relates to the canon. This essay offers such a reading in the hope of advancing discussions of sexual difference in the modernism–postmodernism debate, a project proposed by Craig Owens (61, 77). In an essay on feminism and postmodernism, E. Ann Kaplan similarly suggests that 'we must continue to articulate oppositional discourses' (43). For her, as well as for Owens, such discourse is a precondition to imagining what lies beyond opposition.[2]

Two revisions of *Don Quixote*, neither by Cervantes, highlight these issues of sexual difference and opposition. 'Pierre Menard, Author of *Don Quixote*', a story by Jorge Luis Borges, relates the attempt of the early twentieth-century writer Pierre Menard to recreate, word for word, the text of Cervantes's *Don Quixote*. Menard, the narrator reports, 'did not want to compose another *Don Quixote* – which would be easy – but *the Don Quixote*'. He plans to achieve this goal without forgetting European history between Cervantes's time, 1602, and his own, 1918. The problem is to re-create the exact text within a twentieth-century perspective, not to translate the text into contemporary terms: 'Any insinuation that Menard dedicated his life to the writing of a contemporary *Don Quixote* is a calumny of his illustrious memory.' Borges describes Menard's project in this way: 'To be, in some way, Cervantes and to arrive at *Don Quixote* seemed to him less arduous – and consequently less interesting – than to continue being Pierre Menard and to arrive at *Don Quixote* through the experiences of Pierre Menard' (48, 49).

This plot is an exemplar of the missing contents Lyotard identifies in the narratives of modernity. Menard attempts to write a text, already in existence, in which the original assumptions, historical context, and quest are no longer alive. In fact, the allusion to

Cervantes's *Don Quixote* constitutes a second level of missing contents, since that story centers on the pursuit of knights, armor, chivalry, and the worldview they represent – missing contents that are still presentable in Cervantes's time, at least as objects of satire and as vehicles of moral instruction. Indeed, Borges's story almost perfectly illustrates Lyotard's theories on the condition of modernity. Menard, explaining his project, remarks: 'To compose *Don Quixote* at the beginning of the seventeenth century was a reasonable, necessary and perhaps inevitable undertaking; at the beginning of the twentieth century it is almost impossible. It is not in vain that three hundred years have passed. ...' Thus, as Menard confesses, missing contents are unpresentable, and yet the longing for them informs his project. Perhaps no statement more poignantly expresses the futility of this longing than the narrator's flat description of Menard's efforts: 'He dedicated his conscience and nightly studies to the repetition of a pre-existing book in a foreign tongue' (51, 54).

As it turns out, Menard does succeed in re-creating several pieces of Cervantes's text: 'the ninth and thirty-eighth chapters of Part One of *Don Quixote* and a fragment of the twenty-second chapter' (48).[3] Yet he also does *not* succeed, because the two apparently identical texts differ in style, theme, textual ambiguity, and other elements determined by and within the works' separate historical contexts. For instance, when Cervantes wrote the words 'truth, whose mother is history' in the seventeenth century, he was composing, according to the narrator, a 'mere rhetorical eulogy of history'. The same words written by Menard – who, as a contemporary of William James, defines history not as an 'investigation of reality, but as its origin' – mean something else entirely. While the 'text of Cervantes and that of Menard are verbally identical', the narrator comments, 'the second is almost infinitely richer' (53, 52). This judgment aside, Borges's point is that although Menard has, after great effort, reproduced the letters that blacken some pages in *Don Quixote*, he cannot reproduce the text. It has passed over to the unpresentable. It has become unrecoupable missing contents. The imagination informing this story is deeply nostalgic, as is much of Borges's fiction. His stories relate quests that look backward toward some teleological sense of reality or truth, for which, in the domain of modernity, it no longer seems reasonable to search.

Like Borges, Kathy Acker centers a narrative on Cervantes's text, appropriating the title *Don Quixote*. While Acker's *Don Quixote* also concerns the unpresentable and missing contents, it does not call nostalgically to the unpresentable, does not silently invoke lost or disappeared master narratives. Although the missing contents in Acker's work are also unpresentable, they are composed of the not yet presented. Rather than look backward, her narratives look forward.

Acker's quest novels obsessively depict the search for individuality, for selfhood, in the context of the cultural construction of identity. For this search to proceed, Acker's protagonists must move beyond the border of culture to conceive of themselves as individuals, as other than compliant products of their culture.[4] This quest, like the one Borges depicts, is unreasonable; it cannot be completed, for even in Acker's delirious narratives, it is impossible to step outside culture and thus to shed the culturally constructed self.

During a moment of revelation in the abortion scene that begins Acker's *Don Quixote*, the protagonist resolves to embark on such a quest for selfhood. Dressed in green paper and positioned on the operating table with knees raised as masked medical figures prepare to invade her body, she is struck with the sudden knowledge that her identity is not her own. This understanding moves her to adopt subversive strategies to disengage from the forces that have compelled her identity: 'When a doctor sticks a steel catheter into you while you're lying on your back and you do exactly what he and the nurses tell you to ... you let go of your mind. ...' Once she can conceive of surrendering the constructed self, she can also formulate the quest to acquire her own 'name': 'She needed a new life. She had to be named' (9–10).[5]

The quest for a new life and a name structures several of Acker's works. Yet unlike male quest novels, such as *The Magic Mountain* and *A Portrait of the Artist as a Young Man*, Acker's texts locate the means of acquisition outside culture, since they are unavailable in the context of patriarchy. To constitute the self differently, the quester must find an alternative site for such constitution. Acker moves her protagonists toward this site through the appropriation of male texts, a strategy she explains in the epigraph to part 2: 'Being born into and part of a male world, she had no speech of her own. All she could do was read male texts which weren't hers.' The male texts represent the limits of language and culture within which the female quester attempts to acquire identity. Once inside the male text, the quester, by her very posture, subverts it: 'By repeating the past, I'm molding and transforming it.' In the Borges story, replication is the issue. For Acker the appropriation of *Don Quixote* is a strategy of subversion. Her description of the textual appropriation used by Arabs applies to herself: 'They write by cutting chunks out of all-ready written texts and in other ways defacing traditions: changing important names into silly ones, making dirty jokes out of matters that should be of the utmost importance to us ...' (39, 48, 25).[6]

Acker's purpose in appropriating well-known texts is profoundly political. Through plagiarism, Acker proposes an alternative to the classical Marxist explanation of the sources of power. With Jean Baudrillard she believes that those who control the means of representation are more powerful than those who control the means of production. Plagiarism undermines the assumptions governing representation. Sherrie Levine, an artist who also uses appropriation, explains: 'The whole art system was geared to celebrating ... objects of male desire. Where, as a woman artist, could I situate myself? What I was doing was making this explicit: how this oedipal relationship artists have with artists of the past gets repressed; and how I, as a woman, was only allowed to represent male desire' (96–7). In plagiarizing, Acker does not deny the masterwork itself, but she does interrogate its sources in paternal authority and male desire. By placing the search for modes of representing female desire inside male texts, Acker and others clearly delineate the constraints under which this search proceeds. She also suggests that the alternative nature of, and location for, the missing contents in women's texts is in the not yet presented.[7]

Modernism and postmodernism reveal a pattern of bifurcation: two unpresentables, two sets of missing contents. As male texts look backward over their shoulders, female texts look forward, often beyond culture, beyond patriarchy, into the unknown, the outlawed. Marguerite Duras, commenting on this disengagement from master narratives, remarks, '[T]o put society into question is still to acknowledge it. ... I mean the people who do that, who write about the refusal of society, harbor within them a kind of nostalgia. They are, I am certain, much less separated from it than I am' (qtd. in Suleiman 15). Such separation is evident not only in Duras's work but in many other female texts of modernity; in Acker's narratives, for instance, the protagonists repeatedly demonstrate the inadequacy of patriarchal culture, past or present, as the arena for identity. The liberating image common to these writers is the nomad who seeks sanctuary in the interstices of culture and replaces Oedipus as the protagonist of culture and the unconscious. Nearly all Acker's central characters are nomadic. In Marilynne Robinson's *Housekeeping*, the protagonist, Ruthie, feigns suicide in order to live as a drifter. It gives her license to become 'strange' without having that strangeness defined and perhaps tempered and shaped by society.[8]

Before Duras, Acker, and Robinson, a generation of women innovators set the precedent for these contemporary nomads (see Friedman and Fuchs, 'Contexts'). In Djuna Barnes's *Nightwood*, the character Robin, whose various identities are shaped by the nearest dominating presence, maintains at the core a 'desperate anonymity' (168). Like strangeness and nomadism, anonymity is a strategy to elude cultural construction, a precondition for raising the not yet presented in these women's texts. Robin's husband, Felix, a man obsessed with the past, observes that Robin's 'attention had ... been taken by something not yet in history. Always she seemed to be listening to the echo of some foray in the blood that had no known setting ...' (44). Barnes engages in a critique of the backward oedipal glance with her portrait of Felix's son, the child of a man stuck in this glance:

> [A]s time passed it became increasingly evident that this child, if born to anything, had been born to holy decay. Mentally deficient and emotionally excessive, an addict to death; at ten, barely as tall as a child of six, wearing spectacles, stumbling when he tried to run, with cold hands and anxious face, he followed his father. ...
>
> (107)

The dual central characters in Jane Bowles's *Two Serious Ladies* also follow strange, nomadic paths (Friedman and Fuchs, 'Contexts' 20–2). The non sequiturs of their conversation, their paradoxical pronouncements, the eccentric movements through time and space are motivated less by loss than by hope. Reviewers have characterized the novel as unusual, even bizarre. Edith Walton, for example, finds it pathological, noting that '[t]here is hardly a character in the book who could be called really sane', while John Ashbery remarks, 'No other contemporary writer can consistently produce surprise of this quality, the surprise that is the one essential ingredient of great art' (30). Although *Two Serious Ladies* offers both plot and recurring images, its main structural materials are sentences reminiscent, though not imitative, of Gertrude Stein. These sentences often occur in discrete, monadic units, not dependably connected to what precedes or follows, and only haphazardly make sense. Yet they are resonant and nervously interesting. For instance, Miss Goering, one of the 'serious ladies' of the title, muses, 'Most people have a guardian angel; that's why they move slowly.' In a political discussion she cautions, 'Just remember ... that a revolution won is an adult who must kill his childhood once and for all.' One feels that these statements are penetrable with effort but that such penetration is not the point. A man at a party asks Miss Goering, with seeming disingenuousness, to spend the night at his house because, as he says, 'We have an extra bedroom.' Although he is sincere, Miss Goering speaks to what she assumes is his subtext: '[I]t is against my entire code, but then, I have never begun to use my code, although I judge everything by it' (12, 143, 19).

Readers who surrender to this vermiculate reasoning cannot reliably use it to calibrate anything else in the text. It is neither a proper window to the figure of Miss Goering nor a mechanism to untie textual knots. Bowles's husband, Paul, has revealed that Bowles named her character for the murderous Nazi Hermann Goering. Yet this information does not illuminate. In contrast to surrealism's yoking of two disparate images to yield a meaning-charged third image, Bowles's yoking of the Nazi with her character seems baldly bizarre, though not strictly meaningless. The meaning is simply not revealable in the available context. Although her images and sentences deliberately resist obvious hermeneutics, whether of surrealism or psychoanalysis, they seem to seek resolution in a logic not yet grasped. Unlike male texts, which force the condition of strangeness on the characters, Bowles's and other women's texts seek that condition, for only in the domain of anonymity, strangeness, orphanhood, nomadism, or madness does it seem appropriate to await and perhaps awaken the not yet presented, which for these authors composes the missing contents in Western culture.

In an essay on the writer's block that afflicted Bowles for decades, Millicent Dillon describes the notebooks Bowles filled with fragments of her unfinished novel, *Out in the World*. Dillon, revising the ideas advanced in her biography of Bowles, speculates that the fragments represent a 'mode of expression that was attempting to manifest itself through [Bowles] but that she could not accept':

The cast of her mind and feelings was expressing its intention in this form – through fragmentation and repetition – but she took the result to be only failure. If it is true that her work was psychically blocked, it is also true that had she been able to view this fragmentation as a valid expression of her own narrative vision, the fragmentation could have led her to further development. ... I now see the history of her later writing as a flight from the form that she was being impelled toward by her very nature.

('Experiment' 140–1)

In fact, when her husband suggested, 'Just for the first page have the character come in, see this, do that', Jane would answer, 'No, that's your way, that's not my way. I've got to do it my way and my way is more difficult than yours' ('Experiment' 140). Both Jane and Paul Bowles placed themselves in the avant-garde, but Jane's way involved an element unknown to either of them: the not yet presented to which Jane could not commit herself but whose absence is strongly felt in most of her narratives, including *Two Serious Ladies*.

Although Paul Bowles sets many of his stories in an exotic Arab Moroccan culture that he paints as dangerous to certain unworthy Westerners, Western culture, nevertheless, calibrates the stories' underlying sensibility and values. In his most celebrated story, 'A Distant Episode', a professor of linguistics – made arrogant by his ample Western purse, his status as an American professor in a 'primitive' culture, and most of all his knowledge of the local dialects of Moghrebi – easily falls prey to a group of thugs, the Reguiba, who, with deft ironic cruelty, cut out his tongue. They turn him into a dancing clown and subsequently sell him to a wealthy client. In the process, the Professor, as he is called, loses memory, consciousness of his humanity, and language. Unable to understand what is said to him, he is transformed into a sleeping, eating, defecating, dancing machine. When, at the story's climax, he reawakens to language and thus to his situation, his recognition sends him howling with bereavement into the sunset. Like much of the literature of modernity, this narrative centers on unrecoupable loss, which Paul Bowles offers as the defining condition of modern life. He moved to Morocco to escape his culture; he clothed his narratives in strange and sinister details. But as 'A Distant Episode' suggests, the missing contents in his vision – unlike his wife's vision but like the vision of other male authors of modernity – are to be found in the past, a past that is decidedly Western.

The narrative of *Two Serious Ladies* concerns oedipal missing contents, as Mrs Copperfield, the novel's other main character, reveals when she articulates her longing to replace God the Father, who seems to have disappeared:

> When people believed in God they carried Him from one place to another. They carried Him through the jungles and across the Arctic Circle. God watched over everybody, and all men were brothers. Now there is nothing to carry with you from one place to another, and as far as I'm concerned, these people might as well be kangaroos; yet somehow there must be someone here who will remind me of something … I must find a nest in this outlandish place.
>
> (40; ellipsis in text)

Bowles's narrative juxtaposes two quests, Miss Goering's for sainthood and Mrs Copperfield's for happiness, that differ in form and substance. Both characters, however, act in ways that contradict their declared objectives. Miss Goering, for instance, moves near a glue factory on Staten Island, where she engages in a number of dull, accidental liaisons. Mrs Copperfield becomes compulsively attached to a prostitute while on vacation in Panama with her husband, whom she abandons. The characters meet twice, once at the beginning of the novel and once toward the end. Each time, the plot neither compels nor justifies their meeting. Although both questers are quirky and both share a fondness for non sequiturs, their stories have little in common, not even on the level of metaphor. When they meet again at the end of the book, their statements to each other seem just short of random. Yet the inconsistency, randomness, and contradiction contribute to the narrative's seductive and liberating strangeness. Near the end of the novel, Mrs Copperfield declares, 'I *have* gone to pieces, which is a thing I've wanted to do for years. I know I am as guilty as I can be, but I have my happiness, which I guard like a wolf, and I have authority now and a certain amount of daring …' (197). Mrs Copperfield resists the nostalgic, self-declared quest to find a substitute for the missing God the Father in favor of a more fruitful route to happiness, 'going to pieces'. Similarly, Bowles's writing repeatedly falls to pieces, refuses to organize itself according to nostalgic scripts, and, in spite of the author herself, moves with unconscious daring toward something she cannot name. This proposing and then resisting nostalgic scripts is Bowles's signature quality, evident in the eccentric movement of her unresolved narrative logic. In the final lines of *Two Serious Ladies*, Miss Goering reflects, 'Certainly I am nearer to becoming a saint ... but is it possible that a part of me hidden from my sight is piling sin upon sin as fast as Mrs. Copperfield?' (201).

Unlike Bowles, Anaïs Nin quite consciously and stubbornly pursued the not yet presented, an endeavor that caused her great suffering since the literary circles in which she moved often dismissed her efforts as trivial and nonliterary. Nin's search was confined to the psyche, as mediated by psychoanalysis, out of which she hoped to draw the return of the repressed, her version of the not yet presented.[9] Although this repressed, by its very nature, does represent a 'past' of sorts, it has never occupied the symbolic and thus does not resemble Lyotard's unpresentable, which previously provided the dominant cultural narratives. In a rhapsodic passage of her 1937 *Diary*, Nin describes her vision:

> I mastered the mechanisms of life the better to bend it to the will of the dream. I conquered details to make the dream more possible. With hammer and nails, paint, soap, money, typewriter, cookbook, douche bags, I created a dream. ... Through the markets, the whorehouses, the abattoirs, the butcher shops, the scientific laboratories, hospitals, Montparnasse, I walk with my dream unfurled, and lose myself in my own labyrinths, and the dream unfurled carries me. ... I am passionate and fervent only for the dream, the poem. ... Something is happening to me of which I am not afraid; it is an expansion of my consciousness, creating in space and loneliness. It is a vision, a city suspended in the sky, a rhythm of blood. It is ecstasy. Known only to the saints and the poets. ... I may explode one day and send fragments to the earth.
>
> (2: 152–3)

As this passage suggests, Nin uses a variety of metaphors to tease the not yet presented onto her page – metaphors from religion, psychoanalysis, poetry, politics. Her most persistent terms come from female anatomy. In fact, Sharon Spencer has called Nin's feminine writing 'music of the womb'. The literary men Nin knew, including Henry Miller and Edmund Wilson, saw her diary as a waste of her creative powers and energies. They used the image of the womb to argue the diary's insular inadequacy as art. Lawrence Durrell cautioned, 'You must make the leap outside of the womb, destroy your connections' (qtd. in *Diary* 2: 232). He urged that she rewrite *Hamlet*, a telling recommendation for a modernist since *Hamlet* is an exemplary representation of how the future is propelled by the past, by the power of the dead father. Such a recommendation was insensitive to Nin's project, which was to excavate woman's consciousness. In a statement that anticipates the imagery with which Hélène Cixous and contemporary feminists describe feminine writing, Nin writes:

> Woman never had direct communication with God anyway, but only through man, the priest. She never created directly except through man, was never able to create as a woman. ... Woman's creation far from being like man's must be exactly like her creation of children, that is it must come out of her own blood, englobed by her womb, nourished with her own milk.
>
> (*Diary* 2: 233)

A second prominent image for the domain out of which the not yet presented is summoned is madness. In *House of Incest*, Nin links madness to freedom: 'There is a fissure in my vision and madness will always rush through. ... Lean over me, at the bedside of my madness and let me stand without crutches' (39). Her sense of the not yet presented is consistent with the ideas put forward in *The Newly Born Woman*, by Hélène Cixous and Catherine Clément, who speak in psychoanalytic terms about the identification of women with the fissures in the social structure: 'Women bizarrely embody this group of anomalies showing the cracks in an overall system' (7). Nin searches for women's expression in the imaginary zone, a repository for what culture excludes. Bordering on obsession, the not yet presented is the most compelling force in Nin's writing. As *House of Incest* draws to a close, Nin offers an image of a dancer 'listening to a music we could not hear, moved by hallucinations we could not see' (71).

Nin's *Spy in the House of Love* follows the pattern of male identity-quest novels until the final passage. The protagonist, Sabina, who is dubbed 'Dona Juana', seeks her identity through a series of lovers, each of whom speaks to an aspect of her but none of whom helps her to coalesce the fragments of herself into a whole. She metamorphoses into another role – mother, seductress, sister, mother earth, wife – as each lover appears to her in his role of Don Juan, Wagnerian hero, father, brother, artist, or musician. Unsuccessful in establishing her identity conventionally – that is, in relation to a man, as Virginia Woolf famously observed that women characters generally do – she is admonished, 'Yours is a story of non-love ...' (117). Yet this identity quest has a deviant ending: the protagonist does not resign herself to convention or receive punishment for her sins (as does Don Juan), nor does she come to an understanding of her task (as do Stephen Dedaelus and Hans Castorp). She remains fragmented; a state of irresolution is preferable to any of the old scripts, none of which serves her purpose. Her remedy, as the last line of the novel suggests, is to stay sick: 'In homeopathy there is a remedy called pulsatile for those who weep at music' (140). Homeopathy attempts to cure patients by prescribing small doses of what made them ill. Sickness, in the context of patriarchal culture, may show the way to another kind of health.

The work of HD, as replete with allusions to Western texts and myths as are the works of Joyce, Pound, and Eliot, also refuses the poignant solace of oedipal nostalgia. Indeed, critics have associated HD's use of myths, ancient history, and hieratic symbols with the modernist (male) mainstream, but for the most part they concentrate on biography. Her prose fiction, which constitutes almost half her canon, is deeply autobiographical, as the introductions by her daughter, Perdita Schaffner, to several volumes attest. When viewed through a modernist lens, however, her narratives – despite their allusive tapestry – follow the female paradigm of missing contents. In *The Waste Land*, Eliot slices through the millennia with a sexual theme because one of his purposes, modulated by nostalgia, is to demonstrate the vulgarity of contemporary life, the superiority of high culture. For instance, the 'change of Philomel, by the barbarous king/So rudely forced' is, nevertheless, transfigured: 'yet there the nightingale/ Filled all the desert with inviolable voice' (56). No such transfiguration, Eliot implies, results from or accompanies contemporary instances, such as the sordid 'seduction' of the typist by 'the young man carbuncular' or Lil's abortion (62). Eliot measures the poverty of modern life by such losses. HD does not approach the past with reverence, as Eliot does, but views it, in Henry James's metaphor, as the carpet in which to discover a figure illuminating contemporary life. Eliot and HD share a mythic method and a sense of missing contents, but their purposes in this method, as well as their construction of these contents, differ along gender lines. Both seek revelation in summoning the past, but they deviate in their configuration of revelation. For Eliot the revelation is religious and transcendent; for HD, particularly in *Palimpsest* and *Hermione*, it is psychological and concerns earthly life. While Eliot's pilgrim – whether in *The Waste Land* or in *Four Quartets* – seeks higher ground, HD's protagonists search for a way to be in the world.

Palimpsest, HD's first published novel, proceeds in three sections, each of which depicts a woman's quest. The three protagonists (Hipparchia, Raymonde, and Helen), each a version of a single persona, are linked by similar doubts and strivings through twenty centuries, from 75 BC to 1926; the three sections also share a pattern of repeated allusions and images. HD, influenced by her tenure as a patient of Freud, uses myth and ancient history to describe the territory of the unconscious, a place for excavating the object of her protagonists' quests. Each of the three sections of *Palimpsest*, whose title describes the book's method of superimposing one narrative on another, begins with the protagonist expressing doubt, which leads to her self-abnegation; the course of self-abnegation is then refused as she moves, or is moved, toward hope for affirmation. In the process, each protagonist rejects ordinary life to pursue a goal she cannot define, a decision that makes her an outsider and renders her strange in the context of her society. Each section more clearly articulates the object of the quest, although this object is never precisely identified. Part 1, set in Rome in 75 BC, focuses on the visionary poet Hipparchia, who follows the example of her mother in renouncing the conventional female role and chooses to 'cast [her] lot with cynics, not with women seated at the distaff' (3). Part 2 also centers on a woman writer, Raymonde, an American poet living in postwar London. In the third metamorphosis, the text's persona appears as Helen, a woman on an archaeological expedition to Egypt in 1925. Expanding on the thoughts of Raymonde, Helen articulates her quest: 'She wanted to dive deep, deep, courageously down into some unexploited region of the consciousness, into some common deep sea of unrecorded knowledge and bring, triumphant, to the surface some treasure buried, lost, forgotten' (179). Clearly, this quest for missing contents enters new territory ('unrecorded knowledge') for its 'treasure'. And although what is being sought may have been 'buried, lost, forgotten', it is definitively not the comforting embrace of the father but something that, despite the efforts of visionary women questers (Hipparchia and Raymonde) through the millennia, has not yet surfaced.

The narratives of Joyce Carol Oates, though variously experimental, are fairly faithful to the practice of realism in the late twentieth century. But even Oates invests her texts with a sense of the not yet presented when she offers her characters hints of an option that has yet to materialize. In her bildungsroman *Because It Is Bitter, and Because It Is My Heart*, she builds steadily to a poignant sense of missing contents as she chronicles the lives of two young people in the 1960s and 1970s, an African American man who goes to Vietnam and a white woman who gets married. Oates undermines a satisfying sense of closure in the achievement of these ordinary destinies by infusing the text with irresolution and frustrated yearning. She separates her two central characters from the rest of society and links them immutably to each other by making them coconspirators in the accidental death of a classmate, the circumstances of which they never reveal publicly. Oates also provides them with somewhat unusual longings for working-class inhabitants of a small town. Jinx, the African American youth, longs for a college basketball scholarship, and Iris secretly longs for Jinx, with whom she is in love, although she sets her course more conventionally toward college and marriage. They wage the typical battles of their class: for Jinx, against bigotry, a community hostile to success, the lure of drugs; for Iris, against violent street life, inertia, indifferent and incapable parents addicted to alcohol and gambling. But their real nemesis is nastier than these predictable barriers. Jinx has all the ingredients for success: a caring, hardworking mother, a stable family life, intelligence, talent, and ambition. Yet for Jinx to succeed, he must betray his brother or watch his brother betray him. Rather than choose, he surrenders to failure and to the prescribed role for young African American men at the time – probable death in Vietnam. Iris, who is a virtual orphan (her mother dies of a liver disease related to her alcoholism, and her gambler father abdicates his parental responsibility), marches determinedly, if half-heartedly, toward conventional success but never feels identified with it. In the last line of the novel, she asks her future mother-in-law and the dressmaker adjusting her wedding gown, '*Do you think I'll look the part?*' (405). Both characters yearn to be protagonists in the master narrative chronicling their rise to success, their achievement of self-produced identity, their arrival in the middle class. Jinx learns that this narrative does not account for the complications of his life; it is not devised for him. Iris, although she has fought to enter this narrative, finds that she cannot believe in it, so she walks perfunctorily through its chapters. The master narrative fails Jinx and Iris because it is defunct, even irrelevant, in the world of the author and the world of the narrative. The novel provides this insight and moves toward it not with nostalgia but, particularly for Iris, with a sense of intense yearning for possibilities that have not yet come into range. As an inhabitant of a realistic novel, Iris cannot embark on a nomadic quest for the not yet presented as Ruthie does in Robinson's postmodern narrative *Housekeeping*. Nevertheless, Oates has made the missing contents in Iris's world almost palpable.

Although Deleuze and Guattari target late capitalist rather than patriarchal oppression in summoning a figure to oppose Oedipus, they also put forward the nomad (among others). Michel Foucault summarizes their reasoning:

> The first task of the revolutionary ... is to learn ... how to shake off the Oedipal yoke and the effects of power, in order to initiate a radical politics of desire freed from all beliefs. Such a politics dissolves the mystifications of power through the kindling, on all levels, of anti-oedipal forces ... forces that escape coding, scramble the codes, and flee in all directions: *orphans* (no daddy-mommy-me), *atheists* (no beliefs), and *nomads* (no habits, no territories).
>
> (xxi)

They consider a variety of writers who seem to have broken out of the oedipal stranglehold: 'Strange Anglo-American literature: from Thomas Hardy, from D. H. Lawrence to Malcolm Lowry, from Henry Miller to Allen Ginsberg and Jack Kerouac, *men* who know how to leave, to scramble the codes. ... They overcome a limit, they shatter a wall, the capitalist barrier' (*Anti-Oedipus* 132–3; emphasis mine). Deleuze and Guattari propose that the schizophrenic writer Antonin Artaud is one of the few who escaped the oedipal economy, but most of the nomadic writers they are able to summon do not live up to the nomadic rhetoric. These writers 'fail to complete the process, they never cease failing to do so. The neurotic impasse again closes – the daddy-mommy of oedipalization, America, the return to the native land – or else the perversion of the exotic territorialities, then drugs, alcohol, or worse still, an old fascist dream' (*Anti-Oedipus* 133). Indeed, Allen Ginsberg's Whitmanesque claim to the 'native land' and his Eastern 'exotic territorialities'; William Burroughs's use of drugs and alcohol; Jack Kerouac's pro-McCarthyism, pro-Eisenhower conservatism, and anti-Semitism; and, of course, the beats' pervasive misogyny all suggest that the understanding shaping these writers' nomadism is different from, and ultimately less radical than, the understanding of the women writers discussed in this essay. One wonders what Deleuze and Guattari would conclude from a study of the nomadic patterns of women writers. From the vantage point of the 1990s, Kerouac's *On the Road,* in particular, seems fecklessly rebellious. In fact, the work of the beats, generally, is infused neither with nostalgia for the unpresentable nor with yearning for the not yet presented. The master narratives, strangely, seem more alive in the beats' work than they do in works of modernity. They are the contexts of the beats' rebellion. The beats, in their very opposition, legitimate master narratives and thus position themselves, in some ways, outside modernity.

From the first generation of innovative women writers, female texts generally show little allegiance to the past. Stein's texts, unlike the works of her contemporaries Pound, Eliot, and Joyce, do not engage in nostalgia for the fathers' texts and myths. Stein captures the obsessiveness of this backward look in 'Patriarchal Poetry':

> Patriarchal Poetry.
> Their origin and their history.
> Patriarchal Poetry their origin and their history
> their history patriarchal poetry their origin patriarchal
> poetry their history their origin patriarchal
> poetry their history patriarchal poetry their origin
> patriarchal poetry their history their origin.

(115)

With the word *their,* Stein proposes a schism between her texts and patriarchal texts. She sets hers free from tradition, free from '*their* history their origin'; her texts are formally nomadic, spinning free of nostalgic modes. They resist nostalgic resonance, resist the imposition of narrative, resist outside attempts to construct them according to familiar orders and patterns. In 'Rooms' of *Tender Buttons*, she writes, 'Act so that there is no use in a centre' (498; see DuPlessis). Her works, when compared with the works of male modernists, focus on the present without bearing the burden of regret for what has passed. Stein does not elaborate the present as a tragic condition of no choice or as a condition to escape; rather, it is a place of hope and sometimes joy. There is hardly a nostalgic moment in her work. In *The Mother of Us All*, Susan B. (Anthony) asserts, 'We cannot retrace our steps,' though, she adds with irony, 'going forward may be the same as going backwards' (201). Even in the most radical expressions of rebellion and discontent, male texts of modernity are suffused with nostalgia for a past order, for older texts, for the familiar sustaining myths. This shared sense of order, these shared texts and shared myths bind male postmodernism to male modernism and male modernism to the long reach of the male Western narrative tradition. Male texts of modernity have little trouble acquiring membership in the canon. Despite the different sociological and historical positions they represent, they have similar memories, similar allegiances, the same father, and the same laws.[10]

In 'Composition as Explanation', Stein writes:

> Those who are creating the modern composition authentically are naturally only of importance when they are dead because by that time the modern composition having become past is classified and the description of it is classical. That is the reason why the creator of the new composition in the arts is an outlaw until he is a classic, there is hardly a moment in between. ...
>
> (514)

It is instructive that many male modernists and even contemporary postmodernists like Pynchon are already, in Stein's terms, 'past' and thus classical or, in current terms, canonical. It is instructive, too, that few female modernists or postmodernists, including Stein herself, are 'past'. They – Stein, Barnes, Bowles, Nin, Acker – remain outlaws, outside the canon because there is little in the backward, oedipal glance for them. Instead, they aim their gaze unabashedly and audaciously forward.[11]

NOTES

1. To simplify terminology, I follow Jardine's example and use the term *modernity* to designate the literature usually included under the rubrics 'modernism' and 'postmodernism', but in passages requiring a distinction, I use *modernism* or *postmodernism*, assigning these terms according to common practice.
2. For the idea of nostalgia as a strategy to resist feminism, see Doane and Hodges. In a 1983 essay, Owens proposed introducing sexual difference into the modernism–postmodern debate. By now, this introduction is well under way. See, for instance, Friedman and Fuchs, *Breaking*; Jardine; Suleiman; and Waugh. I am grateful to Charles B. Harris for directing me to these points in Owens and Kaplan.
3. In reading this manuscript, Sharon Magnarelli observed that one of the passages Menard succeeds in replicating – part of Cervantes's ninth chapter – concerns a truncated text. Cervantes's narrator is unable to conclude the adventure introduced in the previous chapter because he does not have the rest of the text, but he finds a manuscript that translates the text from the Arabic. The chapter offers a *mise en abime*, since the Arabic translation makes the story's completion possible and at the same time involves the text and the reader in a series of backward glances. Thus, in Borges's tale, Menard reproduces a reproduction, replicating a text that is itself a replication.
4. For an interesting exploration of a view more radical than Acker's, one arguing that women do reserve an essential, female aspect not liable to patriarchal imprinting, see Fuss.
5. I have adapted some of the material on Acker from Friedman.
6. Acker's use of Arabs to illustrate her point is significant since they, like women, represent an 'other' of Western culture.
7. Winnett proposes that the paradigms of female writing differ from those of male writing; her excellent discussion focuses on the problem of applying an oedipal paradigm of pleasure to women readers (see esp. 505–7).
8. On Acker's nomads, see Dix, who uses the theoretical model provided by Deleuze and Guattari in *A Thousand Plateaus*. Robinson's *Housekeeping* can also be described as a quest for the mother. Unlike Pynchon's *Vineland*, it does not turn into a quest for the father, a figure whose absence in Robinson's narrative gets very little attention. See Ravits.
9. Nin writes, 'I took psychoanalysis and made a myth of it' (*Diary* 2: 152).
10. Jameson makes a similar observation, though, like most other critics, he assumes that male modernism speaks for all modernism: 'Not only are Picasso and Joyce no longer ugly; they now strike us, on the whole, as rather "realistic"; and this is the result of a canonization and an academic institutionalization of the modern movement generally …' ('Postmodernism' 56). Lyotard observes, 'The activity men reserve

for themselves arbitrarily as *fact* is posited legally as the *right* to decide meaning' ('One Thing' 119).

11. I am grateful to Marjorie Perloff and Miriam Fuchs for their thoughtful readings of this essay in draft form. A shorter version of this paper was presented at the American Literature Conference in San Diego, May 1990. It was originally published in *PMLA* 108 on 2 March 1993.

WORKS CITED

Acker, Kathy, *Don Quixote*, New York: Grove, 1986.

Ashbery, John, 'Up from the Underground', rev. of *The Collected Works of Jane Bowles, New York Times Book Review*, 29 Jan, 1967: 5+.

Barnes, Djuna, *Nightwood*, 1937, New York: New Directions, 1961.

Barthelme, Donald, *The Dead Father*, New York: Farrar, 1975.

Baudrillard, Jean, 'Simulacra and Simulations', *Selected Writings*, by Baudrillard, ed. Mark Poster, Stanford: Stanford UP, 1988: 166–84.

Borges, Jorge Luis, 'Pierre Menard, Author of *Don Quixote*', *Ficciones*, 1956, trans. Anthony Bonner, New York: Grove, 1962: 45–55.

Bowles, Jane, *Two Serious Ladies*, 1943; *My Sister's Hand in Mine: An Expanded Edition of the Collected Works of Jane Bowles*, New York: Ecco, 1978: 1–201.

Bowles, Paul, 'A Distant Episode', *Collected Stories: 1939–1976*, Santa Barbara: Black Sparrow, 1981: 39–50.

Cixous, Hélène, and Catherine Clément, *The Newly Born Woman*, trans. Betsy Wing, Minneapolis: U of Minnesota P, 1986.

Deleuze, Gilles, and Félix Guattari, *Anti-Oedipus: Capitalism and Schizophrenia*, 1972, trans. Robert Hurley, Mark Seem, and Helen R. Lane, New York: Viking, 1977.

—— *A Thousand Plateaus*, trans. Brian Massumi, Minneapolis: U of Minnesota P, 1987.

Dillon, Millicent, 'Jane Bowles: Experiment as Character', Friedman and Fuchs, *Breaking*: 140–7.

—— *A Little Original Sin: The Life and Work of Jane Bowles*, New York: Holt, 1981.

Dix, Douglas Shields, 'Kathy Acker's *Don Quixote*: Nomad Writing', *Review of Contemporary Fiction* 9.3 (1989): 56–62.

Doane, Janice, and Devon Hodges, *Nostalgia and Sexual Difference: The Resistance to Contemporary Feminism*, New York: Methuen, 1987.

DuPlessis, Rachel, 'Woolfenstein', in Friedman and Fuchs, *Breaking* 99–114.

Eliot, T. S. *Four Quartets, Collected Poems* 173–209.

—— *T. S. Eliot: Collected Poems, 1909–1962*, New York: Harcourt, 1963.

—— *The Waste Land, Collected Poems* 51–76.

Foucault, Michel, Introduction, Deleuze and Guattari, *Anti-Oedipus* xv–xxiv.

Friedman, Ellen G., '"Now Eat Your Mind": An Introduction to the Works of Kathy Acker', *Review of Contemporary Fiction* 9.3 (1989): 37–49.

Friedman, Ellen G., and Miriam Fuchs (eds), *Breaking the Sequence: Women's Experimental Fiction*, Princeton: Princeton UP, 1989.

—— 'Contexts and Continuities: An Introduction to Women's Experimental Fiction in English', in Friedman and Fuchs, *Breaking* 3–51.

Fuss, Diana J., '"Essentially Speaking": Luce Irigaray's Language of Essence', *Hypatia* 3 (1989): 62–80.

HD [Hilda Doolittle], *Palimpsest*, 1926, rev. ed. Carbondale: Southern Illinois UP, 1968.

Jameson, Fredric, Introduction, Lyotard, *Postmodern Condition* vii–xxii.

—— 'Postmodernism; or, The Cultural Logic of Late Capitalism', *New Left Review* 146 (1984): 53–94.

Jardine, Alice A., *Gynesis: Configurations of Woman and Modernity*, Ithaca: Cornell UP, 1985.

Kaplan, E. Ann, 'Feminism/Oedipus/Postmodernism: The Case of MTV', *Postmodernism and Its Discontents*, ed. Kaplan, New York: Verso, 1988: 30–44.

Levine, Sherrie, 'Art in the (Re) Making', *Art News*, May 1986: 96–7.

Lyotard, Jean-François, 'One Thing at Stake in Women's Struggles', in *The Lyotard Reader*, ed. Andrew Benjamin, Cambridge: Blackwell, 1989: 111–21.

—— *The Postmodern Condition: A Report on Knowledge*, 1979, trans. Geoff Bennington and Brian Massumi, Theory and History of Literature 10, Minneapolis: U of Minnesota P, 1984.

Nin, Anaïs, *The Diary of Anaïs Nin*, ed. Gunther Stuhlmann, 7 vols, New York: Harcourt, 1966–80.

—— *House of Incest*, 1936, Chicago: Swallow, 1958.

—— *A Spy in the House of Love*, 1954, New York: Bantam, 1968.

Oates, Joyce Carol, *Because It Is Bitter, and Because It Is My Heart*, New York: Dutton, 1990.

Owens, Craig, 'The Discourse of Others: Feminists and Postmodernism', in *The Anti-aesthetic: Essays on Postmodern Culture*, ed. Hal Foster, Port Townsend: Bay, 1983: 57–77.

Pynchon, Thomas, *Vineland*, New York: Little, 1990.

Ravits, Martha, 'Extending the American Range: Marilynne Robinson's *Housekeeping*', *American Literature* 61 (1989): 644–66.

Robinson, Lillian, 'Canon Fathers and Myth Universe', *New Literary History* 19 (1987): 23–35.

Robinson, Marilynne, *Housekeeping*, 1981, New York: Bantam, 1982.

Spencer, Sharon, 'The Music of the Womb: Anaïs Nin's "Feminine Writing"', in Friedman and Fuchs, *Breaking* 161–73.

Stein, Gertrude, 'Composition as Explanation', *Selected Writings* 511–23.

—— *The Mother of Us All. Selected Operas and Plays of Gertrude Stein*, ed. John Malcolm Brinnin, Pittsburgh: U of Pittsburgh P, 1970: 159–202.

—— 'Patriarchal Poetry', *The Yale Gertrude Stein*, ed. Richard Kostelanetz, New Haven: Yale UP, 1980: 106–46.

—— 'Rooms', *Tender Buttons. Selected Writings* 498–509.

—— *Selected Writings of Gertrude Stein*, ed. Carl Van Vechten, New York: Vintage-Random, 1972.

Suleiman, Susan Rubin, *Subversive Intent: Gender, Politics, and the Avant-Garde*, Cambridge: Harvard UP, 1990.

Walton, Edith, 'Fantastic Duo', rev. of *Two Serious Ladies*, by Jane Bowles, *New York Times Book Review* 9 May 1943: 14.

Waugh, Patricia, *Feminine Fictions: Revisiting the Postmodern*, New York: Routledge, 1989.

Winnett, Susan, 'Coming Unstrung: Women, Men, Narrative, and Principles of Pleasure', *PMLA* 105 (1990): 505–18.

10

Remembering D-Day: A Case History in Nostalgia

JEAN PICKERING

AMONG MY SOUVENIRS

The war and its aftermath shaped my generation in a number of ways. Its epic scale and scope, seen from a childish perspective, impressed on us a simple patriotic ethic and mythology that were not to be easily or lightly discarded. (How the old emotions welled up again in the Falklands War!)

(Lodge 276)

I begin this essay, which I've been planning since I first visited the *Exposition Permanente du Débarquement* in Arromanches in June 1991, during the 50th anniversary of D-Day celebrations. I have become acutely aware of the ways in which the small world I inhabited at D-Day connects to the present official narrative(s) and the resistance offered to those narrative(s) by my personal history. Out of that resistance comes my understanding of the ways in which national politics molds the uses to which the present puts the past. The premises of my analysis of the Exposition come from the gaps between public memory and my own experience, both heavily influenced by the elegiac nostalgia that colored British national life during and immediately after the war years. I was so accustomed to this pervasive mood that when I read *Brideshead Revisited* in the late 1940s I did not notice how it permeated the novel.

Although I do not think his conclusions would necessarily be transnational, and certainly not universal, I have found useful John Bodnar's terms in *Remaking America: Public Memory, Commemoration, and Patriotism in the Twentieth Century*. The official narrative is produced by the governing classes, who interpret events with the conviction that the national interest is best served by conserving the status quo; the vernacular (that is, the people's) interpretation of those events contests the official narrative; public memory is a mediation of the official narrative and vernacular recollection. Bodnar points out that these two are by no means equally weighted, however; while the particular accommodations vary according to the event in question, generally the official narrative is the more compelling element (13–20). He cites the building of the Vietnam Memorial as the only occasion in the US when the vernacular need for remembrance and mourning has outweighed the official narrative's need for national glory (3–9).

Because it is generally weighted towards the official narrative, public memory puts tremendous pressure on individuals to reassess their own experiences in the direction of the official narrative. While those who live through the events themselves may be able to maintain their interpretations, those without first-hand knowledge of the events tend to dismiss dissenting eye-witness accounts as idiosyncratic, at best a deviation from the typical. I myself have far clearer notions of World War I, which I know only from photographs or written records, than of World War II, into the official narrative of which my recollections intrude to make my sense of the war more uncertain. The generation younger than mine feels the same way about World War II as I do about World War I: several years ago a young man asked me why I was troubled by the newsreel from Hitler's Germany he was watching on the television. 'Can't you see the Nazis are ridiculous?' he said. Such a response could come only from those born into a world where Hitler was always already defeated; for the British of my generation such a reaction is unthinkable because for us the possibility that Hitler might have won has not been erased by his defeat. It may also be that since the re-emergence of fascist demonstrations in the former East Germany the Nazis of the 1930s have begun to look less ridiculous and more threatening.

The personal past, no matter how often rehearsed, is never stable; private memory is constantly assaulted by the revisionary movement of history. Here I am using Pierre Nora's understanding of both terms: 'Memory takes root in the concrete, in spaces, gestures, images and objects; history binds itself strictly to temporal continuities, to progressions and to relations between things' (9). Yet some experiences bolster personal memory in its resistance both to public memory and official narrative. Trying to write about this museum has brought home to me the specifics of how my ambiguous relations with nationalism buffer the pressure of public memory to subsume my personal recollections. Born in London in 1933, I became a US citizen in April of this year after 40 years residence in North America.[1] But the ambiguity of my national identification is situated in a web of other ambiguities, particularly those of the class, gender, and pedagogical ideologies of my childhood. These ideologies have all been modified through further accumulations of experience – increasing knowledge of all kinds, change of domicile, motherhood, familial losses, and what is known in the trade as 'professional growth'. In recent years this growth has undercut my early literary training, which was heavily influenced by the New Critical implication that Art – and Knowledge as well – stands like religion outside the conditions of production and consumption. Poststructuralist theory has reinforced the ironic, critical spirit I contracted in the working-class borough where I grew up, whose inhabitants, alert for hidden agenda, habitually scrutinized official pronouncements. This attitude persisted even though admission to the local girls' grammar school subjected me to middle-class values, one manifestation of which was a determined attack on my working-class vowels. This improvement program had its effect: I was delighted when my erstwhile playmates accused me of becoming a toff.

The *Exposition Permanente du Débarquement*, which I visited again in July 1992, has made me scrutinize my relationship to nostalgia and official narrative. My deliberations have been focused by the 50th anniversary of D-Day celebrations. For various reasons I decided against going to Normandy. I could hardly believe how much, when 6 June came, I minded not being there. I had such a feeling of being left out – which was fed by my feelings towards the end of the war, when I was old enough to understand what was going on but too young to contribute in any significant way.

In retrospect it seems to me that the rhetoric of the war made my generation identify ourselves as British rather than primarily as, say, Londoners or members of the working class. We were urged by posters everywhere that careless talk costs lives; we didn't see how, kept in the dark as we always were about everything adults thought important, we could know anything useful to the enemy. One of our teachers, however, explained that if we told our friends when our fathers were home on embarkation leave, an eavesdropping spy might learn about British troop movements, thus endangering all the men on board, our fathers included. Then there were active ways to contribute: we could save food scraps for the pig-bucket and take fat from the kitchen sink to the butcher's to be made into soap. I collected shrapnel to be recycled into shells and nagged my great-grandmother to give up the eight-pound chunk that had torn out the corner of her bedroom one night while she was in bed. Young as we were, our labour was useful to the na-tional war effort.

Marginal on account of my age and gender to the war itself, I was nonetheless disinclined to see myself as underprivileged on account of my girlhood. I compensated for the erasure of people like me from the official narrative by reading into war narratives a place for myself. The local library had a series of books for adoles-cent boys about the valorous exploits of Royal Air Force pilot Freddie Farmer, who along with his side-kick Dave Dawson seemed to be single-handedly fighting the battle in the skies. I in-vented the only role I knew how to imagine – *sweetheart* as I would have called it then – exploiting the imaginary situation as best I could by keeping both brave, gorgeous flyboys dangling until I could decide which deserved me the most. Even though women were being conscripted, were serving as anti-aircraft gun crews and military nurses, these roles were not called to my attention in what I considered the most prestigious medium of communication. Perhaps there were books about Jenny the Landgirl or Alice of the ATS, but I never saw them. A boy I knew caught me selecting one of these 'boy's books' and tried to bully me into choosing a girl's. He felt strongly that I was stepping outside my proper gender identification, which for some reason he saw as an infringement on his personal prerogatives. If he had known what use I was making of his sacred texts, perhaps he would have been less offended by my presumption.

The role I wrote for myself was a variation of the one I learned through the songs of the period. Although women I knew were munitions workers, landgirls, WAAFS or WRNS, conscripted into various services as substitutes for the men who were at the front or in the pilot's seat, the songs of the war years cast women as be-reaved sweethearts; the 15-year-old Vera Lynn (only a few years older than I, and from the same primary school) with the throbbing voice of a sexually mature woman sang *We'll Meet Again*, *I'll Be Seeing You*, and *Silver Wings in the Moonlight*. Ironically, lunch-time concerts featuring such singers and such songs were frequently broadcast from munitions plants, whose workers were almost entirely women. Perhaps these songs were really for the men being sent away to fight – to convince each one that at home was a soft compliant yearning-towards-him woman of his very own, who depended on him for protection from the enemy.

In the fall of 1944 the school went to a special showing of Laurence Olivier's *Henry V*. This film recuperated an originary story of British imperial expansion to promote the support of a class-fractured nation for a war that was to trigger Britain's decline as an imperial power, a retrospective irony of the first order. Although I did not at the time understand that it was placing the D-Day invasion of France in a long and noble story of British pre-eminence, it did give me a better grasp of nationalism than the patriotic songs we sang in school. From that time I began to associate the idea of *nation* with war.

Nostalgia came several years later, also associated with war – though World War I rather than World War II. It too was introduced through literature. Our reading in the immediate postwar years was heavily weighted towards loss, death, nostalgia, at least in part because Britain was still depressed by the immense losses of World War I. During World War II there was a tremendous reluctance to engage in military actions that would endanger large numbers of men because the nation was still acutely remembering the losses of World War I.

In the early years of the war I had no understanding of this wound festering in the national memory. Although during the Battle of Britain I lived in a heavily-bombed area near the docks, I had a poor grip on the idea of death. No one I knew intimately had died either through accident or natural causes. The first time I remember being forced to contemplate death came on Armistice Day 1943: our teacher made us stand for two minutes' silence for the 'fallen' of World War I. I was appalled at how long two minutes was when one didn't have anything to think about. I tried to keep my mind blank – what was death but an absence, after all? – but it was impossible. I began to understand the magnitude of the casualty list only years later, at the same time realizing why I was the only child I knew who had two living grandfathers (both had served overseas, but neither ever told war stories). Even the war memorial in Central Park, East Ham, carried no emotional charge for me. I did however notice in 1946 when the casualties of World War II were engraved on the same column that the number of the borough's fallen had been far greater in World War I. A few years later it occurred to me that using the same memorial constituted a tacit acknowledgment that the two wars were so closely related that they in fact constituted a single war.

In spite of the cenotaph, I had no sense of loss attached to war until World War II was over. When in 1947 I learned to mourn for the war dead, it was the dead of World War I. The World War I poets were very big in the late 1940s. My classmates and I learned poems by heart and, afflicted by adolescent emotions, mourned the putrefaction of so much young beautiful male flesh, which in spite of our gushing hormones did not seem to us as though it had ever been very real, as though it had only ever existed in marble. This post-World War II experience of World War I provided the generating site of nostalgia for me; the regrets for those whom age would not weary nor the years condemn inscribed me with nostalgia (never mind that those eternal youths were of my grandfathers' generation!).

During the early postwar years I learned to feel nostalgia for a lost homeland that wasn't even mine. I saw *Casablanca* within a couple of years of its release. I was moved by the scene in Rick's cafe where the (woman) guitarist strikes up *La Marseillaise* as resistance to the German military. This reaction persists to this day, fed by other experiences: going to Paris in 1949; reading *Le Silence de la Mer* in the same year and later Simone de Beauvoir's description of the liberation of Paris; watching the newsreel of Paris rejoicing in its liberation, including a rousing rendition of *Le Marseillaise* led by de Gaulle, with in the foreground two small boys, aged about seven, flinging themselves weeping into each other's arms. In fact my response to the *Casablanca* scene has grown even more emotional: I have learned that the actors playing the patriots were French citizens who fled the German occupation. (Never mind that those patriots didn't scrutinize their relationship to the subject population of Casablanca, which has had to wait much longer for its liberation!) I still weep when the guitarist strikes up the *Marseillaise*. So now I feel nostalgia for the official narrative of a nation neither the one I grew up in nor the one I have adopted. It occurs to me as I write that in both these cases of imaginary nostalgia sexuality was a big factor: the story line of *Casablanca* embodies in addition to loss of nation the renunciation of love, which was the only form of the sexual imaginary available to me and my classmates.

It was years before I felt the pain of loss I had come to call nostalgia outside a literary context, this time likewise associated with ideas of *nation*. In my 29th year I began to suspect that the nation I thought I knew was an imaginary construct. I had believed that Britons never would be slaves, that the military existed to protect women and children and so forth. In the summer of 1961, while reading William Shirer's *Rise and Fall of the Third Reich*, I began to think that although my father, suddenly conscripted into the RAF, had indeed been an RAF fitter in Canada from 1941 to 1944, the most likely reason for his presence there was that the Government expected the Germans to invade Britain. Even at the time he was drafted I had been aware of the possibility of invasion: I knew that the beaches of the east coast, where we had spent the fall of 1939 in an extended holiday when our inner-city borough's schools were closed, had been shrouded in barbed wire ('fat lot of good that'll do against a tank', I'd thought) and that place names had been removed from road signs and station platforms (to confuse enemy paratroopers). Nor, I had inferred, was my father's case unusual. Had large numbers of men been shipped to places like Canada in order to stage a come-back later? This would have left me, my mother and sisters at the enemy's mercy with only the Home Guard for protection. Would my mother, my grandmother and great-grandmother as well be expected to fling Molotov cocktails at the well-armed invaders? Suddenly the cynical tone in the voice of the male relative who, saying good-bye to my father on his embarkation leave, had remarked, 'If they do invade, don't you come liberating us!' made sense. I did not sleep for three nights after I read Shirer. *Betrayal* is not too strong a word for what I felt.

Later there were discoveries of other betrayals, though none could be so devastating. I was saddened to discover that *Henry V* had been made as propaganda (Barker 184), funded by the Government to be released coincidentally with D-Day. Subsequently I learned of other literary conscripts. H. E. Bates, called to military service, was commissioned and stationed at a base in Essex, his mission to write fiction about the Air Force: his 1942 *The Stories of Flying Officer X* was the fruit of his service to the nation. In May 1994 I learned that the Government commissioned from Alfred Hitchcock several movies to show in liberated France while the Allies were advancing on Germany, but because the films, rather than offering a version of the official narrative, showed the ambiguity of war, His Majesty's Government would not release them (Nye).

My surprise that artists had been recruited for the war effort was naive, but I attribute it in part to my education. My teachers at the grammar school were avant-garde in literary matters; they had been much influenced by I. A. Richards and promulgated what in the US has been called New Criticism, with its ideology that aesthetics is free of political values. I did not notice at the time, any more than my teachers seemed to, that the literature we read violently contradicted that precept.

Class-based betrayals gave me a special kind of pain. The working class of London suffered more bombardment than suburbanites, who had greater resources in the first place. When some of the bombed-out from the East End had been left shelterless for several days without any official attempt to make provision for them, they marched on Whitehall to request help from Parliament. They were turned back by mounted police (Fitz-Gibbon 103) – this in London, where many houses had been vacated by those who could afford to go elsewhere and in a country where stately homes were requisitioned to billet the military. The realization that the improved educational opportunities for working-class children under the Butler Education Act of 1944 had been motivated at least in part by the desire to cull from the working class those most likely to become class leaders was especially painful because I had assumed I deserved such privilege.

The pain of these betrayals has not diminished the emotional draw of imaginary nostalgia deployed to strengthen the ties of the patriotism that sustains nationalism, but for me it has problematized *nostalgia*, which I have identified as appearing in at least two formulations: imaginary nostalgia attached to events one has not experienced and the nostalgia arising in connection with lived-through events, which is fed by the imaginary. There may well be more. The pain of betrayal has strengthened the ironic stance of my class background and given me a double view in all my dealings. The betrayal was structured as a private rather than a public experience. What I thought existed never did exist; what I regretted losing was the frame of mind that made belief possible, that made choices simple and responsibilities clear. This regret is both performative and constitutive: it is both cause and result of nostalgia. Yet why should I perceive 'losing' a frame of mind as 'loss'? Surely to lose one frame of mind is to find another.

YOU MUST REMEMBER THIS

The acceleration of history: let us try to gauge the significance of this phrase. An increasingly rapid slippage of the present into a historical past that has gone for good, a general perception that anything and everything may disappear ... . We speak so much of memory because there is so little of it left.

(Nora 7)

Since 1991 I've considered the ways in which nostalgia has for me mediated ideas of nation and gender. The *Exposition Permanente* was the field where I first scrutinized the shifting relationships among them. The Exposition presents a multiple narrative embracing both official narrative and public memory, which stretches far back into the past and reaches towards a future controlled by that past. It is a narrative whose ambiguities and ironies trouble me.

The museum has no written history and no apparent affiliation. It is 'owned' by the *Comité du débarquement*,[3] a local elected committee founded in 1945 and still headed by the original chairman, who was a major force in the planning and building. The museum does not interrogate itself; rather it endorses the notion that it is a transparent medium for conveying the facts of the D-Day landing. It wants to make visitors feel what it was like to be there, thus attempts to give an overall picture of the 'débarquement' as planned. The film shown in its theatre, provided by the British Admiralty and made from contemporary film clips, minimizes the casualties and scenes of horror, as did the theater newsreels shown to US audiences, who did not see such footage for years afterwards.

The museum overlooks the bay of Arromanches, where the remains of the floating Mulberry harbor built for the D-Day landing (towed across the channel in sections and assembled in a matter of hours) still sit on the beach. It is, in Pierre Nora's words, a *lieu de mémoire*, a site of privileged memory established out of a sense that 'without commemorative vigilance, history would soon sweep it away' (12). The fundamental purpose of 'the *lieu de mémoire* is to stop time, to block the work of forgetting, to establish a state of things, to immortalize death' (19). A site of privileged memory, the *lieu de mémoire* – 'a moment of history torn away from the movement of history, then returned' (12) is 'created by a play of memory and history', its only difference from the *lieu d'histoire* it supplants being its intention to remember (19). At Arromanches the *lieu de mémoire* is still in dialogue with the *lieu d'histoire* it will eventually erase – perhaps, as those who remember the event it commemorates are rapidly dying off, has already substantially erased. In Nora's arresting phrase 'Memory [is] seized by history' (13). This seizure admits both intentionality – self-consciousness – and nostalgia. The *lieu de mémoire* is thus saturated with latencies of nation and gender.

Such supplanting of the *lieu d'histoire* by the *lieu de mémoire* is already the pattern of the neighboring countryside. Normandy is replete with cemeteries – the American cemetery is five miles away with British and German cemeteries nearby. There are cenotaphs everywhere, from the stylus at Omaha Beach to the village erections at crossroads, for example the memorial at Creully to the 76th and 77th Yorkshire Dragoons, 'to all the dead and those living who, captured at Dunkerque, when freed, fought alongside their comrades to liberate Creully' (my translation).

Further east small graveyards with crosses freshly white-washed border the road from Calais to Paris. Throughout Normandy road signs act as reminders of older wars, Honfleur, Harcourt and Crecy for example. Twelve miles away is the museum housing the Bayeux tapestry, which narrates the Norman invasion of England.

It is the intention of the museum to remember, and yet to do more than remember; its duty is 'to make the younger generations aware of what happened here in Normandy on a certain day in June 1944'. The official narrative – of epic language and proportions – 'immortalizes the memory of those who came from the sea and who, at 20 years of age, gave their lives to liberate Europe from the yoke which oppressed them' (*Arromanches* 8). The museum makes special provision for school parties, offering guided tours in French, English, German and Spanish. It sends out colorful posters, brochures and 'teaching aids' – the latter a questionnaire to prepare children for what they see (those well-prepared behave better than those who are not). The questionnaire comprises 20 questions mainly about the building of the artificial port and about the *débarquement* itself: 'Whose idea was it?' 'How many Phoenix blocks were used to build the sea wall?' 'Where and when did the Polish troops land?' It is full of memory aids to a certain version of the day the museum cryptically announces across the marquee: '6 6 44'. To the left of the entrance fly the flags of the nations that participated in the landing: France (as in Free French), the United Kingdom, Canada, the United States, the Netherlands, Poland,

Belgium, Luxembourg. Across the street a souvenir shop boasts the name OVERLORD, the code name for the D-Day operation, in letters a foot high. Just inside the foyer a large map pinpoints the military cemeteries and the important battles fought in the region from Crecy on, amongst which the D-Day battles find their place. This map attempts to integrate the D-Day enterprise into the official narrative of the countryside, which goes back far into the past and impelled by the museum's intention to 'immortalize the memory' reaches towards the future.

The first time I entered the museum my response was unequivocal: I was invaded by the familiar. *Recognition* is perhaps the best word to name what I felt, but it was recognition of a kind that made me perceive the museum not so much as an image of a past to which I was returning but as an image of my mind projected on the world.

Beyond the turnstile there is an attempt to place the viewers within the narrative. The main exhibit is a model of the floating harbor that faces a plate glass window giving an unobstructed view of the remains of said harbor. The model, donated by the British government, is a reproduction of the original model from which the harbor was built; it too appears to float. Along the walls over the display cases and above the visitors' heads are blow-ups of photographs taken during Operation Overlord. Some of the most arresting are of the faces of troops standing on deck as they cross the channel. These faces are young – very young – and earnest, as though they know their place in history: the sons of fathers and grandsons of grandfathers who fought at Ypres, at the Somme, at Abbeville. That place in history was being prepared for them even before they were born, even before the punitive terms of the Armistice of 1918 had been drafted – that Armistice so much on the minds of the British public during World War II.

Display cases show various artifacts: uniforms (on mannequins) and medals, military-issue plates and spoons, snapshots of individual men and their letters and diaries. The personal belongings of 'ordinary' men predominate, especially in the selections of letters, which show obligingly humorous lower-class attitudes, vocabulary, spelling, and sentence structure.

Two letters from 14261722 Trooper Lang Esq, as he styled himself, of HQ Squadron, 8th Armoured Brigade, BWEF, roused me more to pity and anger than any other item in the museum. One was to his mother, the other to his sister Kathleen. I retain the original spelling, punctuation, paragraph format and line-length:

Saturday 15 July 1944
Dear Mother
Just a few lines to let you
know I am still fine and resting in
one of the many fine Normandy
Orchards. ...
    I see you were thinking of taking
a Evacuee in I hope you
don't give yourself too much bother
although the way some of the Northerners
are recieving them they deserve being
sent down to the S. Coast andLondon for
a few weeks of it. All the Blackpool
Landladies according to one paper deserved
shooting in my opinion for the way
they have acted their motto must be
money before lives. The best way is
to take over these holiday resorts
andmake them recieve every body who likes
to come up north. On D. 3 I saw
French people having to leave their homes
andvillages and you realize what
they must feel like to see there homes
destroyed while English people are
sitting back and not trying
help the war effort. I'll be frightened to
show my face if anything happens like
this in Leeds. The Cockneys will be up
and at us. ...
        Cheerio
        Stan

Trooper Land had received a standard British education of the late 1930s and early 1940s, when the school-leaving age was fourteen, when the 'ordinary' boy or girl went into an office, factory or shop. (When the school-leaving age was raised to fifteen in 1947, there was no pretence of its being for the pupils' benefit: it was to keep the youngsters off the job market.) When I read this letter I thought of a series of British wartime newsreels I'd seen the previous year on the Arts and Education channel. I noted one in particular, dealing with what became known as the postwar settlement. It was narrated by a man with an accent I'd grown up calling a BBC voice, the patronizing tone of which I somehow then overlooked. By 1990 I'd been only too aware of the self-conscious superiority of the speaker, who enumerated promises of an end to these foolish class distinctions, two-week holidays with pay for all workers, a national health scheme and improved educational opportunities. I inferred from this newsreel that the governing classes had been aware of how much more they had to gain from winning the war than the likes of Trooper Lang. Neil Rattigan, examining images of class in British wartime films, notes a similar attitude on the part of the governing class; however, he imputes a less self-conscious and sinister motive to those in power than I:

> The ruling class could not anticipate the subordinate classes' willingness to fight for Britain/England. This position was informed by the ruling-class 'belief' that Britain/England 'belonged' to them.
>
> (83)

The governing class might well have essentialized themselves as the real 'owners' of Britain, but this sense of metaphysical entitlement did not, in my view, obscure their clear-eyed observation that they received a larger share of the Gross National Product. Getting less, they thought, the working class had less reason to fight to the death.

The governing class, however, is not at the center of Trooper Lang's universe; his concerns are with the marginal, his sensibilities engaged with people of his own class – the Blackpool landladies, the Cockneys. He does not spare much thought for the distress of the London children evacuated under the government scheme,[4] although it was considerable. The evacuation was organized by the military, who brought to the operation a conviction that the secrecy appropriate for troop movements should be observed in conveying the children. Consequently parents did not know where their children were going – did not know where they were – until they received letters from their children, which in some cases was two weeks later. Those in charge of the evacuation also considered a roundabout route safer, in some instances taking boats along the coast, so that children as young as five might be in transit as much as 12 hours. Nor were any provisions made for feeding them during these maneuvers. Phyllis Pugh of Dagenham reports that she and her sisters went to Great Yarmouth by paddle steamer, a journey of nine hours; disembarking, they were fed a meal of 'cold saveloy [cabbage] and lemonade' – a repast that was repeated during the three days they remained in Great Yarmouth. On the fourth day they were transported to a village where their hosts chose which children they wanted, to the humiliation of those old enough to understand what was going on. Pugh remembers it as 'kind of a slave or cattle market' (14).

In spite of his casual attitude to the idea of evacuees in these letters, Trooper Lang's sympathies lie with civilian victims when he sees them: his comment on the French evacuation during the Allied liberation is one of the few acknowledgements of the suffering of the civilian population anywhere in this museum. Evidence of such suffering is only now becoming available to public memory with the publication of Marie-Laure Osmont's *Normandy Diary* and the showing of George Stevens's movie, *La Marche des Héros*, which lay forgotten for over 40 years. For Trooper Lang, who saw such suffering with his own eyes, the working class, the civilians – the marginal – are at the center of his sensibilities.

Two photographs emblematize French resistance to the German Occupation of Normandy. Two young French pilots pose with the Bucher-Jungman they had stolen at the Caen-Carpiquet airfield on 19 April 1941 and then flew to the Christchurch Air Force base to join de Gaulle in England. Their gallant deed enacts in small the scenario that sent my father to Prince Edward Island in 1941. But the photograph of the gallant flyers includes no suggestion that they were leaving the women and children to live a life which, if not as luxurious as that of the British airmen posted to Newfoundland, at least did not leave them as prisoners of war or as impressed members of the Vichy forces.

The second photograph is a wartime portrait of Paulette Duhalde, who was 'arrêtée par la Gestapo ... sur "dénonciation"'; she was imprisoned in nearby Fresnes until July 1944, when the Germans were forced to retreat, and deported to Ravensbrück, where she died in April 1945 (the month in which the Allies reached Bergen-Belsen). The word *dénonciation* is the only suggestion in the museum that collaboration with the army of Occupation ever occurred. Such collaboration is clearly the obverse of the 'collaboration' the museum celebrates, and has thus been erased in the interests of the official narrative – the narrative rapidly unravelling in the aftermath of the revelations of French accommodations with the Nazis, the most recent of which are Pierre Péan's disclosures in his biography of the President of France, *Une Jeunesse française: François Mitterrand, 1934–1947.*

Some instances of Vichy's cooperation with the Nazis have always been known, if not widely publicized – the Vichy generals' resistance in 1942 to the Allied liberators of Casablanca and Algiers (Brown 439–44), for example – but often specifics of such cooperation have been both suppressed and repressed in French public memory: 'a self-protected silence, though punctuated by scandals and revelations, prevailed for close to fifty years after the Occupation, as if public memory could not tolerate the truth of French complicity in the persecution of the Jews' (Hartman 16). Such erasures from the museum's narrative – like the nation's – are highlighted by the recent reappearance of fascist attitudes uncovered by the break-up of Eastern Europe, when the ghosts of Hitler Youth, beamed from Rostock, appear on TV screens, and the faces of Bergen-Belsen peer out through the chain-link in Bosnia. The absence from the museum's official narrative of any gesture towards the collaboration with the Nazis save the one word *dénonciation* is troubling.

The museum overtly endorses the kind of collaboration represented by the European Economic Community, whose influence makes itself felt in the gift shop, with its scores of books, videos and model kits, all aimed at the Common Market tourist. I visited the museum twice. Each time the visitors included one organized group of tourists. In 1991 there was a group of some 30 British schoolchildren, boys and girls, ten or eleven years old, with three teachers. For these children three kinds of item were especially attractive: the uniforms, the diorama of the battlefield, and the model kits on sale in the museum shop. The uniforms of various participants in the landing were displayed on mannequins. Uniforms of personnel unacknowledged elsewhere in the museum included one of the Czechoslovak Air Force pilots who flew with the RAF, and members of the women's auxiliary forces, both US and British.[5]

The museum makes a specialty of models, including animated ones where the simulated rise and fall of the tide lifts the models of the mulberries. Another item that engaged the children's attention was the model of the harbor and environs, laid out with miniature tanks, toy soldiers and puffs of cotton. Hearing the children's comments gave me an insight into the way nostalgia for what one has never known may be inculcated. Models were a context known to all the children; seeing the space they were in and its history contracted into this scale model reduced the carnage to manageable proportions. They were used to playing with models, thus the D-Day landing, the outcome of which had already determined so much in their lives, seemed to put the past within their control. These models helped to produce a comfortable imaginary nostalgia for the young who had been born into a world where the Allies had prevailed, where the Nazis had always been defeated. I have since seen a 12-year-old joyfully hoist himself into the cockpit of a Messerschmitt in the Imperial War Museum. The difference between his feelings and mine made me understand how history acquires a teleology denied to those who lived through the events narrated by history. The nostalgia available to these children promoted the mechanisms the poets of World War I had set in motion in me. I too had enjoyed heightened emotions in teleological comfort.

In the museum shop the children, both boys and girls, bought model airplane kits. These kits sell very well, without regard to whether they are Messerschmitts or Stukas, Wellingtons or Spitfires. The children need enemy planes to annihilate. They cannot help but construct a narrative of World War II in which the issues are, and always were, simple.

My second visit to the museum was in 1992. A group of men and women in their late 60s to 70s clustered round the model of the floating harbor to listen to a member of the museum staff. He was 30-something and British. The group had clearly booked this presentation ahead of time. He lectured for some 15 minutes on the operations of the harbor; the audience was respectful as he indicated various spots with his pointer and when he finished asked detailed questions whose answers required more pointing. Only the men asked questions. I gathered they were a group of Free French veterans who had participated in the landing. They were completing the big picture, without which their experiences were memories not knowledge. At the end of the lecture they broke into sub-groups of eight men or so with their attendant womenfolk. One such group donned their reading glasses and huddled round a wall case displaying French medals. They discussed the medals at some length, the women from a respectful distance and with an even more respectful silence. (How many of those women, I wondered, had remained in Occupied or Vichy France while their men followed de Gaulle to England?)

While it is tempting to speculate on the differences between the men's and the women's relationships to the past and thus to nostalgia, here I will confine myself to the differences I see between the children's and the veterans'. The children's easy generalizing of the past which should lead to a comfortable nostalgia could never be matched by that of the veterans, whose struggle for psychological and intellectual control of their experience has been veneered by both the guilt and the triumph of their survival. The 50th anniversary of D-Day has brought so much attention to the casualties that the veterans must think more about their fallen comrades than they did at the moment of death, when the survivors were focused on the task at hand and on the dangers before them. As the recent spate of recollections and oral histories suggests, veterans' nostalgia must always be fragmented, unstable, and dearly bought.[6]

These reactions I recognized in the children and the veterans respectively, or perhaps projected on to them, cued by unrelated remarks and gestures. There was good reason for either recognition or projection, as I later realized: the children were approximately as old as I had been at D-Day, my only authentic memory of which is a sky full of planes and later the day's-long noise of bombardment from the south. The children were an image of what I had been, whereas the veterans were only a few years older than I and so my context for D-Day, in spite of gender and national difference, was similar to theirs. In fact, my position that day in June 1992 was more like that of the accompanying womenfolk: they too were standing back observing the men who were asking questions of the guide and scrutinizing the artifacts – a position I took (and am still taking) in relation to the war itself.

Coming up from the sea at Omaha Beach later that day, my traveling companion and I saw two elderly men, one with a pronounced limp, getting out of a red BMW with a Deutsch plate on the back bumper. As we drew level, the German with the limp surveyed with great satisfaction our California clothes and our hair whipping about in the wind. Making eye contact with me, he said wistfully, 'Oh, des Parisiennes!' The look in his eye as well as his tone of voice suggested nostalgia: I envisioned him as one of the German troops who had marched through the Arc de Triomphe under the gaze of the silent crowds of Paris. In spite of ultimate defeat, it seemed, the time he had been part of the Occupation forces was still glorious for him. His nostalgia was so compelling that he had erased all signs of nation and culture.

The *Exposition Permanente du Débarquement* attempts to control the signification(s) of the D-Day invasion, freezing the rhetorical values of the war itself in the version of official narrative current when the landing took place. It attempts to do this not only for the past but for the future, with its emphasis on the education of future generations, whom it does not want to forget 'the real meaning' of D-Day. The emphasis on educating the young is especially prominent in French pronouncements about D-Day, and not only from officials connected with the museum. My local paper carried a report on the 49th anniversary of D-Day ceremonies at Ouistreham, where Prime Minister Edouard Balladur said, 'It is our duty to cultivate the memory of younger generations about those events.' He warned that 'a resurgence of nationalism and right-wing violence in Europe carries "the germs of new violence, new destruction, unworthy of our civilization, unworthy of human nature"' (Burns). These comments resonate uncomfortably with the news that in April 1994 a French court for the first time scrutinized French complicity with the Nazis when Pierre Trouvier, arrested in 1989, was convicted of crimes against humanity and was sentenced to life imprisonment for executing seven Jews in June 1994 (Kritzman 6–7). Validating the official narrative by pointing towards a future that threatens to repeat it, Premier Balladur might have been speaking on behalf of the *Exposition Permanente*.

To dwell on the official narrative is not to minimize the commercial factor, the tourism that especially in the year of the 50th anniversary brought an enormous influx of money into Normandy. The gift shop is the most obvious site where the museum's dual purposes of education and commerce may be observed. Flyers available there recommend Arromanches as the 'starting point of delightful excursions throughout the surrounding region'. Nearby merchants did a good business from the thousands who visited in June 1994 (10 000 were in the American cemetery alone for the D-Day commemoration service). Hotel rooms throughout Normandy were fully booked; some rooms had been reserved for years. In response to this influx of tourists, the disneyfication[7] of the *débarquement* – ostensibly for the children – of the museum was echoed in such *objects d'art* as a local baker's chocolate replica of a Sherman tank ('Sweet' 1994). This manifestation was only a more extreme

version of the disneyfying impulse already expressed in the souvenir shops, of which OVERLORD is the nearest and most visible
example.

IT'S OVER OVER THERE

On Memorial Day 1987 I was moving some books from West
Hollywood to Fresno and stopped near Santa Monica for gas.
While the attendant was washing my windows, he nodded towards
a book I had on the back seat, *VE Day*. 'Would you sell it to me?' I
hesitated. I began to explain my need for it even as I noticed the
purple heart pinned to his shirt and the ribbons showing he'd
fought at the Battle of the Bulge. He told me he was the 'only
American' employed at the station; the other two men, from
Salvador and Guatemala, had the holiday off. 'But somebody's got
to do it.' I thanked him and pulled away from the pump but
stopped at the edge of the lot. How could I refuse a book to
someone to whom I was personally so indebted? Could the UK
have kept out Hitler if the US hadn't entered the war? I got out of
the car and took the book over to him. 'You mean you're going to
give it to me?' We talked for a few minutes: had I ever been to Las
Vegas? If I wasn't married, would I go with him for a couple of
days? I said goodbye. As he turned away, already flipping through
the pictures, I saw that two men of his own age – one with a cane –
were sitting waiting for him just inside the garage. The last view I
had was of three grey heads bent over my picture book.

In the US the television coverage of the D-Day commemoration services suggested that the meaning of the Normandy landing is still
under active contest. It showed public memory still in the making,
providing a working model of how it emerges from the contest of
official narrative and vernacular interpretation. The broad outlines
of the official narrative were established by the Allies at time of the
landing. As the main supplier of the *matériel* for Operation
Overlord, the US has been the major interpreter of the events of D-
Day, which the official narrative consequently presents as both
metaphor of and justification for the global role of the United
States.
    In retrospect it seems that D-Day had been on the public mind of
the United States ever since the 40th anniversary celebrations.

Various items of interest have appeared in the media from time to time, like a news story about 300 men who every 6 June reenact the D-Day landing on a Florida beach (*Morning News*) or programs like Bill Moyers' *From D-Day to the Rhine*, an extended interview with a busload of veterans touring the sites where they had fought in World War II. Moyers' program rehearsed in 1990 some of the features that became even more salient during the 50th anniversary celebrations. He cited the destructiveness of war in rhetorical generalizations: 'These now green fields were soaked with blood'; 'Hitler had told his generals that "Paris must not fall into the hands of the enemy except as a field of ruins."' He attempted to site the destruction of the D-Day landing in the larger historical context of the nearby Bayeux tapestry, embroidered some 900 years before: it is 'one of the most authentic depictions of war that has ever been drawn. Most of the news that goes home is not that detailed, with heads rolling and arms falling off.' He spoke of pictures of atrocities while the veterans spoke instead of a French family asphyxiated at the dinner table and frozen like a wax tableau, or a soldier with a throat wound propped up against a hedgerow while his last heartbeats squirted out blood in four-foot streams. He proffered concepts like *bravery* while a veteran told of reconnoitering for antitank mines without mine-detectors and 'trampling the hell out of every square foot of snow on the goddamned road'. He tried to construct a heroic official narrative while the veterans offered independent scenes of death and survival as their contribution to public memory.

The contest for control of the meaning of the veterans' experience implicit in Moyers' program became more explicit on the 49th anniversary of D-Day when veterans spoke about the ceremonies planned for the 50th, which for many would be the last they attended. Acknowledging that veterans worry D-Day could fade from the public consciousness – or be subsumed into a public memory scarcely distinguishable from the official narrative when he and others stop making the trip to Normandy – one veteran said, 'I haven't a great amount of money to leave anybody, but I'd like to leave them my memories over the years' (Burns).

In the United States the television coverage of the 50th anniversary celebrations was enormous. My local paper listed 33 different programs on the landing and closely related topics for Sunday 5 June and Monday 6 June alone. Special attention was given to the various ceremonies at Arlington National Cemetery, the American

Cemetery at Cambridge, but most of all to the ceremony at the American Cemetery at Colville-sur-Mer, the coverage of which began on 5 June. On the *Sunday Morning* show newsanchor Andy Rooney valorized those 'average Americans' who jumped as paratroopers in the early hours of the morning of the assault on the beach (though he clearly meant to include all the D-Day veterans in his general homage): 'They were not great men, but on that one monumental day in the history of the world, they did that one great thing.'

Rooney's heightened language was low-key beside the rhetorical peaks scaled on 6 June itself. What Paul Fussell has called the '"raised", essentially feudal language' (21) typical of the official narrative of World War I appeared throughout the two-hour broadcast; the following words appearing on the list he cites were called into service again and for similar purposes: *sacrifice, gallant, deeds, naught*. They were reinforced by words of comparable resonance: *tyranny, remembrance, sanctified, enslavement, precious blood, spilled [their] blood, tide of history, great crusade*, the latter Eisenhower's most famous phrase from his most famous speech, to the troops as they prepared to embark for Normandy. Harry Smith, co-host for *This Morning*, produced an unacknowledged echo of Rupert Brooke's most famous poem: 'These 172 acres of French soil will be forever American.' Such words and the periodic sentences in which they appeared bestowed an epic flavor on the speeches of the President, the Medal of Honor recipient, the veterans, the Navy Chief of Chaplains, and sometimes on the utterances of the newsanchors themselves. Together all these speakers rearticulated and reinforced the official narrative, frequently drawing attention to this reinforcement by referring to 'the course of history'. The Medal of Honor recipient interpreted D-Day through a popular US myth: the D-Day landing was 'the new world returning to redeem the old. ... Moreover, it was the new world ... caught up in the ... spirit of freedom ... to support ... the salvation of the old world.' The Chaplain connected 'the sacrifice of those who shared their youth and life blood' with the founders of 'our nation ... , brave souls who declared their reliance on your divine providence' – a providence that foreshadowed the 'rendez-vous with destiny' cited by Charles Durnin, the veterans' representative. President Clinton brought this national narrative up to D-Day, relying heavily on Stephen Ambrose's interpretation of the invasion published only two months before: 'Hitler [was] sure the Allied soldiers were soft,

weakened by liberty and leisure, by the mingling of races and religions. They were sure their totalitarian youth had more discipline
and zeal. ... [But American troops finding themselves without
officers] inched forward, and together in groups of threes and fives
and tens, the sons of democracy improvised and mounted their
own attacks. At that exact moment, on these beaches, the forces of
freedom turned the tide of the twentieth century'.[8] Walter Ehlers, a
veteran making a formal speech at the commemoration, brought
the national narrative up to the present: D-Day 'did not mean
peace, but it marked the stand for freedom that would continue
through the Korean War, the Vietnam conflict, the fall of the Berlin
Wall and the allied containment of Iraq. ... This anniversary must
be not only remembered but a new beginning' (*This Morning*).

This official narrative was supported by commentators who
offered conjectures as to why D-Day had gradually assumed the
primary position it now holds in American history. Cokie Roberts
on *Good Morning America* said, 'A lot of people think that [D-Day] is
the most important day of the twentieth century. It not only has-
tened the end of the war against Germany and fascism, it kept the
Russians from sweeping over Europe and stopped communism,
and it brought American ascendancy in foreign policy in the
world.' Reminiscing about his grandfather, Ike's grandson David
Eisenhower established the material base of this US ascendancy:
'My grandfather wrote later of flying over the beachhead and ...
noticing that, despite the destruction of 50 per cent of our port capacity in a single storm, it caused barely a ripple in our buildup. He
said, "Never before or since in my life have I been so impressed by
the industrial might of America than I was that day to see our port
capacity swept away by a storm and to know that our buildup just
proceeded ... and that we were amassing more *matériel* than
anybody had ever seen in Europe"' (*This Morning*).

The site of the commemoration ceremony itself served to endorse
the official narrative being (re)produced there. Walter Cronkite's
comment on the different burial practices of the US and Britain un-
derscored the visual impression made by the 9386 marble crosses
and stars of David laid out in symmetrical rows in the trim lawns.
He found it 'interesting' that the British practice was to bury the
dead pretty much where they fell 'in numerous small cemeteries'
across the continent rather than assembling them in one place (*This
Morning*). This observation naturalizes the American practice,
which itself acts as a metonomy for the vast resources of the United

States noted by Eisenhower, in fact a metonomy for American hegemony. The repeated references to the blood spilled in the 'mighty endeavor' suggested that just as the dead had earned their spot on French soil (which would thus be 'forever American') so the blood-price had paid for the hegemony the cemetery itself so clearly represented. This signification of the cemetery is to be reinforced by the Wall of Liberty planned for the International Liberation Park next to the Memorial Museum in Caen. The Wall will display the names of all members of the United States Armed Services, some five million of them, who served in any theatre in World War II. The Memorial Garden representing the fifty states is already finished, paid for by the (US) Battle of Normandy Foundation, which sponsored the statue of Dwight Eisenhower in Bayeux dedicated on 5 June 1994 and will also pay for the Wall (Mabel Stover, Pierre Salinger on *Larry King Live*). Together with the cemetery these various monuments to the power of the US reinforce the official narrative as forwarded on the anniversary of D-Day.

This official US narrative being reasserted under the eyes of the nation – indeed, of the world – was at the same time contested in various ways. First, it was interspersed with news clips from parts of the world where armed action was in progress, notably Bosnia, Rwanda and Israel,[9] which interrogated the premise that US hegemony has brought peace and democracy to the world. It was also contested by a theme reiterated several times in news clips that the Russians thought they might have 'gotten a little more credit here today for having decimated the Germans so much to maybe open the door on this front a little bit' (Harry Smith, *This Morning*). The voiceover clip from the original announcement – aimed at Europe – that the landing was part of 'the concerted United Nations plan for the liberation of Europe, made in conjunction with our great Russian allies' gave a certain weight to this suggestion. Another newsclip suggested that the Germans, now allies, might also have been invited, an idea that was thoroughly aired in newspaper commentary on the celebrations.

The official narrative was interrogated also by the appropriations it was undergoing as the nation watched. The 'police actions' characterizing US foreign policy since 1945 – the list of which included the abortive 'Vietnam conflict' – do not have the epic grandeur D-Day has acquired, and point towards the United Nations action in Bosnia that public consciousness tries desperately to ignore.

Although it was mentioned only in passing during the US broadcasts of the commemoration services, much was written in the newspapers about President Clinton's appearances in Europe during this period, the gains or losses in domestic support of his presidency he might make by the way he comported himself there. These speculations in the forefront of the public consciousness demonstrated the way in which the official narrative might be appropriated for the uses of the present, and thus contested the 'naturalness' of the official narrative itself.

The newscasts on all channels were interspersed with elaborate commercials shot especially for this week of celebrations. Actors of the veterans' age were shown in Normandy, on the quiet beaches, in late medieval farmyards, in the pastures with cream-colored Charolais cows, with putative sons and grandsons, who listened while the grandpa character described the events of 50 years ago. These were some of the most attractive visual images on the screen that day. But the beautiful beach, now cleared of Rommel's barricade, is still overlooked by the pillboxes so sturdily made they'll see out centuries before they disappear. The tremendous weight of the official narrative hangs over the scenes commandeered to sell Boeing and AT&T, whose logos were tastefully visible for a mere ten seconds. Nonetheless these commercials offered a powerful commentary on the status of the US as a world industrial power, the ascendancy of which is by no means as certain as it was 50 years ago. Further, as examples of how even vernacular interpretation – itself resistant to the official narrative – can be appropriated, they served as eloquent reminders of how all narratives of the past can be wrenched out of their contexts and (re)presented for present ends, thus undermining the truth-value of narrative itself.

Most of all however the official narrative was interrogated by many of the veterans interviewed live through the extensive broadcasts who, in contrast to those giving prepared speeches as part of the commemoration service, frequently voiced latter-day reevaluations of the enterprise they had survived. Andy Andrews, a machine gunner on Omaha Beach, spoke about his visit to the nearby German cemetery, which contains twice as many dead as the American cemetery: 'The realization really hit me that I had killed so many and because of me, so many were there, and that really hit me for the first time. ... In answer to your question, "How many?" I lost count a long, long time ago.' Ed Manley ruminated on the death of a soldier in his platoon: 'This guy was an all-

American boy. He was engaged to a girl. He wouldn't go to town
with any girls or anything like that. He didn't drink. And this guy's
laying over there, you know. It – he's never really lived, never even
started to live' (*Sunday Morning*). William Preston Jr. developed a
similar point: 'In reminiscences of combat different perspectives
emerge gradually as the events deepen in memory, above all of
those whose lives ended in the sand. ... Having come near death
also induced a desire, which I would not otherwise have imagined,
to live life to the fullest' (46). It was his friend's lost opportunity 'to
live life to the fullest' that Ed Manley mourned.

One of the phenomena emerging from the interviews with veterans and their relatives was the silence the veterans had kept about
their experiences on D-Day. Walter Cronkite confessed that he was
somewhat puzzled by their reticence even with their families, until
he realized they 'did not feel they should reap the glory just
because they had survived. It was, they felt, their comrades who
didn't make it who were the true heroes' (*This Morning*). Rather it
seemed from what the veterans themselves said they didn't want to
talk about glory or heroism at all. Those interviewed during these
two days, whether on television or in the newspapers, as well as
those on Moyers' program four years before, were in elegiac rather
than triumphal mood, remembering the losses of the war, measur-
ing them up against the long lives the arbitrariness of chance had
given them.[10] This sentiment had been voiced in 1972 by Arnold
Toynbee when he spoke of his increasing understanding of all that
the casualties of his generation, friend and enemy, now dead for
over half a century, had been deprived of as he himself experienced
what they had missed: 'The longer I live the greater grows my grief
and indignation at the wicked cutting-short of all those lives' (11).

Most frequently the veterans' resistance took the form of persist-
ing in their specific experiences of D-Day. Television added to
vernacular recollection: footage of the dead on Omaha Beach, never
before shown to a US audience, and of the devastation the friendly
invasion caused to the inhabitants of the countryside (15 000 French
dead by the time the fighting moved out of Normandy) and the
formerly medieval city of Caen (80 per cent obliterated) was aired
for the first time during these two days (*This Morning*).

The veterans did not offer counter-narratives of the war; their
statements did not even acknowledge the official narrative's existence. With the sense of an ending that lingered in the margins of
this commemoration, whether because of their own advancing

years or a suspicion that the world the D-Day landing ushered into being is on the verge of collapse, now resisting the official narrative in this public forum they contributed their recollections to the public memory, as though they had traveled there to testify. Their voices contest the official narrative of heroism and glory, a narrative that has depended on their years of silence. The dead, it seems, have served their country more usefully than the living veterans; without resistance they can be subsumed into the official narrative, all 9386 present and correct, pressed into service to testify mutely to United States hegemony. Whether the public memory will accommodate the resistant testimony of the veterans when they are no longer able to speak remains to be seen.

My meditations on nostalgia suggest that it is a leisure activity. It seems to have something in common with Wordsworth's idea of poetry as 'recollection in tranquility', needing both distraction from immediate concerns and deliberate recollection for its manifestation. Like poetry it is formed by a set of rhetorical practices constructing what Raymond Williams has called a 'structure of feeling'; like all speech acts its manifestations are various and specific to the manifesting subject. Nostalgia as *langue* may be common to all speakers, but the *paroles* are bound by the circumstances of enunciation.

I cannot separate the feeling of nostalgia from ideas of gender and nation. But categorizing these terms through the feeling/thinking divide seems immediately to constitute them as different orders of experience, which I am not so sure they necessarily are. All three are culturally determined concepts, concepts signifying relationships between subjects and their world(s). All are operations, processes; dynamic and fluid, they are contingent on historical factors and structured by the contexts in which they find expression.

The preceding pages are an attempt to outline the circumstances of enunciation provided by my configuration and intellectual history. They show amongst other things both the impossibility of speaking about culture from within culture and the impossibility of speaking from without. It seems to me that nostalgia is a constitutive element of both gender and nationalism, though it does not precede them; none is stable; each is constitutive of the other two; all three are both cause and effect. Modification of one makes changes in the other two. Such imbrication explains why, even

when understood as deliberate indoctrination, nostalgia is impossible to escape. This entrapment is the difficulty of asserting
personal memory in resistance to an official narrative sited in a
nationalism constituted by war, where considerations of gender are
an unspoken presence.

NOTES

1. I spent four years in Vancouver, British Columbia, where as a couple
    my husband and I were *personae non gratae*; Anglophiliac Canadians
    delighted in me but shunned him, whereas the America-lovers adored
    him and were suspicious of me. I was never so conscious of national-
    ity on a daily basis as I was during those four years.
2. For a full account of this unlikely posting, see Bates, *Blossoming*
    179–82; *Ripeness* 5ff.
3. Two letters from the Director, Colonel Gerard Legout (retired), n.d., in
    response to my letters of 12 January and 28 June 1994.
4. For much of the following information I am indebted to a conversa-
    tion with Catherine Woodcock in March 1991.
5. The word *auxiliary* still troubles me: it diminishes the contributions of
    the 350 US women pilots who ferried planes and supplies across the
    US and who only a few years ago had to sue the US government for
    veteran status; and of the British women (aged 17–45, unmarried)
    who were conscripted as members of various services, including anti-
    aircraft gun crews, where they suffered casualties comparable to those
    of fighter and bomber crews.
6. In addition to the reprint of Cornelius Ryan's *The Longest Day* (1959),
    other books recently published that rely heavily on veterans' recollec-
    tions are Ambrose's *D-Day June 6, 1944*; Lewis's *Eye-Witness* and
    Neillands and Normann's *D-Day, 1944*. Recollections have also
    appeared in magazines from *The London Review of Books* or *The New
    York Review of Books* to Sunday supplements like *Parade*. Local news-
    papers have printed the recollections of local heroes and survivors.
7. Disneyfication is apparent in other commemorations of D-Day events,
    such as the commemorative re-jump by 44 veterans of the 101st
    Airborne on 6 June 1994. Nor is disneyfication peculiar to D-Day
    events: the annual Doolittle Flyover, for example, or the tolling the
    boats ceremony with miniature submarines in a motel pool at the
    annual state convention of the submarine veterans of World War II
    (Milos B1). The reasons for participating in such ceremonies are to re-
    member the lost but also to celebrate survival and, as for the children
    who visit the museum, to reinforce a sense of control. The issues
    implicit in disneyfication were epitomized in the objections of histori-
    ans to the construction of a Disney theme park on a Civil War battle-
    ground. David Cullough, president of the Society of American
    Historians, complained that the enterprise would create 'synthetic

history by destroying real history' (Feinsilber). The dispute centered on who would control the meaning of the Civil War and to what end.

8. Ambrose's book, published in April 1994, was just in time to intervene in the national interpretation of D-Day. This interpretation, supported by the nostalgia of the generation old enough to remember the war but not old enough to have fought in it, seems to be on its way to being the dominant one. George Will, for example, wrote a column on D-Day entitled in my local paper 'A Love Song to Democracy'.

9. A similar juxtaposition of official narrative and interrogative news appeared unnervingly in the 6 June 1994 edition of *Time*, where the last page of the lead article, 'Ike's Invasion' (the cover proclaimed Eisenhower as 'The Man Who Beat Hitler') announcing 'You will bring about ... the elimination of Nazi tyranny over the oppressed peoples of Europe and security for ourselves in a free world' was immediately followed by 'Fascism Lives: 50 years later the legacy of Hitler and Mussolini still bedevils Europe', complete with photos of Nazi youth, then and now, and one of neofascist skinheads demonstrating in London (Nelan 49; Jackson 50).

10. A British correspondent tells me that British veterans' groups refused to take part in Government celebrations planned for Hyde Park. The 50th anniversary of D-Day, the veterans said, was no occasion for celebration: their membership preferred to spend the day in quiet remembrance.

WORKS CITED

Ambrose, Stephen E., *D-Day, June 6, 1944: The Climactic Battle of World War II*, New York: Simon & Schuster, 1994.

Arromanches: D-Day – Jour J – 6 juin 1944, Arromanches: Musée du Débarquement, n. d.

Barker, Simon, 'A History of the Present', in Francis Barker *et al.* (eds), *Literature, Politics and Theory*, London: Methuen, 1986.

Bates, H. E., *The Blossoming World: An Autobiography*, London: Michael Joseph, 1972a; Columbia: Missouri University Press, 1972.

—— *The World in Ripeness: An Autobiography*, London: Michael Joseph, 1972; Columbia: Missouri University Press, 1972.

Bodnar, John, *Remaking America: Public Memory, Commemoration, and Patriotism in the Twentieth Century*, Princeton, NJ: Princeton University Press, 1992.

Brown, Anthony Cave, *'C': The Secret Life of Sir Stewart Menzies, Spymaster to Winston Churchill*, New York: Macmillan, 1987.

Burns, Christopher, 'D-Day vets observe 49th year of invasion', *Fresno Bee*, 7 June 1993: A2.

Feinsilber, Mike, 'Civil War historians decry park', *Fresno Bee*, 12 May 1994: A12.

Fitz-Gibbon, Constantine, *London's Burning*, New York: Ballantine, 1972.

Fussell, Paul, *The Great War and Modern Memory*, London: Oxford University Press, 1975.

Hartman, Geoffrey, 'The Voice of Vichy' in Lawrence D. Kritzman (ed.), *Auschwitz and After: Race, Culture, and the Jewish Question in France*, New York: Routledge, 1995: 15–24.

Jackson, James O., 'Fascism Lives', *Time*, 6 June 1994: 50–1.

Kritzman, Lawrence D., *Auschwitz and After: Race, Culture, and the Jewish Question in France*, New York: Routledge, 1995.

Larry King Live, Cable Network News, 6 June 1994.

Legout, Col. Gerard, two letters, n.d.

Lewis, Jan, *Eye-Witness D-Day*, London: Robinson, 1994.

Lodge, David, *Out of the Shelter*, London: Penguin, 1970.

Milos, Charles, 'Sub stories resurface', *Fresno Bee*, 30 January 1994: B1, B3.

Morning News, Cable Network News, 7 June 1992.

Moyers, Bill, *From D-Day to the Rhine*, Public Broadcast System, KVPT, Fresno, 6 March 1990.

Neilland, Robin and Normann, Roderick de, *D-Day, 1944: Voices from Normandy*, London: Weidenfeld and Nicolson, 1993.

Nelan, Bruce W., 'Ike's Invasion', *Time*, 6 June 1994: 36–49.

Nora, Pierre, *Between Memory and History*: Les Lieux de Mémoire, *Representations* 26, Spring 1989: 7–25.

Nye, Doug, 'Hitchcock's war efforts rescued', *Weekend*, supplement to *The Fresno Bee*, 15 May 1994: 8.

Osmont, Marie-Louise, *The Normandy Diary 1940–1944*, trans. George L. Newman, New York: Random House, 1994.

Péan, Pierre, *Une Jeunesse française: François Mitterrand, 1934–1947*, Paris: Fayard, 1994.

Preston, William Jr., 'On Omaha Beach', *New York Review of Books*, 14 July 1994: 46.

Pugh, Phyllis, 'My Memories as an Evacuee', in *On the Home Front: Barking and Dagenham in World War II*, London: Barking & Dagenham Libraries, 1990: 14.

Rattigan, Neil, 'The Demi-Paradise and Images of Class in Wartime Films', in Wheeler Winston Dixon (ed.), *Re-Viewing British Cinema, 1900–1992*, Albany, NY: SUNY Press, 1994: 83–94.

Roberts, C., *Good Morning America*, American Broadcasting Companies, KFSN, Fresno, 6 June 1994.

Ryan, Cornelius, *The Longest Day*, 1959, repr. London: New Oxford Editions, 1994.

Shirer, William L., *The Rise and Fall of the Third Reich*, New York: Simon & Schuster, 1960.

Stevens, George, *La Marche des Héros*, Paris, n.d., 60 min.

Sunday Morning, Columbia Broadcast System, KJEO, Fresno, 5 June 1994.

'Sweet Machine', *Fresno Bee*, 24 April 1994: A2.

This Morning, Columbia Broadcast System, KJEO, Fresno, 6 June 1994.

Toynbee, Arnold, *A Study of History*, New York: Oxford University Press, 1972.

Will, George, 'A Love Song to Democracy', *Fresno Bee*, 6 June 1994: B7.

Index

Index